Kusamira Music in Uganda

Kusamira Music in Uganda

Spirit Mediumship and
Ritual Healing

PETER J. HOESING

UNIVERSITY OF
ILLINOIS PRESS
Urbana, Chicago, and Springfield

Publication supported by a grant from the
L. J. and Mary C. Skaggs Folklore Fund.

© 2021 by the Board of Trustees
of the University of Illinois
All rights reserved
1 2 3 4 5 C P 5 4 3 2 1
∞ This book is printed on acid-free paper.

Library of Congress Control Number: 2021940090
ISBN 978–0–252–04382–6 (hardcover)
ISBN 978–0–252–08581–9 (paperback)
ISBN 978–0–252–05272–9 (e-book)

For my family, with love,
and for healers everywhere.

Contents

List of Illustrations   ix

Notes on Languages and Orthography   xi

Acknowledgments   xv

Introduction: Situating *Kusamira* and *Nswezi* as Repertories of Well-Being   1

1. Ritual Work in Twenty-First-Century Uganda: From Folk Well-Being to Ex-Colonial Professionalization   33

2. Ecologies of Well-Being: Hearing the World through Ritual Repertories   59

3. Possessing Sound Medicine: Gathering Resources, Strengthening Networks, Composing Knowledge   108

4. Sacrifice and Song: Ritual Exchange and the Production of Relational Ideals   128

5. From Tea and Coffee Berries to Beer and Meat: Sound, Hospitality, and Feasting in Repertories of Well-Being   154

Conclusion: Listening to *Kusamira*'s Lessons on Well-Being Now   165

Notes   169

Bibliography   179

Index   191

Illustrations

Figures

1. *Mbuutu*, the large drum that plays the main rhythmic motifs underlying *kusamira* songs and many other Kiganda repertories 13
2. *Nsaasi* (Luganda) or *nnhengo* (Lusoga), the large rattling gourd idiophones used across *kusamira* and *nswezi* repertories 14
3. *Ngalabi*, the long drum used to improvise rhythmic idioms in Kiganda music 15
4. Healer and musician Erukaana Waiswa Kabindi sets up *nswezi* drums 17
5. A forested classroom at PROMETRA Uganda's Institute of Traditional Medicine 53
6. A test plot for medicinal plants at PROMETRA Uganda's Institute of Traditional Medicine 53
7. Small houses under construction for spirits at Munamaizi 56
8. Newly constructed houses for spirits at Munamaizi 57
9. The *balongo* power object 63
10. Twins of the royal enclosure and their homologous domains 80
11. The spirit Ddungu receives offerings and prepares to distribute food to his loyal devotees 93

Map

1. Uganda in East African context, showing contours of Buganda and Busoga 5

Musical Incipits

1. Typical *nsaasi* pattern   16
2. *Nnankasa* pattern for the *mbuutu* drum   16
3. Full *nnankasa* texture typically used for *kusamira* songs   18–19
4. Introductory figure for *nswezi* music played on *kadingidi* drum   21
5. Full *nswezi* texture as is typically used for most *nswezi* songs   21–22
6. Tune for "Ssewasswa"   67–75

Table

1. Kiganda Twin, Sibling, and Parent Names   64

Notes on Languages and Orthography

This book draws on songs and other components of language from two neighboring language groups, Luganda and Lusoga. My usage of these two languages adheres to several features they hold in common. They are classified as Eastern Lacustrine Bantu languages—that is, languages from the eastern part of the region between the Great Lakes of East Africa known as the Interlacustrine region. People write Luganda and Lusoga words phonetically using Latin/Roman script, including just one letter not found in the English alphabet:

ŋ   combines the sound of *n* with the sound of *g*, as at the end of the word *sing*

Luganda and Lusoga are additionally classified by linguists as "agglutinating" languages, meaning that morphemes, which take the forms of prefixes, infixes, and suffixes, join together to create words and sentences. This system operates in both languages according to "classes" of words, which categorize the vocabulary based on prefixes. The following prefixes communicate crucial information:

ba-   people, as in Baganda and Basoga
mu-   the singular form of *ba-*, which can describe someone's ethnicity (e.g., *muganda* or *musoga*) or occupation (e.g., *mugoma*, one who plays *eŋŋoma* [drums], or *muyimbi*, one who sings)
bu-   land or place, as in Buganda and Busoga
ki-   adjectival descriptor for things related to these groups, as in Kiganda music and Kisoga dance

xii   *Notes on Languages and Orthography*

ku-   prefix for verbs (e.g., *kukola*, do, *kukuba eŋŋoma*, beat drums, or *kukon-gojja*, carry something on the head)
lu-   languages related to these groups, as in Luganda and Lusoga

Some prefixes can have additional agglutinative letters, which act as articles:

o-   as in Oluganda (the Luganda language) and *omuganda* (a Ganda person); with verbs, this prefix creates an infinitive, as in *okukola* (to do)
a-   as in Abasoga (the Soga people)

This process works the same way for nouns in other classes:

ŋoma (drum) becomes *eŋŋoma* (a drum or the drum)
nsaasi (gourd rattles) becomes *ensaasi* (a gourd rattle or the gourd rattles)

I sometimes use the noun stem without its initial letter, instead placing the English article before the word, as in "the *ŋoma*." At other times, the word needs no article: Baganda speak Luganda, or Basoga speak Lusoga. Moreover, I adapt these rules of indigenous usage, bending them considerably to fit into English prose. For example, throughout the text I frequently use the verb *kusamira*, which connotes spirit mediumship, in adjectival form: *kusamira* ritual. These admittedly awkward uses do not exist in Luganda or Lusoga, but it would make even less sense to invent adjectival forms for this book.

The transliteration of these languages creates problems for indigenous linguists and foreign scholars alike. In particular, linguists and scholars disagree about whether Luganda and Lusoga should write the letter *r* at all, since its sound in the languages is interchangeable with *l* in idiomatic pronunciation. Although a new system of writing *l* for all such sounds exists in Luganda, it remains controversial. This study adheres to the conventions that most Baganda and Basoga recognize, which govern the use of *r* and *l* as follows:

r after *i* and *e*
l after *a*, *o*, and *u*

Translation causes some recurrent challenges, too, as in the case of singular pronouns, which are gender neutral in Luganda and Lusoga. Unless context clearly indicates gender specificity, then, this book translates these pronouns using likewise neutral language (e.g., s/he, his/her).

Both languages frequently use contractions to reflect elision of sounds in pronunciation. Although the latest ideas from Kiganda linguists support the eradication of all such contractions in written words, this book again sides with the longest standing conventions on this matter, with one exception: a commonly used contraction, *n'g*, was a solution to the lack of a specific letter

Notes on Languages and Orthography xiii

on older keyboards and in early word processors. This obsolete contraction has given way to the more accurate solution, *ŋ*.

As some examples have already shown, some indications apply more fully to one language or the other. In Luganda, double written vowels indicate elongated vowel pronunciation, sometimes with tonal variations; for example, the *i* in *ekintu* (a thing) is pronounced as in *gift*, while the *ii* in *kusiima* (to show gratitude or approval) is pronounced as in *reef*. In Lusoga, the letter *h* appears after some consonants, softening the preceding consonant slightly:

basadha (men)
idha (you come, imperative)

Finally, both Luganda and Lusoga are stressed tonal languages. Syllable tones and stresses change according to the sentence context and syntax. Because no standard system exists for indicating these stresses, and because neither written language uses them in print, I have not included any diacritic stress markings here.

Acknowledgments

This book project has incurred massive debts of gratitude to multiple people and institutions. A few words of thanks will not begin to be enough. I count it a privilege to pay their generosity forward however I can. My wife, Jenn, and our two beautiful children, Grant and Sam, have patiently loved me through field research, write-up, and editorial phases. They serve as constant reminders of why music and well-being continue to fascinate me.

Damascus and Betty Kafumbe were the first Ugandan friends and teachers to foster my research career. Damascus began teaching me multiple Ugandan instruments in 2005, a process that continues to this day. Their wedding in 2006 remains one of the most impactful and memorable rituals I have ever been involved in, and it was a moment of enormous personal and professional growth. They and their families knew it would be that way, and they patiently supported my growth both before and since. The depth of my gratitude to Kakensa and Mukyala Kafumbe is endless.

Thanks to arrangements that Damascus made, Deo Kawalya and Waalabyeki Magoba were my first Luganda teachers. With her weeks-old firstborn son on her lap, Betty Kafumbe sharpened my Luganda skills beginning in 2007, with continuing support from Damascus and others along the way. What a tremendous gift. Mr. Magoba and his wife, Annette, began sharing their home and family with me from our first weeks together in 2006. The cultural education, generosity, and love that Kawalya, the Kafumbes, the Nayigas, the Magobas, and their extended networks of kin on both sides of the Atlantic have poured into this project makes it as much theirs as it is mine. *Mu nju, temuli kkubo, bannaffe. Nneyanzizza, nneyanzeege!*

In ethnomusicology, our terms for the people who help us do fieldwork have shifted: no longer simply informants, they have become field colleagues and interlocutors. Dale A. Olsen appropriately and simply identifies them as our teachers, and like other researchers, he lavishes respect and praise on them. I follow our colleagues in this tradition: these kinds of teachers have offered me the repeated and sustained privilege of their time, expertise, insight, good humor, and patience. I apprenticed Kabona Ssematimba Frank Sibyangu in Kiganda drumming and singing, and he taught me much along the way about the practice he maintains at his shrine. Andrew Lukungu Mwesige Kyambu welcomed me as a *nswezi* drumming apprentice in Busoga, while his brother William, his father Kyambu Ntakabusuni, their dear friend Lukowe Rehema, and a large band of other Lukowe- and Isegya-associated healers taught me about Kisoga musical healing repertories. Dr. Yahaya Sekagya, Umar Ndiwalana, Kasirye Ahmed, and the entire staff and entourage of teachers and attendees at the PROMETRA Uganda forest school offered me not only my first few experiences with Kiganda healing repertories, but also a field site consistently rich with related experiences and lessons. Balikoowa Centurio sacrificed time with his family to introduce me to many gifted healers and musicians scattered across Busoga, including the late Erukaana Waiswa Kabindi. A widely renowned singer who refused to be identified except by her spiritually significant stage name, Nakayima, took me on for an intensive short-term apprenticeship in cultural song practice, and she showed me many of the most significant shrines and ecological features of Buganda over a more sustained series of travels.

Among so many other teachers whose contributions shaped this book, I am also deeply grateful to Zawedde Gloriah, Ssettimba Charles Lwanga, Kaweesa Francis, Kavuma Gerald, Zawedde Prosikovya, Nantongo Sylvia Nakigozi, Nassuna Prosikovya, Nsubuga Francis Bugoya Ssaalongo, Namaganda Agnes, Dr. John R. S. Tabuti, Kijogwa Robert James, Nsubuga Waalabyeki Joseph, Musanje Kyabagu, Sulaiman Kizza, Jjajja Ndawula, Akita Janat, Nabawanuka Nakigozi, Arafat Musa, Mumbejja Buyego, Kiwalabye Robert, Kabona Mugalula Wamala, Banja Nsubuga Jonathan, Cecelia Pennacini, Byoto Ismael Ssaalongo, Twagalane Martin, Nalubega Resty, Kajura Methuselah, Lutaaya Dennis, Kabona Jjajja Mutale, *nswezi* drum maker Ndhote David, Omusiige Ronald Bweete, Jjajja Nakawuka, Desiderio Matovu Kiwanuka Ssaalongo, Lisa Nakawuka, Harunah Mbogga, Albert Bisaso Ssempeke, Hasan Lubowa, Mwalimu Ssenogga, Dr. Grace Nambatya-Kyeyune, Tomusange Kimuli, Anatore Kirigwajjo, Richard Ssenyonga, Gavin Dixon at the Horniman Museum, Heidi Cutts at the British Museum Warehouse, Elin Borneman at the Pitt-Rivers Museum at Oxford, the late Lukowe Kotilda Bibireka, Isiko Nabongho Francis, Kalooli Mulekwa, Lukowe Helus Nabwiire, Lovisa and Kibaale Logose, Kibaale Moses, and Mayanja Peter Dhube. I am also grateful

Acknowledgments xvii

to many others unnamed here whose voices raised thousands of choruses, whose hands sounded many instruments, and whose collaboratively created experiences continue to help so many people live better.

Several mentors, colleagues, and friends deserve special thanks here. Frank Gunderson not only saw me through challenging fieldwork and write-up dynamics, but also showed me a towering example of what it means to be a lifelong student of Africa and African music. Sylvia Antonia Nannyonga-Tamusuza, head of the Makerere University School of Performing Arts and Film and founding curator of the Klaus Wachsmann Audio-Visual Archive, has offered this project a physical and scholarly home time and again. Our work there is still in progress, as the building of effective, sustainable institutions tends to be. Kakensa Nannyonga-Tamusuza has been a trusted adviser and a mentor of surpassing wisdom throughout this project. She, her colleagues, and her students continue to offer insightful critical reflections about it. I am deeply grateful to Joseph Hellweg and Donald Pace for their compassionate mentorship and their stalwart support. My colleagues at Claflin University's Music Department supported me in innumerable ways, and Frank Martin and Alison Mc Letchie at South Carolina State University continue to challenge and inspire me. I thank Frankie Bukeyna Raiderson and Stephanie Annyas for their hospitality and companionship. Lois Anderson, Jonathon Earle, Jennifer Johnson, Marissa Mika, Rachel Muehrer, and Kathleen Vongsathorn have been excellent compatriots and critical sounding boards both in Uganda and in the United States, introducing me to so many other ethnographers and historians of Africa and medicine along the way. Damascus Kafumbe, Jennifer Kyker, Michael O'Brien, and Suzanne Wint have strengthened this research and promoted it in their local intellectual communities, and they continue to motivate me. Although it is unrelated to my daily work, this book has benefited from strong, consistent support at Dakota State University from Mark Hawkes, Ben Jones, Kurt Kemper, David Kenley, Josh Pauli, and Ashley Podhradsky. At University of South Dakota's Sanford School of Medicine, Mark Beard, Jerome Freeman, and Ellie Schellinger have also offered generous encouragement. Holly Hanson and China Scherz have likewise promoted this work and demonstrated the value of ethnomusicology to allied African studies fields for years. I am grateful for their formative questions, to Steven Feierman for his encouragement, to John Janzen and David Schoenbrun for their thorough, incisive reviews of the manuscript, and to Neil Kodesh for his critical input on some of the earlier work that informed this project.

Several people deserve special thanks for their work on the analytic and editorial phases of this project. Laurie Matheson at University of Illinois Press

xviii   *Acknowledgments*

saw its potential as a book, and she has offered countless forms of guidance. She supervises a supremely capable cohort of staff and contractors, all of whom have made the book stronger. My student research assistant and laboratory technician Ar'Darius Stewart offered a range of technical and scholarly assets during a follow-up research trip to Uganda in 2015 and beyond. Likewise, research assistant Amiah Henry made significant contributions to post-fieldwork research. All transcriptions and translations of Luganda songs emerged from sustained collaborative work by Kabona Ssematimba Frank Sibyangu with the author. Damascus Kafumbe, Deo Kawalya, Medadi Ssentanda, and Waalabyeki Magoba have provided a wealth of additional translation and transliteration support. Kinene Peter, Mugerwa Robert, and Kibirige Jimmy copyedited the Luganda songs with Dr. Kafumbe. Minah Nabirye transcribed all Lusoga songs, and Mwesige Andrew Kyambu helped translate them with additional interpretative input and transliteration support from Minah Nabirye and Lukowe Rehema.

Multiple institutions and organizations made this project possible through access to research resources and generous financial support. The Smith Educational Trust bolstered part of my language learning and pilot research in 2006. Florida State University funded language learning with support from the Carol F. and Richard P. Krebs World Music Endowed Fund in 2007, and field research through an International Dissertation Research Fellowship in 2008–9. The Fulbright-Hays Doctoral Dissertation Research Abroad program funded an additional six months of field research from late 2009 through June 2010. From 2006 to 2010, the Makerere University Institute of Social Research, the Centre for Basic Research in Kampala, the Jinja Cultural Research Centre, the Uganda Museum, and the National Archives in Entebbe offered a wealth of library and archival resources, and the Uganda National Council for Science and Technology supported research clearances. A Mellon Foundation workshop called Folklore Studies in a Multicultural World nurtured the writing process for this book. Claflin University supported a return to Uganda for follow-up research in 2013, with funds from the United Negro College Fund (UNCF) and the Andrew W. Mellon Foundation. Additional support from the United Methodist Church General Board of Higher Education and Ministry funded another return in 2015, this time through Claflin's Global Leadership Program. The UNCF Henry C. McBay Research Fellowship funded a major portion of the write-up time on this manuscript. Grinnell College was my temporary home for research and teaching as I edited and refined it. The University of South Dakota Sanford School of Medicine funded indexing and, together with Dakota State University, has shaped a stimulating intellectual home for this study and related discourses. To my colleagues and students and these and prior institutions: thank you!

Kusamira Music in Uganda

Introduction

Situating *Kusamira* and *Nswezi* as Repertories of Well-Being

This book is about music and well-being. More precisely, it is about how music socializes dynamic processes of illness, wellness, health, and well-being in southern Uganda. The people and music of this region define well-being within mutually constitutive ecological, human, and spiritual domains. This is the first comprehensive ethnographic study of musical repertories associated with *kusamira* (mediumship/possession) and *nswezi* (Kisoga mediumship rituals and their drums), two closely related ritual healing traditions in southern Uganda. It is about how the act of performing repertories of well-being articulates categories of illness and wellness. It is about the relevance of ritual performance to well-being and about the transmission of ritual modalities for social good across generations. These are processes of social reproduction, an idea that emerged from anthropologists' and sociologists' efforts to describe how human social groups constantly remake their social structures and patterns, and how, over time, people consciously attempt to preserve and enhance advantages.[1] The performance of *kusamira* and *nswezi* generates ideas about illness and well-being, and repeated performances over time reproduce those ideas with fresh relevance for each succeeding generation. The social reproduction of well-being through these performances suggests enormous potential for *kusamira* and *nswezi* to shape discourses about development in a region where roughly 80 percent of the population relies on traditional healers to provide them with access to primary health-care services.[2]

The central hypothesis of this book concerns how and why people participate in *kusamira* and *nswezi*: Ugandan traditional healing specialists perform repertories of well-being to pursue and maintain well-being, to preserve ideas about illness and wellness, to consider and negotiate the incorporation of persistent influences, and to generate innovative strategies as they navigate changing circumstances. My investigation of this hypothesis will begin from a few observations from the field research that informs the study. First, cultural adepts understand these processes of healing and well-being, preservation, negotiation, and strategic positioning to be fundamentally social. This observation reflects an understanding that has been a mainstay in African studies since the 1980s.[3] Second, the category of the social here includes ecological and spiritual factors, often glossed in this monograph as other-than-human. Historian David Schoenbrun has been publishing on this idea since at least 2016, and more recently he has led us to think about how it informs our understanding of ethnicity.[4] While the mutually constitutive triangulation of social, ecological, and spiritual domains does not make Uganda unique, the contours are certainly distinctive there. Third, and building on the second point, repertories of healing prove efficacious well beyond physiological and biomedical concerns. Traditional healers do of course acknowledge and directly affect physical realities, but often they construe the physical domain as symptomatic of underlying influences, be they human, other-than-human, or some combination. Fourth, dynamic circumstances and processes demand sophisticated networks capable of both proactive mediation and reactive mitigation. This last observation is in response to the literature on cults of affliction, as will be discussed throughout the book.

These four observations on Ugandan traditional medicine demand two equally important analytic assumptions. First, the working notion of repertory in this study expands beyond music and dance to include the complex collection of practices in which healers and associated specialists engage. Second, ideas about efficacy necessitate both inclusion and transcendence of the physical domain. As paradoxical as these ideas might sound as they strike their first notes, this book attempts to render them familiar by examining how specialists perform their repertories alongside their clients and sometimes their patron spirits in the service of efficacious intervention.

These observations and analytic assumptions intersect with some of the guiding questions that informed the field research:

- What are the present expressive contours of the popular healing traditions that people in this region have practiced for centuries?
- Given the current and past social marginalization of these once more public traditions in an African ex-colony, what continuing cultural relevance do repertories of healing retain?
- How do Ugandan healers and musicians understand the intersection of expressive, diagnostic, and therapeutic domains?

Introduction   3

This study considers the practical and theoretical implications of these questions in the context of the present discourse on national development and socioeconomic progress. It is a discourse that considers and sometimes hotly contests what it means to be ill or well, which begs an even more rudimentary question: why, among all the voices concerned with how public health affects Uganda's national progress, should anyone consider a few raucous drums, gourd rattles, and songs? As usual in ethnomusicology, the study and analysis of these musical and healing behaviors concern much more than the facts of their performance. The repertories are vast, and they are embedded in ritual and social life. That basic question about the relevance of songs and their performance is among the motivating impulses of this study, and its responses cannot emerge from a cultural vacuum.

Repertories of Well-Being

In studies of music, oral traditions, and poetry, a repertory often connotes the catalogued works of a single artist, composer, poet, or performer, often within narrowly defined parameters, including geography, language, and time. *Kusamira* and *nswezi* certainly generate repertories in this strict sense of songs and their performances, but here the term takes on additional meanings. Ritual practitioners called *basamize* (people of *kusamira*) and *baswezi* (people of *nswezi*) share these repertories with overlapping professional circles of varying specializations. In the context of southern Ugandan ritual and social life, the terms *kusamira* and *nswezi* refer to overlapping constellations of healing practices and their associated elements of expressive culture. These are not bounded, static categories; like all living traditions, they are dynamic. They encompass highly sophisticated fields of indigenous knowledge, including plant medicine, human anatomy, the etiology of affliction, and interventions that combine these with other domains of expertise and action. All these fields express an ontology that connects human life with the animals, plants, and spirits that Ugandan specialists believe are crucial to sustaining well-being. Thinking about these broad-ranging categories—and the ways they interact—as repertories of medical, sonic, spiritual, and performative practice facilitates analytic perspectives on the creativity of indigenous knowledge production, management, and reproduction.

On a more practical interpretive level, considering *kusamira* and *nswezi* as repertories in this multivalent sense addresses a thorny translation challenge: neither Luganda nor Lusoga has a term for music. People might speak of *nnyimba* (songs) or of *kitone* (talent); of *omunyumungufu* or *kaffulu* (a person adept at something or a master of something); or of *ggono* (a pleasing inflection or ornamentation in music). People with an appreciation for singing or poetry or drumming might remark that a person has many motifs, an expression of admiration for the ability to keep so many variations of rhythm and phrase organized, and the capacity to use them effectively within the musicultural idiom. They might even say that someone makes music with *kawowo* (pleasant odor, scrumptious taste, or a more general sweetness). The expression relates to a sensory concept: the verb *kuwulira* connotes not only hearing, but also smelling, tasting, and feeling things. Luganda and Lusoga often collapse sensory modalities for which English has separate verbs, and yet separation via contextual usage remains possible. Likewise, the noun *mpewo* can mean either wind or spirit, so the question *Towulira empewo?* could mean "Don't you feel the breeze?" or, alternatively, "Don't you feel/ hear/experience the spirit?" Such complex sensory and material concepts become useful for understanding how people think of *kusamira* and *nswezi* repertories and how deeply these repertories can affect people—physiologically and spiritually.

The "linguocentric predicament" around the term *music* also arises because the word itself implies a cosmology rooted in a Western tradition.[5] For the ancient Greeks, the Muses (goddesses) occupied a metaphysical plane (Mount Olympus) and fulfilled an inspirational function for poets, musicians, other artists, and scientists. *Basamize* and *baswezi* operate within a completely different paradigm and draw on their own associated cosmologies. The differences are profound, rendering the Greek etymology of the music concept completely outside the purview of this book. The more productive focus here is to consider how *kusamira* and *nswezi* repertories articulate sensual and spiritual experiences at the heart of what it means for Baganda and Basoga to live the good life, *obulamu obulungi* (i.e., to embody their ideals of well-being and prosperity). This study of *kusamira* and *nswezi* investigates how repertories articulate, index, and socialize this cultural logic of holistic spiritual and physiological well-being.

Geographic and Fieldwork Context

The multisited nature of the field research that informs this book facilitates an understanding of the common elements that emerge in *kusamira* and *nswezi* praxis. These elements reveal as much about the ways that *basamize* and *baswezi* behave and interact as they do about the representative works in their performances that we can reasonably consider as interconnected repertories. *Kusamira* and *nswezi* are related by virtue of the historical, linguistic, and professional connections among their custodians and practitioners. These

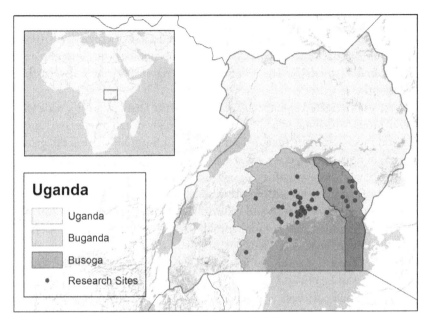

MAP 1. Uganda in East African context, showing contours of Buganda and Busoga. Map by Thomas Nello White with the author.

ritual performers, the *basamize* and *baswezi*, come from two ethnolinguistic groups who occupy the areas of southern Uganda immediately to the west and to the east, respectively, of the river Nile at its source (see map 1). The people to the west are the Baganda, who call their lands Buganda. Their neighbors to the east are the Basoga, who call their lands Busoga. Their languages, Luganda and Lusoga, share broad mutual intelligibility with roughly 80 percent of their vocabulary in common. Likewise, Kiganda and Kisoga ritual practices and repertoires (the *ki-* indicating an adjectival form) overlap considerably. As with their approaches to pronunciation, however, the social articulations of their ritual healing traditions bear notable differences. This monograph considers them together under the rubric of *kusamira* because that is the term both groups use in reference to spirit mediums' possession. However, like other traditional healers in the broader region, they deserve to be heard and taken seriously as medical professionals operating in discrete traditions.

The two regions lie between natural boundaries on three sides. The rolling hills of western Buganda give way to the Rwenzori Mountains farther west. Likewise the low-lying areas of eastern Busoga look east toward the Bugisu region on the foothills of Mount Elgon. The littoral that unites the regions along their common southern edge overlooks Africa's largest body of fresh water, somewhat diminutively dubbed Lake Victoria by British colonizers. Baganda and Basoga call it Nnyanja Nalubaale (lit. "watery place of the *lubaale* [spirits]"). The Nile serves as a natural border between the two regions.

These well-irrigated equatorial areas offer fertile farmlands for a wide variety of crops, which many people—including many urban dwellers of Kampala and Jinja—cultivate for subsistence, cash, or both. Most areas can grow bananas of numerous species, cassava, corn, groundnuts, legumes, potatoes, pumpkins, rice, sweet potatoes, many edible greens, yams, and a staggering diversity of medicinal plants. Southwestern Buganda is home to the most fecund banana-growing hills and valleys, while Busoga has excellent soil for both sweet potatoes and rice, depending to a great degree on topography and proximity to wetlands. Wide availability of these food staples, together with ready access to traditional medicinal expertise, helps shape the social determinants of health and well-being across these two regions.

Most Baganda peel, boil, and mash an unsweet banana (*Musa acuminata*) as their staple food, serving it with a sauce made from groundnut paste. This staple may be eaten on its own, as a base, or in alternation with stews and sauces made with fish, meats, vegetables, and legumes. Most Basoga peel and boil various colors and species of sweet potatoes as their staple, which they eat with a similar variety of sauces and stews. Both groups supplement their diet with other staples including cassava, pumpkin, rice, and yams as arable land and financial resources allow. Commoners treat consumption of animal proteins as a luxury, often reserved for feasting on special occasions or at rituals. In both regions, rituals involve special preparations of some foods, such as roasting banana inside the peel or roasting organ meats as offerings to the spirits.

The exchange of food and other gifts for blessings from the spirits emerges from a broader set of relationships between human beings and their surroundings. Performances of *kusamira* and *nswezi* ritual situate these relationships within a common ontology in the two regions. This ontology includes humans; a creator called Katonda, who occupies the skies; ancestral and other patron spirits, who might dwell anywhere from the landscape or the sea to the heavens to human mediums; and Walumbe, a spirit who is strongly associated with death and who occupies the underworld. As historical literature on these regions has shown, categories of ancestral and other patron spirits in southern Uganda have evolved over time to include the following spirits that make up the two overlapping pantheons:

Introduction

- *cwezi*, pre-Buganda royalist spirits, glossed in Lusoga as *nswezi*
- *mayembe*, "working" spirits that often behave like guards or soldiers
- *lubaale*, Kiganda "national" spirits that the Basoga also recognize as influential
- *misambwa*, once territorial but now widely acknowledged spirits that reside in flora and fauna
- *mizimu*, ancestral ghosts
- *nkuni*, autochthonous Kisoga "firstcomer" spirits
- *majiini* or jinn, known among some Islamic practitioners[6]

This regional ontology lies at the center of this book's inquiries into local categories of personhood, spiritual influence, illness, and wellness. Working within it, *basamize* and *baswezi* organize the production of knowledge about well-being around two interdependent notions:

- *okusiba ebibi*, the process of binding bad things, misfortunes, or bad potentials in order to truncate, restrict, diminish, or banish their power
- *okusumulula emikisa* or *amakubo*, the process of unbinding blessings or pathways to spiritual blessings associated with wellness and fruition writ large

Basamize and *baswezi* recognize that well-being encompasses multiple realms: plants, including crops, medicinal plants, and other flora; animals both domestic and wild that sustain human life either as food sources or as spiritual dwellings; and human clients who seek the guidance of traditional medical practitioners as much for fertility and preventative measures as for illness and misfortune. In both languages, professional healers are called *abasawo ab'ekinansi* (native healers or traditional healers), a term that distinguishes them from *basamize* and *baswezi* as broader categories of ritual adepts. Virtually all ritual actions in *kusamira* and *nswezi* repertories relate to the central concepts of binding and unbinding the potential of flora, fauna, fellow humans, spiritual patrons, and even spiritual dwellings in the landscape, and traditional healers work closely with *basamize* and *baswezi* to manipulate the dynamic circumstances of binding and unbinding.

Like the repertories of song and action people use to influence the dynamics of well-being, these ideas about fixture and obligation are embedded in social relations, the basic unit of which is the clan. Although both regions trace their ancestry through patrilines for naming purposes, neither Baganda nor Basoga use surnames. Instead a person receives one of many names associated with his or her father's clan. This name signals to others a person's membership in the associated clan, and therefore with that clan's totem, which people frequently discuss as part of normal greeting practices. Most totems are animals, though a few significant plants serve as totems, too. With over fifty clans in Buganda alone, this means that most adults in these regions of Uganda carry with them a vast knowledge of clans' associated names and totems. People observe strategic avoidances associated with clanship, including the refusal to eat one's totem and the avoidance of marrying within any given clan. Thus, the system ensures the same fundamentals of exogamy as does a system of surnames, even if the structural details differ considerably.[7] Because people so often understand physical affliction as a manifestation of spiritual—often ancestral—affliction or imbalance of some kind, the clan is an important vector for both etiology and therapeutic mitigation.

Pathways to the Healer's Shrine

The field research for this study has roots in a linguistic examination of the proto-Bantu cognate terms that characterize a broader regional constellation of ritual healing practices. Preparation for intensive study of Luganda and pilot interviews during early field research involved surveying Eastern Lacustrine Bantu languages for terms connoting spirit mediumship, possession, or trance; healing or therapy; illness and wellness; and healers and patients. In searching for terms that described these activities and roles, I focused especially on behaviors that might be construed as musical. Precolonial travel writers, colonial administrators, and colonial-era missionaries, along with the rich ethnographic literature published later, consistently mentioned drumming and singing in connection with ritual healing practices in Uganda, Rwanda, and Tanzania. These descriptions echoed a broader *ŋoma* (drum) concept common across much of sub-Saharan Africa.[8] However, prior to my three extended periods of field research, the question remained unanswered as to what music and sound might have to do with the ancient practice of *kubandwa* (spirit mediumship) as a living tradition in southern Uganda.

In order to understand how these old vocabularies and repertories of ritual healing might manifest in living *kusamira* and *nswezi* traditions—how indeed they might remain relevant in Uganda—I needed to identify the most active custodians of popular healing and find ways to consult them. During a twelve-week period in 2006, I undertook an intensive study of Uganda's most widely spoken indigenous language, Luganda. Concurrently, I sought out knowledgeable interlocutors from across the Interlacustrine region who understood proto-Bantu cognates associated with traditional healing. Many recognized terms like *kubandwa*, perhaps the oldest term associated with spirit possession and spirit mediumship in the region, and *mufumu*, a term that still means "healer" in many of the region's languages. They translated

Introduction

these terms for me, offering more relevant local categories for current practices. Using these proffered terms, I structured a series of formal interviews with linguists and cultural leaders and ran a concurrent series of informal interviews with willing participants in Kampala. In this latter group of interviews, I purposely engaged in a playful line of questioning across a curious, economically and ethnolinguistically diverse cross-section of Kampala, Jinja, and smaller municipalities as far southwest as Masaka.

The results of this preliminary field research were overwhelmingly consistent. While many understood *kubandwa* as a concept, many more agreed that *kusamira* offered a more current and relevant local verb connoting both the specific act of releasing one's usual sense of self to the embodiment of a spirit and the ritual process of engaging in this act. Likewise, most people agreed on the most common venue for *kusamira*, a type of shrine called *ssabo*. I would later discover many variations on this concept throughout Kampala and across both Buganda and Busoga. I discovered that Basoga also use the term *kusamira* for the specific act of spirit possession, but that the *nswezi* rituals in which it occurs derive their name from the drums that accompany them. Although the extant, widely circulated scholarly literature mentioning similar terms remained outdated and lacked musical specificity, these early project consultants uniformly indicated that both *kusamira* and *nswezi* featured interesting sonic elements worth further examination.

By August 2006, the project of outlining the expressive contours of *kusamira* and *nswezi* had presented some clearer challenges than when I had first begun. Ongoing Christian missionary endeavors and public scrutiny of traditional healers promised to make the work of identifying the most active custodians of musical practice in these two regions' popular healing traditions a delicate matter. This challenge was perhaps especially acute for a researcher whose visual identity matches that of so many missionaries in Uganda: it was then and still is completely reasonable for locals to assume that a white male English speaker in Uganda might be a missionary. Healers' associations and professional performing groups would be excellent points of primary access, but the process of building rapport with ritual musicians and finding representative samples of ritual musicking would require a far deeper engagement with local languages and their speakers.

Returning to Uganda during the fall rainy season of 2008 after another period of intensive language study, I set out to observe and participate in the music of popular healing, to interview healers and musicians, and to understand what constituted a representative sample or event. The contours of that participant observation had clear boundaries. I sought musical apprenticeships with a series of willing teachers who negotiated a mutually agreeable

10 *Introduction*

rate of compensation for lessons, with additional provision for travel to field sites. At those sites my participation was primarily musical and verbal. The act of providing gifts of food and contributions to group meals was standard, but no more or less frequent than the acceptance of abundant, warm hospitality of meals and lodging. Respectful participation in prayers and songs offered other means of participant observation. Multiple visits to research sites helped build rapport, often leading to audio- and videorecording where permissible. Many interviews with healers employed the technique of free listing, incorporating cognate terms from ritual and traditional spiritual life. Even in the first handful of these interviews, I quickly realized that the internal diversity of the two traditions called for an ambitiously multisited ethnographic approach. Extended apprenticeships with singular healers, performers, or communities—an approach that other ethnographers had used for deep and meaningful engagement in Zimbabwe, Malawi, Niger, and Côte d'Ivoire—threatened in the Ugandan context to obscure a robust variety of spirits, mediums, and musical configurations that might be considered representative of *kusamira* and *nswezi*.[9]

This project required not just one or two but multiple apprenticeships, sometimes overlapping. Author, folklorist, and beloved radio host Waalabyeki Magoba has been by far the longest-serving ambassador of Kiganda culture among these. He worked in tandem with linguist Deo Kawalya to create opportunities for practical language application in a variety of contexts. He opened his home and brought me into his family's cultural life. He tutored me in the performance of *kulanya*, a form of self-introduction originating between commoners and royals in Buganda and practiced at pre-wedding introduction rituals. As an experienced researcher, widely traveled recordist, archival collector, music teacher, and leading teacher of student groups in national school music competitions, Centurio Balikoowa spent much of his time during school holidays in 2008–9 sharing his recordings with me and taking me to meet healers throughout Busoga. Experienced healers named Yahaya Sekagya and Ndiwalana Umar helped me understand the conceptual categories of Kiganda *kusamira* and introduced me to hundreds of fellow healers through PROMETRA, the NGO for which they both worked. Andrew Lukungu Mwesige, the son of a prominent healer named Kyambu Ntakabusuni in an area of Busoga near Busembatia, became my primary *nswezi* drumming and singing teacher and an important interlocutor with fellow *baswezi*. The late Erukaana Waiswa Kabindi, a *muswezi* healer to whom Balikoowa had introduced me in 2006, explained many of the subtleties of *nswezi* divination, plant medicine, and musical ritual. Combined with lessons from Mwesige and Kyambu, Kabindi's guidance elucidated an ecologi-

Introduction   11

cal context for Kisoga understandings of physical and spiritual wellness as articulated through *nswezi* music. Prominent Kiganda traditional musicians Ssematimba Frank Sibyangu and Nakayima became my primary Kiganda *kusamira* drumming and singing teachers, inviting me to join them at sacred sites and ritual events in Buganda, and sometimes inviting me to perform with them at weddings and funerals. Bwette Ronald, the custodian of an important *mmamba* (lungfish) clan estate, and Lisa Nakawuka, the granddaughter of the main spirit medium at the same estate, introduced me to that medium and her community of devotees. They patiently helped document the landscape of the estate and its spiritual dwellings through hand sketches and audio recordings out of respect for a local moratorium on photography and videography. In doing so, they gave important ecological context for the songs people sing at that estate and in so many other *kusamira* rituals.

During a combined total of two years that I spent living and working in southern Uganda between 2006 and 2015, this series of apprenticeships significantly unbound and opened to me the intertwined constellations of *kusamira* and *nswezi* praxis across nearly fifty discrete field sites scattered throughout Buganda and Busoga, both inland and along the Nnyanja Nalubaale littoral (see map 1). They familiarized me with interlocking social networks of practitioners, adepts, and professionals from highly localized healers' associations to international NGOs to Ugandan government ministries. They clarified local categories of illness and wellness. This book binds those categories within a rich tradition of scholarship on social reproduction, an idea that the ethnography and history of healing in Eastern and Southern Africa has established as the theoretical underpinning of medicinal knowledge-making in the region. Anthropologist John M. Janzen and his critics view *ŋoma* as the symbol that binds and contains widespread notions of "fruition."[10] These ideas organize the social power of healers and healing into the drum as a symbolic container of spiritually erudite fecundity. This book interprets knowledge-making as a process that healers and musicians jointly brew and beat into *ŋoma*. Following the Janzen school, I view *ŋoma* as a powerful container of medical and spiritual knowledge. The methodological and theoretical contributions of this study depend on analysis of the powerful sounds and understandings that emerge from that very same instrument and from the voices it accompanies.

The Music: Instrumentation, Idioms, and Heterophony

A focus on the specifics of sound avoids reducing *ŋoma* performance to some mysterious African rhythmic stereotype or to a guiding cultural impulse that holds sway over huge, diverse populations. As references to extant literature throughout this book demonstrate, ethnographers and historians of Uganda have long recognized the importance of musical performance across multiple domains of social and political life. Ethnomusicology is the study of how and why people create and experience music, why it matters to them, and why all of that matters to the world."[11] My ethnographic motivations begin with human creative agency, understanding that people shape cultural contours, not the other way around. An ethnomusicology of *kusamira* begins with people singing and playing songs as an analytic focus rich with possibility, considers the meanings and impacts of those sounds in and on their immediate social, spiritual, and ecological contexts, and critically assesses their potential to affect a broader world.

In both Buganda and Busoga, repertories of well-being are first and foremost song traditions, which helps explain why this book places so much analytic emphasis on songs and their meanings. Song style in both areas involves a leading solo role and a responding choral role. The former often alternates among knowledgeable singers, sometimes even within the same song. The latter choral role is the responsibility of virtually every other person present. Exceptions for children and spirit mediums are common, but spirits just as routinely join the chorus by singing or dancing through their mediums, and children's enculturation frequently includes listening or beating gourd rattles during songs.

The typical instrumentation for Kiganda ritual performance involves, at minimum, a main drum called *mbuutu*, a singer who leads the responsorial singing, and a few other singer participants, some of whom generally play gourd rattles called *nsaasi* (Luganda) or *nnhengo* (Lusoga).[12] *Mbuutu* is a large drum, roughly 40–50 cm (16–20") in diameter and 60–80 cm (24–31") tall. Its tuning mechanism includes many short tensioners (roughly 12–15 cm [5–6"] in length) made from twisted strips of hide. These secure a large hide batter head, scraped of its hair, to an even larger hide that encloses the smaller bottom of its stemless goblet shape (see figure 1).

Nsaasi are made from dried gourds that range from roughly 12 to 30 cm (5–12") at their widest, but even the largest among these can taper down to less than 5 cm (2") at their narrowest. Filled with hard seeds and stopped at the open end with barkcloth, these idiophones—large and small—can produce volume rivaling even the large *mbuutu* (see figure 2).

From there, households, shrines, or musicians who come might add any or all of the following drums:

Introduction

FIGURE 1. *Mbuutu*, the large drum that plays the main rhythmic motifs underlying *kusamira* songs and many other Kiganda repertories. Image used with permission. Center for Music of the Americas Photo Archive, Florida State University College of Music.

- *Mpuunyi* is an onomatopoeically named drum that one player uses to keep the pulse (*puun, puun, puun*). *Mpuunyi* is often a slightly smaller drum than the *mbuutu*, with longer hide tensioning strings, roughly 20–40 cm (8–16"), which contribute to its lower sound. Its enclosed, stemless goblet-shaped construction is otherwise similar to the *mbuutu*.[13]
- *Namunjoloba* is a smaller drum, roughly 20–35 cm (8–14") in diameter and 35–45 cm (14–18") tall, with construction more like the *mpuunyi* than the

FIGURE 2. *Nsaasi* (Luganda) or *nnhengo* (Lusoga), the large rattling gourd idiophones used across *kusamira* and *nswezi* repertories. Image used with permission. Center for Music of the Americas Photo Archive, Florida State University College of Music.

mbuutu. While players use hands on all other drums in this battery, the *namunjoloba*'s player uses sticks (*minyolo*) to play a standard set of offbeat variations.
- *Ngalabi* is a long, narrow, tubular drum (roughly 15–25 cm [6–10"] in diameter and often over 100 cm [39"] tall) that flares just before the batter head at the top and out to a kind of foot to stabilize the bottom (see figure 3). It is the only drum in this battery with an open construction at the bottom.

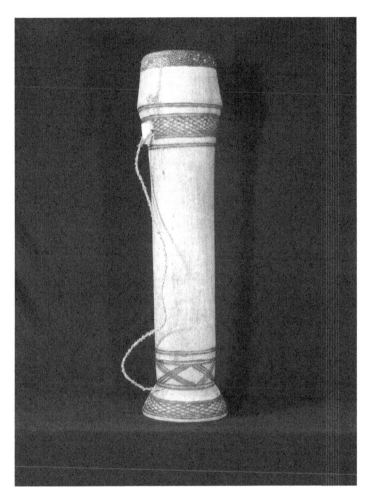

FIGURE 3. *Ngalabi*, the long drum used to improvise rhythmic idioms in Kiganda music. Image used with permission. Center for Music of the Americas Photo Archive, Florida State University College of Music.

It also features this group's sole reptile batter head, which makers cut from the hide of a monitor lizard (*Varanus albigularis*). This distinctive playing surface, together with the sophisticated techniques known to its players, makes possible a range of pitch and articulation options for idiomatic improvisations. Its player uses these in musical discourse with both leading singer and chorus.

Handclaps and loud rhythmic activity from gourd rattles, often played by multiple singers, round out a boisterous battery. With the exception of *ngalabi*, all the drums use a convex goblet-shaped wood shell with both ends covered in membranes of cowhide, the hair of which remains on the bottom part but is removed from the batter heads. *Ngalabi*'s tubular wood shell and lizard-hide batter head give it a much different timbre.

Songs begin with singers and add other instruments as available. The gourd rattles are most often the first instruments to enter after a leading soloist establishes an exchange with respondents. They play a basic pattern that has many variations, a few of which appear in musical example 1.

MUSICAL EXAMPLE 1. Typical *nsaasi* pattern.

Drummers derive the standard *mbuutu* rhythm for the vast majority of the Kiganda repertory from a suite of idiomatic *baakisimba* variations common across the rest of Kiganda music. *Baakisimba* has a long history of its own, closely linked with the royal court of Buganda.[14] The term offers one of many strong linkages between *kusamira*, histories of migration, and agrarian life: *kusimba* means to plant, and the crop referenced by the infix *ki-* is *matooke*, the unsweet banana that Baganda use for their main staple food. It is not native to Buganda, but because it grows well in the fertile soil there, it has become the ubiquitous symbol of Kiganda culinary and cultural identity. *Nnankasa*, one of the three main rhythmic *baakisimba* idioms, forms the basis for a compound duple meter (see musical example 2).

Songs built on a simple duple platform use a different base rhythm, but since *nnankasa* is prevalent in the repertory, analyses of Kiganda songs as-

MUSICAL EXAMPLE 2. *Nnankasa* pattern for the *mbuutu* drum.

Introduction

sume it as a standard governing meter except where otherwise noted. It is so firmly embedded in the Kiganda *kusamira* repertory that when Basoga *baswezi* sing Luganda songs at *nswezi* rituals, they imitate the *nnankasa* rhythm. In Kiganda *kusamira* songs, the pulse drum and handclaps lend weight to every third beat, with some variations. The small drum called *namunjoloba* adds a layer of offbeat interest (see musical example 3, where it enters in measure 7). The long drum called *ngalabi* (which also enters in measure 7 in this example) adds one more layer of complexity by playing idiomatic rhythmic motifs. Like those improvised by singers and poets, these motifs are called *bisoko*. The entrances of these instruments might happen in virtually any order depending on their physical availability and on the attention and energy of available players, who might well be alternating their participation with other tasks.

Kisoga *nswezi* rituals differ from Kiganda rituals in their instrumentation, even if the governing metric concepts based on compound duple time bear some similarities. Songs still begin with singers and gourd rattles (here called *nnhengo*), but the *nswezi* drums that people use for rituals of the same name differ in construction and use. Their wood shells still have flat bottoms, but their contours follow a conical V-shaped line rather than the rounder goblet shape (see figure 4).

FIGURE 4. Healer and musician Erukaana Waiswa Kabindi sets up *nswezi* drums, while some of his grandchildren look on. Photograph by the author.

MUSICAL EXAMPLE 3. Full *nnankasa* texture typically used for *kusamira* songs.

MUSICAL EXAMPLE 3. Continued.

20   *Introduction*

These drums still have cowhide covering both the bottom and the top of the shell, but unlike with Kiganda hand drums, makers usually leave the hair on the batter heads to be beaten away by *minyolo* (drum sticks). Regardless of the number of instruments accompanying any given song, people play *nswezi* drums with these sticks. Smaller gatherings or events where the musicians had to travel with instruments in tow might only use a single drum, and might use a combination of hands and sticks, but midsize and larger gatherings use a set of four or more drums. In any case, the governing musical meter remains compound duple, with the gourd rattle patterns resembling those described above. The rhythmic possibilities for a single drummer using just one drum derive from those of the larger set of two players and four drums of varied pitch. Again, the drummers enter following the initial calling motif, which is given by a solo singer to a responding chorus. Both drumming roles (one higher, several lower) involve introductory motifs that players can layer into the texture either sequentially or simultaneously. The highest drum—onomatopoeically dubbed *kadingidi* after its main rhythmic motif—begins as is shown in musical example 4. The three (or sometimes more) lower drums in the *nswezi* set begin with a different introductory motif (see musical example 5). The full texture appears with a few idiomatic variations, played mostly by the person beating the three lower drums.

Meanwhile, atop these energetic rhythms, the singers in both regions rarely harmonize. Responsive choruses sometimes double their lines at the octave. The use of a small buzzing aerophone called *kagwala* (pl. *bugwala*) by *baswezi* sometimes produces homophonic textures at a fourth or a fifth, but those sonorities tend to revert rather quickly to octave doublings. The overarching choral texture that results from these brief variations in both regions more closely resembles heterophony, a musical feature that invites comparison with *kusamira* as a social practice in southern Uganda.

As its Greek etymology suggests, *heteros* refers to something other, something different or varying from the main *phono*, a sound or voice. Heterophonic music features only slight, complementary variations, as opposed to the more significant and sustained differences that account for homophonic harmony in many other choral traditions. Musicians make these variations via articulation, ornamentation, fleeting harmonization, timbral variety, or slight adjustments to the words. Singers can, in theory, interpret a given tune homophonically or heterophonically. Spontaneous participation within the idioms of *kusamira* and *nswezi* music frequently results in heterophonic textures: a corpus of over three hundred unique *kusamira* and *nswezi* songs (as demonstrated in an even larger corpus of recordings that I collected,

Kadingidi

(ka - din - gi - din - gi - din - gi - di...)

MUSICAL EXAMPLE 4. Introductory figure for *nswezi* music played on *kadingidi* drum.

MUSICAL EXAMPLE 5. Full *nswezi* texture as is typically used for most *nswezi* songs.

MUSICAL EXAMPLE 5. Continued.

transcribed, translated, and interpreted for this study) establish heterophony as the all-but-ubiquitous standard. As this book argues, heterogeneous social articulation of *kusamira* and *nswezi* aligns with the heterophonic musical textures their practitioners produce. In other words, although *basamize* and *baswezi* demonstrate broad practical similarities across southern Uganda, their repertoires of well-being elucidate important subtleties and variations in their constellation of diagnostic, etiological, ecological, musical, therapeutic, and spiritual systems.

Introduction

Broader Impacts of *Kusamira* for Ethnographic Theory

To be clear, the parallels between heterophonic sound and heterogeneous process emerge as coincidental, and yet sound structure reflects social process in a way that usefully informs critical engagement with ethnographic theory. Steven Feld's contributions to thinking about sound structure as social structure offer one starting point.[15] Multiple points of comparison and contrast arise between Kaluli aesthetics and repertoires of well-being in southern Uganda. Notably, for example, they both incorporate significant ecological and spiritual components. Victor Turner's work on ritual offers another starting point in his movement beyond the structuralist roots of his Africanist predecessors toward situations, symbols, and processes. Richard Jankowsky's work is useful here. He follows both Turner and Bruce Kapferer in characterizing ritual processes involving possession or trance as "dynamic." Ethnographic evidence from *kusamira* and *nswezi* events supports that assertion. Jankowsky examines "compositional elements that shape perception, transform experience, and generate meaning," and he broadens from there to situate the aesthetics of musical production and ritual process as mutually constitutive.[16]

Given the prominent use of the word *kusamira* among both *basamize* and *baswezi*, and considering the term's strong connection to musicking and other acts of spiritual invocation, *kiganda* and *kisoga* iterations of the *ŋoma* tradition suggest a similar relationship between musical aesthetics and dynamic ritual processes. As with so many verbs in Luganda and Lusoga, the infinitive form, *okusamira*, can also be used as a gerund or even contextually as a noun, and the stem generates additional adjectival, verbal, and nominative forms. To examine these forms closely is to introduce the processual heterogeneity and the musical heterophony of ritual invocation. The verb form *okusamira* parses as follows:

oku-, the prefix indicating an infinitive verb
-sam-, a stem with varied connotations
    serve as a bodily medium for a patron spirit
    bark like a dog, which some mediums do at the moment of possession
    sit on one's heels
    accept blessings
    grow new bark (as on a tree)
    pierce lower lip; scarify, or bleed
-ira, an adpositional suffix that gives a sense of actions and things related to the actions and connotations named here.

The resulting meanings of *okusamira* resemble something like "to exhibit the qualities of being possessed," or of "getting blessed," or of "growing new bark," all intransitive verb meanings associated with this infinitive. For example, "ono asamidde" could carry those layers of meaning, translating as both "that person has demonstrated the qualities of mediumship possession" and "that person has grown new bark," meaning that the medium had taken on the physical features and mannerisms of something else, namely a patron spirit. Baganda and Basoga use the term *kusamira* as a synecdoche, generalizing its literal meaning to the many other actions—musical and otherwise—that invite spirits into human mediums, engaging them in ritual work and play. So the linkages between these meanings and associated musical and ritual practices truly do embed musical repertories in dynamic ritual processes.

Taken together, the meanings of *kusamira* as the umbrella term for these repertories of well-being generate other terms as well. Some have already been noted above, like *basamize* and *baswezi* for the practitioners of the traditions. Of particular interest here is *okusamiza*, the process of initiating someone into the associated practices. Whether such a person commits at a personal level to ancestral and other patron spirits or travels the demanding path toward semiprofessional or professional status as a traditional healer, the notion of "growing new bark" proves apropos. A possessed medium adopts the mannerisms and outward gestures of the occupying spiritual force. Initiates and regular practitioners of possession don different clothing and headwear. These and other features of mediumship generate revised social identities for mediums, who acquire new expertise that affects their communities, often significantly changing how those communities perceive them. So perhaps the first contribution of *kusamira* to ethnographic theory is the understanding that while its dynamic ritual process does shape perception, transform experience, and generate meaning, it also does something even more significant in the lives of its practitioners: practicing and living in *kusamira* transforms people and communities.

These terms occupy a central place in the ritual and social lives of healers because *basamize* and *baswezi* do not separate categories for illness and wellness from the influence of spiritual powers. On the contrary, they treat social life, spiritual life, and well-being as mutually inclusive. Their use of *kusamira* to connote a broad range of diagnostic and therapeutic activities, their clients' enormous investments of time and resources in those activities, and their strong belief in the efficacy of ritual healing practices all bear out the sociocultural importance of spiritual influence. Virtually every stage along the diagnostic-therapeutic trajectory involves actions and sounds worth careful consideration. These features enrich our understanding of what Byron Good sums up as a "folk model" of illness and wellness—or a folk etiology, the study of what causes illnesses.[17] In this case, such a model constitutes

Introduction

a complex set of etiological notions about how people in southern Uganda relate to flora, fauna, and spirits. As Ugandan repertories of well-being demonstrate, the broader consideration of etiological notions among *basamize* and *baswezi* involves an understanding not only of how spirits influence illness, but also of how animals, plants, spirits, and communities influence and promote wellness.

Victor Turner's work on Ndembu ritual made such important contributions to understanding the relationship between illness and spiritual life in Southern Africa that it has become difficult for many ethnographers to see other *ŋoma* traditions as anything but what he calls "cults of affliction," groups primarily motivated by the tendency of spirits to cause illness and to demand sacrifices through their mediums.[18] The soundscapes of *kusamira* and *nswezi* offer a slightly different folk model of both illness and wellness. People's initial reason for seeking the assistance of a traditional healer often remains firmly in the category of afflictions, which, as healers explain to their clients, have spiritual components. However, were we to focus only on the containment of affliction (through the binding of negative potential) in drawing a trajectory from diagnosis through therapeutic intervention(s) to sacrifice and other forms of ritual work, our model would remain only half complete. *Basamize* and *baswezi* share a common commitment to unbinding the spiritual blessings that facilitate well-being, and to celebrating the openness of pathways that allow those blessings to flow freely. Many people therefore regularly visit shrines, offer sacrifices, and maintain spiritual relationships in order to promote a free-flowing stream of blessings and prosperity, regardless of whether an affliction had motivated previous visits. Many children and young people grow in these traditions, paying tribute to patron spirits, participating in the activities of sacrifice, and thanking them for their blessings, without ever having experienced prolonged spiritual affliction. In addition to their influence over affliction and healing, these spiritual relationships contribute more generally to a high quality of life, glossed as *obulamu obulungi* (the good life).

All the same, embarking on an often protracted path of inquiry about wellness can indicate that such blessings have been somehow obstructed: clients do seek guidance from traditional healers for physical afflictions, misfortunes, relationship problems, or protection from witchcraft; for common ailments like eczema or malaria; and for sexually transmitted infections like syphilis. Because so many healers have some training as both herbalists and spiritualists, many people exhibiting symptoms of HIV/AIDS seek traditional healers' nutrition advice and their plant medicines for symptomatic relief. Regardless of what ails the clients, however, they quickly learn in these interactions that virtually all human problems can benefit from addressing underlying spiritual causes. Whether or not healers find that spirits caused the problems, they generally agree on processes of ritual inquiry that offer important physical, metaphysical, and social means of pursuing solutions.

Among these means, divination constitutes an area of expertise that many healers offer their clients. For Baganda and Basoga, divination or *kulagula* is quite often the first ritual act that clients witness. Both languages use the term *kulagula* to denote prophecy, soothsaying, and divination, powers that—according to historian David Schoenbrun—have long "revolved around the central theme of speech."[19] He asserts that both *kulagila* (to promise) and *kulagula* (to make divination) "had their origins in the complex meanings attached to the powers of speech expressed in the ancient meanings of 'to promise,' 'to say farewell,' 'to teach,' 'to show,' and 'to command,' all meanings that Eastern Lacustrine Bantu speakers could have expressed with forms of the root *kulaga.*"[20] *Balaguzi* (diviners), most of whom have broader expertise in plant medicine and spiritual healing, perform professional services that combine these meanings.

Discussing the rationale for seeking the services of a *mulaguzi* (diviner), healer and professional musician Ssematimba Frank Sibyangu explained a range of possibilities worth repeating here:

> When you go to begin *kusamira*, you go to a diviner, and he throws the divining objects and he says to you that, "a guardian [spirit] is disturbing you, but a guardian of the clan." Because now [in addition to] guardians of the clan, we have guardians of the blood pact, we have those of the in-laws, [and] you have the guardians of ours here in Buganda.[21]

Ssematimba's description of a scenario that would likely proceed toward a sustained commitment to mediumship reflects a complex set of possibilities for the healer to sort out in divinatory diagnosis. First, wellness clearly depends on the fulfillment of responsibilities to kin and clan. Other social commitments follow closely behind, beginning with the blood pact. Still others involve what John Roscoe (writing in 1911) called "national gods" and what ritualists generally refer to as "royal" spirits. Writing a century after Roscoe, Neil Kodesh offered a detailed treatment of these and other classes of spirits in the Kiganda pantheon, with particular attention to *lubaale*, *misambwa*, and *mizimu*.[22] Regardless of where in the taxonomy a healer's client finds his or her spiritual affliction, virtually all their practices highlight the importance of social relationships to a strong sense of identity, which *kusamira* and *nswezi* ritual construe as crucial to wholeness of personhood and alignment with broader cosmic forces.

Introduction 27

Ssematimba's frequent mention of clanship and blood pacts throughout our interviews reinforces this assertion, demonstrating the belief (shared widely across both Buganda and Busoga) that alienation from kin and clan not only causes illness but also constitutes a form of illness. This belief is one of many things about *kusamira* that takes on qualities peculiar to the ethnolinguistic groups who practice it and yet is sufficiently adaptable to be considered a "transposable disposition."[23] In the Kiganda case, the healers and clients who view alienation from kin and clan as illness illustrate the continuing relevance of an observation that Kodesh makes about the historical links between healing and social authority. Kodesh writes that healing became "central to the functioning of the kingdom" through its close association with the Kiganda system of clanship and social organization. This important contribution to understanding Buganda's history remains relevant to Uganda today. Ssematimba's assertions about this same history persist in conceptualizing the health of Baganda persons as inextricable from the health of Buganda kingdom and of its leader, the Kabaka. Just as Kodesh links historical healing practices with broader regional perspectives, current divination practices in both Buganda and Busoga demonstrate that spiritual ethnicity and social responsibility inform Kiganda and Kisoga notions of wellness and personhood. In other words, whereas Kodesh asserts that public healing in "the distant Ganda past" supported the kingdom's achievement of "political complexity," current practices of spiritual healing, often transposed across these two regions, outline different—if sometimes intersecting—contours of personhood and postcolonial politics.[24]

In the early stages of diagnosis, though, client concerns have little or nothing to do with political ideology or complex ritual understandings of personhood; clients typically seek out a diviner for much more mundane purposes. In a shrine at the estate of a celebrated healer named Kabona Jjumba in Kirowooza, Mukono District, one woman said she had come for help with her husband's sexual frigidity.[25] Others, per Ssematimba's narrative above, seek explanations for problems they cannot understand but know might relate to kin, clan, or community. He and other healers do sometimes trace these afflictions to disgruntled spirits that clients must then propitiate through sacrifice, a formulation consistent with the classic *ŋoma* model. "If you agree with the ancestors and give them what they want," Ssematimba explains, "you can do what? Get peace. Here in Buganda . . . But if s/he does not agree with the ancestors one time . . . then they eat rubbish, there in the dust bin, and they eat. [Those are] crazy people."[26] The rationale for adhering to custom links directly to the consequences of breaking with custom. On the day I met Kabona Jjumba, he was visited by a client who had undergone a similar experience: he could not focus on his studies, he began acting "like a madman," and his family would sometimes find him wandering the streets, shoeless and shirtless.[27] This notion of consequences goes beyond the idea that a person might find himself eating rubbish or wandering aimlessly without knowing why; as Ssematimba emphasized (partly through his shift from second-person to third-person perspective), refusing to cultivate healthy relationships with ancestral and other patron spirits is something only crazy people do. A stark irony resounds through attempts by mainstream news media, high-profile politicians, outspoken conservative clerics and their followers, and some allopathic medical professionals to cast *kusamira* as a manifestation of insanity: the frequency with which people consult traditional healers precisely to avoid insanity runs demonstrably high. It is entirely possible to make such a commitment to one or more patron spirits before encountering any of these problems, and many who grow up in these traditions do just that. Perhaps as in human relationships, breaking a commitment can have more potential for harm than refusing to make a commitment in the first place. In other words, while the motivations for initial consultation sometimes align well with the "cults of affliction" model, the character of ongoing, long-term engagement with the spiritual components informing a person's quality of life suggests an adjustment of that model to account for both binding and unbinding, affliction and well-being.

From Divination to Diagnosis to Intervention

The technical aspects of divination offer valuable perspectives on the variety of diagnostic practices in the region and an opening into the broader sound world of *kusamira*. A comparison of techniques within and across Buganda and Busoga will situate musical sound as one tool among several that healers use to invoke ancestral and patron spirits. This crucial point about the relationship between music and invocation in particular and between music and spirit possession or trance more generally builds on several important ethnographic and theoretical observations. First, a rich ethnomusicology of possession and trance in the 1980s firmly established that a frequent correlation with music did not imply causality in either direction. John Blacking argued that context and intention mattered as much as musical factors in Venda rituals.[28] Gilbert Rouget suggested that although music often supplies an effective means of "manipulating the trance state," it accomplishes this not by triggering trance but by "socializing" it.[29] Second, more recent ethnomusicological literature on music and spirit possession has moved from what

Introduction 29

Richard Jankowsky has characterized as two alternating extremes—scientistic universalizing studies at one end and intensively reflexive or positivist studies at the other—toward an analytic middle ground.[30] Jankowsky capitalizes on theoretical contributions by Turner, Blacking, Rouget, Paul Berliner, Ron Emoff, and Bruce Kapferer, among others, to argue that "scholarly fixations on the mechanisms of trance" should not divert us from the analytic priority of asking how the aesthetics of music articulate epistemology.[31] Emoff's work in Madagascar meanwhile offered a valuable interpretation of how music in *tromba* spirit possession recollects histories to inform and empower present generations.[32] This book focuses squarely on the capacity for repertories involving divination and trance ritual to produce knowledge within specific cultural contexts. Domain specialists accomplish this by illuminating complex local categories of illness and wellness on their way to promoting and reproducing social relations that support well-being according to those categories.

In Buganda and Busoga, I observed two main techniques for divination. One involves throwing objects and reading the resulting symbolism. The objects might be shells, coins, seeds, and other things of varying significance, or they might be *engatto za Muwanga* (the shoes of Muwanga), which are small squares of leather that diviners read much like they would interpret other divinatory items. These techniques involve sound only as a result of throwing the items. The other technique, by contrast, involves shaking a gourd rattle. Often combined with the scent of home-cured pipe tobacco, the sound offers an important expression of hospitality for spirits, who, healers and clients hope, will indicate their desire for social interaction, their need of musical or physical actualization, or perhaps the causes of an affliction or misfortune. The latter technique was by far the most common in both regions among the healers I consulted, but throwing objects for divination was often at least present and available as a method as well. Both cases offer entry points into the sonic world of *kusamira* and *nswezi* repertories of well-being.

The enormous social force of these repertories resides in their capacity to mediate among multiple, competing entities. They reveal so much about the links between clanship and kinship, cosmology and ontology, and illness and wellness precisely because of this mediating capacity. The literature has often highlighted this power without taking music seriously as a focus for inquiry. Victor Turner's *Drums of Affliction*, though an enormous contribution to understanding the structural and symbolic aspects of ritual performance, says little about the actual sounds those drums make. Likewise, John M. Janzen's study of *ŋoma* offers important analytic perspectives on the drum as both symbol and container of therapeutic power, but neither musical tools for analysis nor fine-grained local ethnographic specificity about musical sound were within its purview. Kodesh clarifies the link between clanship and public healing: his work listens beyond royal spheres of influence to narratives from healers' shrines that, he writes, "were not of the center but nevertheless became central to the functioning of the kingdom." This study is therefore motivated not only by these important narratives and contexts, but also by their sonic elements. Working at this intersection is a conscious focus on ethnographic frontiers suggested in part by Paul Stoller's notion of "sensuous ethnography," or ethnography that is attentive to the senses, particularly (in this case) that of hearing.[33]

Taken together with the topic of spirit mediumship, such consideration of a specific, intangible sense in ethnography is no simple matter. Jankowsky incisively observes that the study of mediumship, possession, and trance has intersected with the study of music to produce what he calls ethnomusicology's "crisis of experience."[34] Jankowsky plays productively here with George Marcus and Michael Fischer's ideas about the crisis of representation in ethnography, ideas that have been a touchstone for so many studies in ethnomusicology since the late 1990s.[35] Among the few scholars in the last twenty years to take music seriously as an analytic focus in the ethnographic study of mediumship or trance, Jankowsky cultivates an intimate appreciation for music's mediating tendencies. He follows anthropologist Michael Herzfeld by insisting on a "militant middle ground" between Adeline Marie Masquelier's caution about "reducing musical spirit possession to ritualized practice" and an alternative neglect of important analytic links between words, sounds, spirits, and things in the performance of healing.[36] With Herzfeld, Jankowsky is right to assert that this middle ground is not neutral space, to take the lived realities of spirit mediumship at face value in favor of magnifying the ability of embodied experience to generate meaning.[37] He is right to argue that the performative aspects of musical spirit possession do not negate their efficacy or power, and to suggest that purposeful care of artistry in the production of ritual might well suggest that the opposite is true. For just as Janzen has defined health as being "embedded in a set of structured relationships, rights, and practices rooted in a worldview of values, truths, and ideals," and just as he has pointed to the roles of healers in "adaptive systems" that account for social and spiritual ecologies, the present study shows that musicians and healers occupy a space somewhere between and among all those socially embedded entities. "Healers, when they are at their most effective," argues Steven Feierman, "play a mediating role in society."[38] The same assertion applies to musicians, particularly when they work within therapy management groups alongside healers.

The Path Ahead

This book is structured to analyze those mediating roles relative to the central argument. The attempt to interpret coffee berry exchange, other forms of hospitality, divination, the brewing of banana beer, animal sacrifice, foodstuff offerings and distribution, and ritual musicking as connected forms of ritual work presents a fascinating challenge in the space of a monograph. Yet all are linked within a repertory of practices concerned with well-being. Diachronic thick description of a single representative ritual trajectory would not only risk exhausting readers (listeners), it would also present far too narrow a representative slice of experience. On the other hand, a synchronic approach risks overgeneralization; it could flatten the rich complexity of these two traditions, the diverse event possibilities, and the variety of procedural approaches. Janzen once made a compelling argument to offer "a synthetic picture of an institution"; as he explained, doing so "is correct not because it reflects the statistical averages of all practices but because it explains the underlying logic."[39] But presenting only such a synthesis would mute the powerful impact that *kusamira* and *nswezi* have on such a broad cross-section of the Ugandan population. So, motivated by Herzfeld's and Jankowsky's notions of powerful middle ground, this book revolves around the core ideas noted here about how and why people perform these repertories, synthesizing *kusamira* as a social institution while selecting particularly illustrative or audible specific examples from the field research.

Chapter 1 proceeds with a look at the mediating roles that healers and musicians characterize as ritual work. It sets those actions against the current backdrop of a twenty-first-century ex-colony, considering how new and distinctive ways of organizing healers intersect with the historically tenacious practices of healers, their clients, and their other colleagues who specialize in ritual musicking. Its central premise is that performing songs constitutes a form of ritual work that, within broader repertories of well-being, reveals distinctive ways of thinking about illness and wellness. This chapter thus lays a foundation for considering why such knowledge production matters in present Ugandan, regional, and international discourses of public health.

Chapter 2 examines how repertories of well-being facilitate, generate, and manage knowledge relative to ecologies that incorporate humans, flora, fauna, and spirits as overlapping domains. It complicates a presently fashionable but ultimately reductionist view of *kusamira*, which tends to collapse far too much complexity into characterizations of traditional healers as herbalists. In pursuit of a more robust assessment, I posit interdependent domains of local ecology as crucial to expressions of risk and abundance that inform a wide variety of healing practices. These go well beyond a monolithic characterization of traditional medicine as plant medicine. In its broad-reaching implications, this chapter frames the three that follow.

Chapter 3 considers three different ways that people who perform repertories of well-being gather and distribute resources. A look at shrines, spirit mediums, and power objects finds that they all contribute to projects of binding/gathering and unbinding/distributing that people use to maintain well-being, preserve ideas about illness and wellness, manipulate influences, and innovate under dynamic conditions. Particularly in its discussion of spirit mediums and power objects, the chapter gets specific about those conditions, about their stakes, and about the mediating role of music in them.

Chapter 4 focuses on sacrifice, a widely misunderstood concept in Uganda's popular news media. The realities of sacrifice support mutual aid among human communities and transactional relationships with spirits. Supplicants exchange sacrifices with patron spirits for their blessings, each motivated by a need to understand and reinforce their respective place in the ecological and relational sphere. These exchanges point back to the dual potential for risk and abundance, another reflection of the high stakes negotiated through the performance of ritual repertories.

Chapter 5 examines abundance, arguing that sound is an important component of producing not only practical resource networks, but also ideals around community and well-being. Songs celebrate those ideals in combination with the sharing of foodways and hospitality. These lead back to the initiating actions of ritual gathering, which, like music, dance, and other components in the repertories, constantly produce and reinforce the aesthetic and conceptual contours of well-being.

A conclusion finally considers what contributions ethnographic listening might offer to discourses of well-being, particularly those that concern popular practices and public health. While not necessarily intended to be prescriptive, the reflections do attempt to provoke new directions in those discourses.

1. Ritual Work in Twenty-First-Century Uganda

From Folk Well-Being to Ex-Colonial Professionalization

The social nature of African healing, particularly ritual healing, is by now a well-rehearsed theme in a vast body of literature that cuts across Africanist ethnography, historiography, and public health scholarship.[1] By comparison, allopathic physicians and clinical systems have expanded their emphasis on patient engagement and social determinants of health relatively more recently.[2] In all these contexts, the social behaviors that shape health and well-being motivate keen interest, often because human behavior proves as challenging to understand and measure as it is formative for health outcomes. Within such an expansive domain, this chapter examines who traditional healing specialists are in southern Uganda by focusing on a common component of their work: they perform music with clients as an important feature of their broader repertories of health-related behaviors and interventions. In other words, people perform music as a form of ritual work within repertories of well-being that reveal sophisticated ways of thinking about illness and wellness.

Examining music as ritual work will mean considering three main questions:

1. What tools do the "things of tradition" provide for Ugandan healers, and how do they understand them relative to their times?
2. What features of the present moment in Uganda's development shape these tools and understandings?
3. How do these tools and the present moment render musical performance both influential and efficacious in Ugandan repertories of well-being?

The first question permeates this entire book. It emerges from the repetitive mention of two phrases by ritual healing specialists: the "work of the ancestors" or other spirits, and "the things of tradition."[3] The things of tradition include ancestral and other patron spirits, the songs that venerate them, other methods of invocation, hospitality for human and other-than-human familiars, bodily practices of possession, other physical practices of spiritual and environmental interaction, bodily and social practices of semiprofessional and professional mediumship, the gathering of spiritual information about specific interventions, the gathering of physical medicines, and methods and modalities of sacrifice and celebration. This inclusive—but not comprehensive—list only begins to introduce the concept, but it establishes some concrete notions of what it means to do ritual work.

Labor histories in the region emphasize the creative sociopolitical power of (largely precolonial) collectives that understood the social basis of health and healing.[4] More recent colonial and postcolonial discourses have imagined that such social processes can be directed from places of administrative objectivity, a top-down model that the professionalization of traditional healing in Uganda since the 1960s reveals to be impossible.[5] On the contrary, because the production of medical knowledge and the reproduction of well-being emerge from social processes, we must look to their most social components—namely the ritual performance of song and work—to learn about them.

What does it mean to be a professional in an ancient tradition of ritual work and folk wellness that is so frequently influenced by a current sociopolitical landscape of international aid and development? This chapter turns from the intersections of agriculture, pastoral life, and spiritual healing toward a more recent pair of discursively linked domains: ritual work and professional healing. The work of ritual healing has, in the twentieth and twenty-first centuries, transformed for some from a commitment to community into a professional endeavor that seeks respect from political authorities and legitimacy through networks of those who perform similar labor. Despite these habits of professionalization, connections to larger, older social structures of mutual aid produce knowledge about health and healing. These links socialize well-being in ways that place the relatively recent shift toward professionalization against the backdrop of Uganda's most durable practices of mutual aid, community participation, and identity.

From (In)Visibility to Audibility: Traditional Healers in the Ugandan Ex-Colony

Recent historical scholarship on East Africa has drawn attention to the importance of "public healing" by analyzing oral narratives about the distant past and relating them to political and social phenomena. Work by Renee Tantala and Neil Kodesh has emphasized hearing oral narratives in order to understand history, a turn away from visual metaphors and toward aural perception, opening new avenues for scholars of indigenous and ritual healing.[6] Kodesh and other scholars of the history of public healing in Uganda offer a partial response to Steven Feierman's concern that at several points in their history public healers have "become invisible."[7] Just as Kodesh and Tantala emphasize utilizing aural perceptions of public healers in order to understand their past, it has become more urgent now than ever for healers and their associations to make their voices heard while remaining somewhat out of view, to interact with public servants while continuing their practices away from other forms of public scrutiny. Their shifts encourage structures of support for organizations that value rather than degrade the possibilities that traditional healers offer.

As David Schoenbrun observes, the powerful spiritual forces on whom *basamize* and *baswezi* call in ritual have undergone a slow redefinition over the last six hundred years; once understood as entities capable of potentially beneficial impact, they are now perceived by many people to be forces with destructive proclivities, even demons.[8] Visual narratives in tabloids like *Red Pepper* and sensationalist images in television news media have exacerbated this process by recycling footage and photographs to cover widely circulating allegations that traditional healing somehow involves bodily mutilation and human sacrifice. It is possible that the impulse to treat traditional healing with this level of suspicion offers a critical commentary on the transformation of a once public resource into a monetized profession. This trend is complicated by overlapping missionary efforts to demonize pre-Christian traditions and likewise by Muslim imams who speak out against practices they characterize as illicit. A shift in emphasis from visibility to audibility for Uganda's indigenous healers seeks correctives for this ongoing deployment and consumption of neocolonial perception.

This analysis neither minimizes the real threat of bodily violence present in some specious ritual practices nor detracts from at least some legitimate reporting on the issue. To be clear, charlatans exist in Uganda just as they do elsewhere. In extreme cases, they promise riches in exchange for severed body parts or human sacrifice. In a series of articles for the Pulitzer Center that drew wide criticism for ethical negligence, Italian journalist Marco Vernaschi documented both the problem of child sacrifice and efforts to eradicate it.[9] Vernaschi made no attempt to highlight the related matter of sensationalist reporting practices, and the Pulitzer Center has since apologized for his contributions to that problem.[10] Dozens of articles by journalists and citizen media alike from 1999 to 2016 detail these tragedies, but even rare retrac-

36   CHAPTER 1

tions like the Pulitzer Center's have done little to mitigate the devastating impact these stories have had on traditional healers. Many such stories simply amplify rumors, and others have later been discredited as fabrications trumped up by overzealous critics of traditional healing.[11] The matter is not as simple as some publications make it appear. The question is not whether all traditional healing practices are either destructive or helpful, but rather how do traditional healers mitigate potentially harmful natural, human, and spiritual power in pursuit of healing and well-being for their communities?

Fraudulent healers raise entirely separate questions that lie beyond the purview of this book, and yet narratives about them definitely affect an ongoing redefinition of healers' powers to manipulate spiritual relationships and human well-being. This impact in turn affects the public perception of healers and a great many decisions that professional healers make regarding the visibility of their practices. For example, some allow photographs and video, others only audio recordings, and still others no electronic documentation of their practices at all. Some invite all into their presence; others carefully define and restrict who may pass beyond the initial threshold of their compounds or their shrines. For a category of people once characterized quite accurately as public healers and who still offer primary health care services to a huge swath of the Ugandan public, these considerations frame their shift toward less visible spaces. The same factors also enliven the focus here on how healers nevertheless remain persistently audible.

Public performances of spirit possession ritual in East Africa predate the colonial encounter by at least four hundred years.[12] Over the past hundred years, the visibility of ritual practitioners in Uganda has undergone major shifts. However, their continuing activities testify to the value that people in this region place on spiritual healing as a form of local knowledge and indigenous scientific practice. Healers' associations and NGOs in contemporary Buganda and Busoga have begun to reshape the public impact of these practices. These groups move local dialectics of wellness into broader discourses on indigenous knowledge and public health.

This recent history emerges from several historical trajectories for *kusamira* practitioners. European explorers and colonial administrators commented on the boisterous public presence of visually distinctive popular healers during the late nineteenth century.[13] After Uganda became a British colony in 1900, administrative policies and Christian missionary work pushed *kusamira* into less public settings. Ritualists appear in colonial-era literature as "secret societies" and "African gypsies," clandestine groups whose activities Europeans conflated with witchcraft.[14] Uganda's 1957 Witchcraft Ordinance made a distinction between the two types of practitioners by excluding "*bona fide* spirit worship or the *bona fide* manufacture, supply, or sale of native medicines" from the definition of witchcraft.[15] This ordinance made little difference in the popular imagination, however: even today, articles in sensationalist print media and websites in Uganda and abroad continue to conflate the two. This coverage is overtly exoticizing and neocolonial in its gaze. One story (in the far-right US outlet *Breitbart*) even used an unrelated image of bare-breasted women covered in white body paint and dancing. The conflation of traditional healing and witchcraft is aimed at linking alleged child sacrifice to politics.[16]

Independence in 1962 eased relatively short-lived colonial legal constraints enough to facilitate the founding of the first healers' associations, but when President Milton Obote abolished traditional kingdoms in Uganda in 1966, many other cultural institutions also suffered. During the 1970s, Idi Amin's regime undermined the budding government support that Obote's administration had encouraged for the fledgling independent nation's health-care system.[17] It was not until the early 1990s that foreign investment and emerging political leadership renewed efforts to foster meaningful health-care sector collaborations with indigenous healers. NGOs that promote traditional medicine have since expanded their activities. Uganda has seen immense growth in the number of publicly recognized local healers, especially those who register with these organizations.

What are healers' motivations for aligning with healers' associations and NGOs during the past two decades? How do the groups affect healers' public influence? How do they link local practices with a broader discourse on the value of indigenous knowledge? As these groups move between government collaborators and critical nongovernmental enterprises, they consciously push for a respectful approach to indigenous knowledge in the health-care system. They encourage shifts from the unwieldy media coverage toward environments in which they can exercise more control over the discourse. Eschewing the negative visibility of media coverage, these associations promote audibility for indigenous healers. They make their voices heard through focused attempts to professionalize indigenous healing according to local definitions of healing practices and through a ubiquitous and recognizable musical repertory for spiritual healing. Their current efforts to be heard are consistent with a tendency in ritual practice to manipulate paths toward healing through song.

Development-era public infrastructures for integrating indigenous knowledge into the national health-care system had antecedents in two broad categories: the NGOs' efforts to raise awareness of indigenous methods, and government-funded initiatives related to plant research. Examples of the latter include efforts to test local plant species for medicinal use as early as 1962 at the Natural Chemotherapeutic Research Laboratory (NCRL), and instruction on indigenous medicine in the Makerere University School of Medicine beginning in 1988.[18] These early pushes to assimilate both plant medicine and local techniques into clinical and hospital systems have yet to give way to robust competing efforts to professionalize indigenous healing in its original context, the healers' shrines (*amassabo*). In the present era of development politics, the dialectical tension between the grassroots-level (and NGO) professionalization of indigenous healing and the government-supported institutional reform continues to shape the social production of well-being in Uganda.

Such tensions prove more complex than any simple binary between NGOs and government ministries, however. Efforts to improve health care in Uganda have involved sophisticated networks of funding, ideas, implementation models, and medical expertise. In this environment, *basawo abekinansi* (indigenous healers) have become interlocutors who still act as primary care providers for many Ugandans. An organization called Uganda n'Eddagala Lyayo (Uganda and Its Medicines) was founded in 1962, the same year that NCRL/NCRI started testing local plants for chemical efficacy. Now joined by many other NGOs, Uganda n'Eddagala Lyayo remains the oldest association of indigenous healers in Uganda today. The healers associated with these organizations define current primary care practices in healers' shrines and in clinics and hospitals. So, even though the government/NGO dialectic gets more complicated, it remains provisionally useful for examining Ugandan health care in these two very different kinds of places: shrines operate in villages and urban spaces alike, and by contrast, cities with sufficient resources and trading centers along major arterial roads have a variety of clinics and hospitals.

Healers' associations promote diverse healing practices and multiple approaches to networking that embrace all kinds of venues for healing. Amid political volatility in the 1960s and 1970s, Uganda n'Eddagala Lyayo continued to grow. The organization made a permanent home at Mengo Social Centre (within walking distance of Makerere University), and by 1991 it claimed to have more than thirty thousand members.[19] Other efforts moved in different directions. The proliferation of healers' associations later in the twentieth century advanced the organizations in both number and focus. Healers organized themselves at the level of subcounty, county, and sometimes district for networking and referral purposes. These local offices sometimes maintain a record of the traditional healers operating within their administrative divisions, but they do not track healing activities; their records are typically both incomplete and inconsistent from one area to the next. A number of national and international organizations have also sprung up to offer healers professional legitimacy through registration with a nationally unified entity. For example, an NGO called Traditional and Modern Health Practitioners

Together against AIDS (THETA, est. 1992) received major start-up funding from Médecins sans Frontières (Doctors without Borders) and the Rockefeller Foundation to train local healers and their communities in HIV/AIDS awareness and prevention. This effort followed broader trends in the NGO sector and community-driven health education that helped Uganda become a model for success in the fight against HIV and AIDS in the 1990s.[20] Other examples include the apparently short-lived Jami-Tiiba Society (based in Nairobi, but with registered healers as far west as the River Nile), the National Council of Traditional Healers and Herbalists Associations (NACOTHA), the Uganda National Integrated Forum of Traditional Health Practitioners, and the Uganda chapter of an international NGO called Promotion des Médecines Traditionnelles (PROMETRA Uganda). NACOTHA began as an organizational rally toward unity for the many healers' associations that sprang up in the 1980s and 1990s, but it has more recently operated as a healers' registry organization in the vein of Uganda n'Eddagala Lyayo. Now both groups behave somewhat like brokers of legitimacy: they have worked to convince the Ministry of Health and the Ministry of Gender, Labour, and Social Development (commonly known as the Ministry of Culture) that healer registries are mutually beneficial for healers and government. So far, however, healers remain ambivalent about registries and directories, often fearing that governmental efforts in this arena will too easily lead to impractical forms of bureaucratic control.

Struggles for Control and Productive Simultaneities in the Ugandan Ex-Colony

The healers associated with these organizations shape current primary care practices in healers' shrines as well as an ever-developing relationship with the national health-care system as imagined by clinics, government ministries, referral hospitals, and universities. Until 2019, the Ugandan government had yet to endorse any organization to register healers in an official capacity.[21] The development of the National Integrated Forum represented a shift in that it sought to bring government, NGO, and healers' voices into a discourse about regulation without necessarily attempting to circumscribe what the consensus body perceived as individual healers' legitimate activities. Unlike government ministries, it operates on the assumption that most healers derive their legitimacy from community trust, not from a certifying authority or governing body. Notably, even when the government moved beyond the National Integrated Forum and NACOTHA to set up an official registering body, passage of the bill took no fewer than six years between initial introduction of a draft bill in 2013 and passage of a revised version in 2019.[22]

In a 1985 article commissioned by the *African Studies Review*, Steven Feierman wrote about public health issues in Africa: "No narrow bureaucratic decree can impose a solution," he asserted. "Health care, like health, is resistant to directed change from above."[23] Some researchers have contended that Uganda's biggest successes in controlling infectious disease, particularly HIV and AIDS, have drawn on culturally sensitive health-care reform, cooperation with indigenous healers, and the use of music for health education.[24] Whereas music definitely serves as a symbol and source of authority among parties vying for influence in the social reproduction of health, estimations of the government's interest in indigenous healers and their contributions (musical or otherwise) have been exaggerated. Just as Feierman suggested, Ugandan officials and international entities attempt to impose decrees or place demands on indigenous healers, especially when doing so is politically expedient, but they find themselves unable to rein in or control the dynamic practices. The African Union, for example, laudably encouraged nations to examine the place of indigenous healing traditions in national health-care systems as part of a "Decade of African Traditional Medicine" between 2001 and 2010.[25] Despite the Ugandan Ministry of Culture's vision of "a culturally vibrant, cohesive and progressive nation," cohesion on this issue remains an elusive goal fraught with multiple, competing agendas.

If one thing is clear, it is that healers regulate themselves and stubbornly resist any kind of government oversight, often fearing that bureaucrats will eventually attempt to prohibit their practices. That concern was baldly on display during a meeting I attended in February 2009. Traditional healers met with the Ugandan Ministries of Health and of Gender, Labor, and Social Development. During discussions on a range of matters relevant to both policy and practice, fears of outright bans on traditional medicine came up frequently.

Professionalization and self-regulation since independence have been marked not only by struggles over political power in African states, but also by the rhetoric and foreign capital influx of international development. Important questions about public health arise here. What does it mean to be a professional indigenous healer in this era? What ambitions shape the language and the actions—including performances—of healers who struggle for control of their practices? What could traditionalists' approaches to the HIV/AIDS pandemic and other pervasive infectious diseases like malaria demonstrate about the efficacy of educational performance and about indigenous approaches to healing and palliative care? Is it possible to separate methodological criticisms of indigenous healing from misplaced neocolonial or theocratic anxieties? These questions reveal a discourse of public healing that reinforces Feierman's dictum: health and health care are social processes by definition. By extension, public healers' most social processes—namely the performance of indigenous healing rituals and the policy wrangling that surrounds them—generate a wealth of knowledge important to a consideration of public health and well-being in Uganda. The central role of performance in Ugandan traditional repertoires of healing praxis renders musical repertories an excellent avenue for understanding a local cultural logic of illness and wellness.

The present study acknowledges the fundamentally social basis of an indigenous repertory for the performance of ritual healing that predates the colonial period by several hundred years. Various attempts at regulation show a progression of struggles to control Uganda's national discourse on traditional medicine. Typical efforts at colonial marginalization gave way to attempts by healers' associations to professionalize the practices and, then, to a stalemate among healers' associations, NGOs, government ministries, and communities. It is not yet clear whether the Ugandan Parliament's 2019 intervention—the passage of the Indigenous and Complementary Medicine Bill—will break or reinforce that stalemate.

Adapting Homi Bhabha's model of a postcolonial Third Space, I theorize the alternating ambivalence and structural violence of opposing voices in this discourse not in terms of the hybrids that Bhabha imagines, but rather as simultaneities somewhat closer to what Anna Lowenhaupt Tsing has called "productive frictions."[26] Uganda's narrative is distinctive, though: a return toward the end of this chapter to the ritual methodologies in *kusamira* and *nswezi* repertories shows how these frictions occur among social actors who, like spirit mediums, often occupy multiple roles. This theoretical motif of the study emerges from a homology between the aesthetics of plurality in *kusamira* and *nswezi* performance—particularly musical heterophony—and the apparent social necessity for various simultaneities in the indigenous well-being of ex-colonial Uganda.

Healers' wariness of government control, together with the rich literature on ritual healing and resistance in Africanist ethnography and historiography, raises theoretical questions for analyzing the performance of healing and the social production of well-being in ex-colonial Uganda. Why have so many efforts from both within and without Uganda's indigenous healing community ultimately fallen short of integrating long-present notions of folk well-being into a system of national health care? What could those behind these efforts learn from those who perform traditional repertoires of well-being? How might a serious consideration of music and healing in the Ugandan context affect national policy and postcolonial theory?

What the rapid proliferation of healers' associations makes clear is that bureaucrats have much to learn from the large number of Ugandans who turn

42 CHAPTER 1

to local traditional healers to provide their primary health-care services.[27] Just as ethnographers and historians gain much from listening to the shift from healers' once public visibility to their current insistence on audibility both in the shrine and in discourses of public healing, and just as communities have long heard drums beating and songs rising from shrines in their villages and urban boroughs, bureaucrats must not turn a deaf ear to the *ŋoma* that have shaped the social reproduction of well-being in this region for hundreds of years. "Those drums are backward," I heard one ritual participant say at a site that had moved from animal-hide drums and horns fashioned from dead ungulates to drum sets, guitars, and amplified voices. "We've developed them."[28] Prior to 2019, the monitoring and regulation discourse among ministries suggested a similar tone. The Indigenous and Complementary Medicine Bill promised new directions, but it remains unclear whether these regulatory norms will work.

Until fuller implementation reveals more, *basamize* and *baswezi* continue to operate in an ex-colonial Third Space.[29] They function as persistent traditionalists who participate in current discourses. Together with the other voices in those discourses, they motivate the present rhetorical move from thinking about postcolonialism to considering the stain of colonial rupture in an ex-colonial context. Their performances of healing repertoires reflect Bhabha's noted "split in the performative present of cultural identification," which he divides between traditionalist "stable system[s] of reference" and "new cultural demands."[30] In critical engagement with Bhabha's suggestion that hybridity is the dominant product of this Third Space, other ethnographers have effectively argued that ritualists employed "mestizo logics" to navigate it.[31] What an ethnomusicology of *kusamira* and *nswezi* performances shows, however, is different: rather than hybridity or mixture, Ugandan traditionalists' repertoires of well-being produce simultaneities, like what Anna Lowenhaupt Tsing has called the "frictions of encounter" between cultural regimes that generate gaps even as they circulate knowledge.[32] Although they might well have begun to seek a mutually agreeable hybrid system, NGOs, healers' associations, and government ministries have thus far been slow to do so.

For the moment, that process of political abrasion remains productive and reproductive of the priorities and systems that produced it in the first place. *Basamize* and *baswezi* remain effective not because they hybridize or syncretize, but most often because they insist on being heard with the amplified force of accessible tradition in Ugandan life. Because they clearly engage both traditionalist and progressive voices (demanding both stable reference and solutions to problems of the moment), they offer opportunities to observe simultaneity, an alternative outcome for the Third Space. The examples pre-

Ritual Work in Uganda 43

sented here reinforce John M. Janzen's assertion that those productions and reproductions constitute discursive and social strategies.[33] In sonic terms, these encounters remain true to their heterophonic musical performances. Performers understand the power of standing between tradition and development in their many forms, between the harmful impact of the bad things they combat and the healing power of the blessings they pursue, between the realm of spirits and the world. For generations, their ability to negotiate those interstices through ritual performance has facilitated their power to manipulate dynamic factors that affect well-being, and the same capacity will continue to reproduce indigenous knowledge systems of illness and wellness for the foreseeable future. Healers' and patients' embrace of simultaneities has constituted an important coping mechanism throughout Uganda's colonial and ex-colonial history of inconsistent public health management.

The Social Basis of Ugandan Health, Past and Present

When asked about the provenance of their healing repertories, *basamize* and *baswezi* frequently respond that their great-great-grandparents taught them these "things of tradition" or simply that they are "of/from the ancestors."[34] Often they report having learned about combinations of medicinal plants or the preparation methods for a specific ailment from either a living relative or an ancestor in a dream. Others gain part of what they learn more directly, from patron spirits who speak to them through their mediums during ritual. Most if not all undergo one or more lengthy apprenticeships with more experienced healers, and frequent rituals offer healers constant opportunities for engagement with what could otherwise be an esoteric body of knowledge. Regardless of modes of transmission, a strong sense of continuity pervades traditions believed to have roots in the distant past, and yet people adapt and change these practices constantly. The result is an accumulative tradition of ritual healing in which people archive medicinal knowledge socially through performative repetition, organize it locally through idiomatic musical iteration, and deploy it according to the needs of specific people and situations.

It will be useful at this point to review the contours of this accumulation, beginning with the conceptualization of illness and wellness. *Kusamira* and *nswezi* practitioners conceive of holistic wellness as crucially dependent on two things: the eradication of bad things (*ebibi*) and the promotion of blessings (*emikisa*). *Ebibi* include such occurrences as physiological illness, misfortune in love or work, pestilence or infestation in crops, animal or human infertility, mental illness, or a spiritual disturbance that manifests in abnormal behavior. Avoiding or eradicating such bad things might be a preemptive act, as in the binding of newborn twins' cast-off umbilical cords

44   CHAPTER 1

to prevent known possibilities for negative spiritual intervention, or it could follow a more diagnostic or therapeutic trajectory. Musical calls for spiritual guidance are common to both approaches.

The eradication of bad things, however, accounts for only half the process; people must also seek blessings, *emikisa*, from patron spirits in order to promote the good life. In both preemptive and diagnostic/therapeutic contexts, adepts consult patron spirits through their mediums after calling them through songs. Beyond these contexts, people use similar methods to call patron spirits for the purpose of offering gratitude for blessings already received. Virtually all such cases share a few common features that require communities to work together to promote positive spiritual relationships.

The social nature of the process helps explain how public healers traditionally operated unlike professionals in any other category.[35] They maintained valuable knowledge for their communities. For example, prayer and song continue to function alongside other offerings to propitiate spirits or simply to make them more welcome. Interventions often involve more formal sacrifices, which can appease angered spirits, remove negative spiritual influences, or convey gratitude for positive relations. Spirits request these sacrifices with a high degree of specificity regarding the number, type, and sometimes even color of animals to be sacrificed, and they might make additional requests for foodstuffs. Invariably, sacrificial offerings get fed to spirits first, then distributed by the spirits—through their mediums—to ritual attendees. As chapters 4 and 5 demonstrate, these exchanges involve a repertory of songs to thank spirits for blessings. Experienced ritualists in the distant past did not share their knowledge of these processes on a pay-for-service basis in the same way that traditional healers sometimes do now. Rather, they did so because it served a communal good. Communities ensured that they shared resources with these healers just as they offered generous gifts of hospitality, food and drink, clothing, and shelter to other human guests or to their patron spirits. Today, healers and guilds of healers operate somewhere between the money economy (which has its own fascinating history entangled with well-being in Uganda and the region), traditional gift economies, and newer forms of developmentalist gift economy.[36] Professionalization has meant that healers often alternate between accepting cash payments or mobile money transfers; trading their services for goods like crops, small animals, or airtime; and sharing in the feasting that so often follows ritual sacrifices. As discussed in chapter 4, these exchanges remain inextricable from ideas about civic duty and ethical participation.

Regardless of the motivations for performing a given ritual or the available means of funding it, people still tend to consult local experts to assist in questions about well-being and ritual proceedings. Traditional healers, now professionals, often serve as primary health-care providers for many

Ugandans. Uganda's Ministry of Health estimates, following the World Health Organization, that the ratio of traditional medical practitioners to population in Uganda is between 1:200 and 1:400, compared with a doctor/patient ratio of 1:18,000.[37] According to PROMETRA, the traditionalists they work with normally train in a series of master/apprentice relationships to become one of five types of healers:

- *ab'empewo* (spiritual healers)
- *abayunzi* (bonesetters)
- *abazaalisa* or *abamuleerwa* (birth attendants)
- *ab'emitwe* (mentalists)
- *abatabuzi b'eddagala* (herbalists)

In practice, most professional healers use some personalized combination of these five skill sets, often specializing in one or two. The social habits of ritual gathering and performance render boundaries between the five domains porous. During field research across nearly fifty communities in southern Uganda, I encountered only two healers who did not have at least some experience with spiritual healing and its associated rituals: one in Buganda and one in Busoga. Some knowledge of plant medicine was also ubiquitous: virtually every healer involved in this study had some experience with plant medicine, and nearly all understand plants to have specific, powerful associations with patron spirits.

These two pillars of indigenous medicine in Uganda—herbalism and spiritualism—are both inherently social *and* ecological. Spirits occupy social and conceptual/ecological/cosmological space. If they are ancestral spirits, they are socially linked to their devotees through kinship ties and through lands of common residence, affinity, or inheritance.[38] Social relations that people establish and maintain with nature spirits or "working" spirits through ritual resemble other social interactions; people greet one another, exchange gifts, enter into other reciprocal social transactions, and generally try to maintain positive relations. They often occupy physical spaces within family compounds that integrate symbolic elements of the surrounding landscape and involve families and nearby social groups in cooperative construction. The production and transmission of esoteric knowledge about medicinal plants follows social pathways that reflect human and spiritual networks. These are often forged along biological grandparent/grandchild lines and then replicated through spiritual grandparent/grandchild relationships (though as I have noted elsewhere, sometimes the spirit/medium relationship can be cast in marital terms).[39] Like other elements of ritual life, such relationships are frequently associated with common clan membership, even if the knowledge transmitted remains applicable well beyond the confines of a shared totem.

"Living Positively": Indigenous Music and Medicine in the Time of AIDS

One challenge that moves far past the boundaries of kinship—and that Ugandan ritual healers frequently encounter—is the necessity for palliative care of clients living with HIV and AIDS. Organizations that train or retrain traditional healers to deal with HIV/AIDS have proliferated rapidly, and their varying approaches to this training offer one indication of how they perceive socially acquired knowledge of local plant medicine and indigenous spirits: the more committed these organizations are to clinical medicine, the less cachet local knowledge of traditional medicine seems to hold for them (even if such knowledge can mean real, measurable improvements in patient care and quality of life). And yet, HIV/AIDS treatment is one of the most common points of intersection among medical professionals in clinics and hospitals, rural health workers (who usually work for NGOs), and traditional healers with varying affiliations. The act (on the part of a traditional healer) of referring a patient to the hospital for treatment neither renders the healer's knowledge useless nor severs their therapeutic relationship with the HIV-positive client. On the contrary, the management of such a widespread affliction has become both a key area for examining the mechanisms of development and a prime indicator that health and wellness are necessarily social endeavors. This may be particularly true in a context in which monetary resources are scarce but natural and human resources are abundant.

Evidence of these claims about social well-being in this context can be found in two main forms: the "edutainment" that transmits information about HIV and AIDS to public audiences, and the rubric of "living positively" that characterizes palliative management of the disease. The latter in particular points up the role of what John M. Janzen calls "therapy management groups."[40] These networks incorporate healers, patients, families, and communities to foster a transformation, as Lotte Meinert writes, "from biological survival to living a life."[41] Noting their social, communicative, and expressive functions, Gregory Barz and Judah Cohen have called such networks part of a "culture of AIDS in Africa."[42]

In his 2006 monograph *Singing for Life*, Barz highlighted the value of song and musical drama as entertaining educational offerings in Uganda's battle with HIV/AIDS. "The great progress of the system adopted in Uganda for AIDS prevention," wrote Barz, "was largely due to the effective transmission of medical and social information through well-established traditional social networks."[43] His study emphasized performance among NGOs, women's groups, and other grassroots organizations. Writing a few years after Barz,

Daniel Reed identified "edutainment" as a common feature of development-era parlance in Africa.[44] Both Barz and Reed demonstrate that this entertaining deployment of educational outreach says as much about African communities and their expressive cultures as it does about the influence of NGOs and international aid organizations. For our purposes, these performances reaffirm what Steven Feierman and John M. Janzen had proclaimed decades earlier: health and health care—in Africa especially—are fundamentally social processes.[45] As Fraser McNeill and Deborah James show, some organizations have been highly effective in using local understandings of illness to mobilize peoples' responses to AIDS and HIV.[46] An examination of those local understandings promises deeper insight into what motivates patients and healers for the ritual work embedded in repertoires of well-being.

This book aims to show how these social processes of well-being have been performed through *kusamira* and *nswezi* musical repertoires. My field research on those performances, however, revealed something more complex than just the social components: the other-than-human aspects (what in other contexts we might call ecological or natural and spiritual phenomena) loom large here. The remainder of this chapter, then, has two goals:

- to demonstrate how those repertoires and their overlapping complexities remain relevant to current discourses of development
- to examine why participants in those discourses—particularly those in the public sector and NGO circles concerned with HIV/AIDS—should listen carefully to those who perform repertoires of traditional healing

Beyond their important social interventions, these practitioners provide symptomatic relief through plant medicines in tandem with forms of social and spiritual support that comprise a continuum of diagnosis, therapeutic intervention, and palliation. The palliative approach to HIV/AIDS known as "living positively" emerges from a much older tendency toward positive intervention among *basamize* and *baswezi*. A strong tradition of scholarship on "cults of affliction" casts African healing first as a means of coping with affliction and then as a form of resistance. The affliction model grew out of an interpretive anthropological tradition focused on ritual structure and rites of passage.[47] These were particularly important analytic steps, as Janzen observes, for unpacking the nuances of ritual structure and later, in Max Gluckman's work, differentiating ritual and societal roles.[48] As important as this scholarly trend has been to the study of ritual and healing, it also creates potential for binaries that betray the complexity of ritual traditions. Affliction literature may offer sophisticated understandings of the structural elements of ritual, but it still casts ritual performance as motivated by the mitigation of

48   CHAPTER 1

affliction. A related body of literature on religion and resistance offered some
important social referents to triangulate illness and wellness with historically
grounded elements of social structure, with a third stream offering interesting
semiotic possibilities.[49] This is not a case for discarding the scholarship on
affliction or resistance. It is rather an attempt to ground a critique of them
in the notion that ritual performs highly sophisticated, culturally informed
versions of well-being just as it does affliction and resistance.

In the sections below, then, I turn to a notion of indigenous well-being in
this present era of international development. Through a case study of one
particularly impressive effort to professionalize Ugandan indigenous healing,
I demonstrate the social processes of generating and transmitting knowledge
about health and health care and substantiate the claim that these processes
emphasize well-being in an overtly positive manner. Both the processes and
their emphasis on well-being reveal a strong sense of agency among healers
and their clients: these are not African victims of circumstance, affliction, or
marginalization, but rather self-determined healers and patients taking control
of their well-being and their quality of life. Barz and Reed have already thoroughly documented edutainment and other support repertories that surround
the notion of "living positively." Here, I examine the integration of a range of
traditional medical services into a culturally sensitive training module directed
by a Ugandan healer with both biomedical and traditional expertise.

New Struggles for Control in Uganda

As noted above, Uganda has a rich history of professionalization among
healers' associations designed for various, sometimes competing purposes
relative to indigenous medical knowledge. The Uganda chapter of the international NGO PROMETRA espouses a model unique among all these
organizations. Whereas Uganda n'Eddagala Lyayo and NACOTHA register
healers and broker legitimacy, the National Integrated Forum facilitates a
national discourse on traditional medicine, and smaller NGOs like THETA
focus on specific diseases, PROMETRA combines nearly all these activities under the umbrella of a holistic and respectful approach to the active
development of traditional medicine. Country director Dr. Yahaya Sekagya
explained in an interview his transition from a previous position at THETA
to his work with PROMETRA:

> They train traditional healers in Western diagnosis. I didn't like that, but I didn't
> know how to improve it as a model until I trained as a healer. Then I started
> with PROMETRA Uganda. You see, there's no system in place for traditional

healers, so it took time to find out what was right, how to approach traditional medicine respectfully.[50]

Sekagya was particularly uncomfortable with the way that THETA traded on healers' shortcomings to attract funding from large international donors like Médecins sans Frontières and the Rockefeller Foundation. Recognizing that healers of all kinds must continually pursue professional development, he wanted an organizational model that built on indigenous healers' strengths rather than exploiting their weaknesses.

Prior to training as a traditional healer, Dr. Sekagya had trained as a dental surgeon, so by the time we met, he was well acquainted with professional development needs among both allopathic and naturopathic physicians in Uganda. He helped get PROMETRA's Uganda chapter registered as an NGO in 2001. PROMETRA Uganda began a comprehensive program "to promote traditional medical knowledge and practices for improved health through mutual cooperation amongst health systems."[51] For Dr. Sekagya, this mission appropriately emphasized the potential for indigenous healers to cooperate more fully, and ultimately to have their contributions valued as much as those made by doctors trained in medical schools. It is a discrete focus from PROMETRA International's mission "to preserve African traditional medicine, culture and indigenous science through research, education, development, advocacy and service; and to improve the health and well-being of Africa and the Diaspora." PROMETRA Uganda continues to work through a peer education model that—even as it promotes collaboration among physicians of all types—favors local discourses of illness and wellness over governmental and other forms of hierarchically controlled medical systems in its pursuit of indigenous practice and innovation.

According to its staff, PROMETRA's activities involve four interdependent areas of engagement:

- organization and mobilization of traditional healers
- training and networking
- treatment and care
- research and information management

These scalable efforts began modestly, but in its first fifteen years, PROMETRA Uganda engaged nearly twelve hundred indigenous healers in peer education and professional development. It has managed this growth with support from PROMETRA International, whose funding partners include the Ford Foundation, the Global Health Council, the UN Development Program, the US Agency for International Development, and the Kellogg Foundation.

In contrast to entities like district offices, Uganda n'Eddagala Lyayo, and NACOTHA, which—prior to the 2019 establishment of the National Council of Indigenous and Complementary Medicine Practitioners—registered healers in attempts to broker their legitimacy, PROMETRA Uganda is more interested in fostering grassroots mobilization efforts. The goodwill and voluntary participation of over a thousand traditional healers facilitated the publication of what PROMETRA claimed as early as 2004 to be the country's most comprehensive district healer directory.[52] As of 2021, no ministry, NGO, or individual has contradicted that claim, which typifies other indicators of PROMETRA's effective approach to engaging traditional healers in development discourse. At the local level, PROMETRA organized healers from Mpigi District's sixteen subcounties to form the Buyijja Traditional Healers' Association, which has become the anchor constituency for most of PROMETRA's other areas of healer and patient engagement. More broadly, it has involved some of the same healers in national and international discourses on traditional medicine.

PROMETRA's grassroots approach to comprehensive integration of traditional medicine into the public health sector has produced some suspicion regarding governmental and organizational attempts to control healers' activities. Sekagya's reactions to would-be power brokers illustrates his perspective clearly. For example, one day a messenger from the Ministry of Gender, Labour, and Social Development (Ministry of Culture) entered the PROMETRA offices in suburban Kampala. After handing Sekagya ten copies of the contemporaneously published National Culture Policy, he produced a summons from the minister of culture. PROMETRA was instructed to send a representative to a meeting of healers' associations, heads of Buganda's clans, and representatives from the army and police to address issues of healer regulation. Sekagya's brief exchange with the messenger from the Ministry of Culture follows.

> *"Nearly ten years ago," Sekagya explained, "the [African Union] began their 'Decade for African Traditional Medicine.' Now we are entering into the tenth year, and what has Uganda done? They're responding now to a crisis, and if we respond in that way, we cannot be principled. Where was the government for this whole decade?"*
>
> *"The problem," replied the man from the Ministry of Culture, "people are not working together. Healers/herbalists, the Ministry of Health, and the Ministry of Culture. We have to work together, those three, and this might be the beginning of another ten-year process."*
>
> *"If you're asking us to come together on something [for which] the healers don't even know where they fall, won't you bring us more havoc?"*

A well-rehearsed ministerial response echoed the tone of the minister's summons. "You, the ones who have been in the field with untarnished records," he said, "will be the ones to help us sort out who are the bad ones and who are the genuine traditional healers and herbalists."

The meeting was supposed to be one week later, but even after the ministry's in-person delivery of invitations, it made a late-breaking schedule change. When it finally happened in February 2009, the gathering brought together Sekagya's worries, the minister's good intentions, and the ministry's poorly organized efforts to approach these problems. Attendees argued for several hours before the deputy minister recommended the formation of a government-run umbrella registration of individual healers, even those already associated with a reputable NGO. She left the group with a strong impression that this decision was probably made before the meeting ever happened. She made no meaningful attempt to respond to concerns raised in the meeting. Perhaps the most obvious of these was that the existing National Integrated Forum and NACOTHA could have been obvious partners in such a process since they had both already undertaken healer registry efforts. Given the broad organizational and individual healer engagement in the healer directory, and its direct involvement in convening the National Integrated Forum, PROMETRA Uganda might well have been a logical third partner. However, Dr. Sekagya's responses to the ministry were just one indicator of PROMETRA's disinterest in the ministry's hasty tactics. Sekagya predicted that this impasse would arise: he did send a representative, but he refused to spend his own time going to hear a ministerial decree that he apparently knew would have no realistic hope for timely follow-through.[53]

Sekagya likewise lamented other attempts to control healers. Whether based on administrative divisions or local healers' associations, international NGOs or cults of personality, the process of gathering people in order to control their actions was and is, for Sekagya, an inexcusable denial of the dynamic nature of Uganda's healing traditions. His perspective typifies the paradox of fierce independence and inevitable interdependence of *basamize* and *baswezi*. It also reinforces Steven Feierman's observation that bureaucratic decrees have little impact on the fundamentally social processes of health and healing.

PROMETRA's day-to-day operations offer a window into how those processes currently look. The description below draws on direct observation that began in 2008, and the systems remained consistent through my most recent site visits in 2015. A partnership with the Buyijja Traditional Healers' Association, PROMETRA's Institute of Traditional Medicine includes large outdoor classroom spaces and test plots for herbal medicines under the canopy of a lush forest (see figures 5 and 6).

The institute has become the locus of training, networking, treatment, and care activities. Located near Buyijja village in Buwama subcounty about forty miles southwest of Kampala, this facility fosters the kinds of master/apprentice relationships that have historically characterized indigenous healing in this region, but on a much larger scale. The training program gives novice and intermediate practitioners access to experienced healers two days a week for three years. In the first year, healers learn over four hundred discrete medicinal plant species. The second year consists of anatomy, physiology, disease etiology, and therapy. In the third year and beyond, each healer specializes in one of the previously mentioned five areas: spiritual healing, bonesetting, labor and delivery, mental illness, or herbal medicines. By building its training program around a local taxonomy of healers and their practices, rather than around imported terms and practices of diagnosis, PROMETRA Uganda makes contemporary processes of development culturally legible to a growing population of practicing healers, relevant to them as professionals, and respectful of their existing practices. Dr. Sekagya and the organization maintain that any training module founded on the devaluation of indigenous medicine will be less sustainable than a model that builds on local strengths. Moreover, this locally relevant model also endows PROMETRA Uganda with the organizational capacity and focus for enormous impact not only on local clients, but also on doctors, clinics, hospitals, and international funding agencies.

In Buyijja, PROMETRA's healers and healers-in-training provide a weekly clinic offering traditional medicine to nearby clients. While this formal clinic happens on Wednesday when the healers gather for training, the production of plant medicine and the presence of at least some healers continues through the rest of the week. The constant activity of the facility is important: illness knows no regular schedule, so an iron-deficient pregnant woman, someone seeking a plant-based antidiarrheal compound, or a child with malaria can seek care without having to make the journey to Kampala. That model of proximity aligns with the traditional development of local popular healers: just like similar healers in other developing economies, these remain the most widely available, convenient, and cost-effective primary care providers for a majority of Uganda's rural population.[54]

FIGURE 5. A forested classroom at PROMETRA Uganda's Institute of Traditional Medicine. Photograph by the author.

FIGURE 6. A test plot for medicinal plants at PROMETRA Uganda's Institute of Traditional Medicine. Photograph by the author.

54   CHAPTER 1

Ritual Musicking as Ritual Work

Training days often end with music and dance activities that address the concerns of people living with HIV/AIDS, whom PROMETRA Uganda staff refer to as PLWHAs or "people living positively." Often these same clients will arrive along with several healers on the Tuesday evenings before training days for similar activities, which staff and clients call "HOPE" activities.[55] A wide range of smaller organizations feature both drama troupe edutainers and ritual practitioners, often with personnel that overlap as they do for PROMETRA Uganda. In contrasting cases like the Lubowa Traditional Healers' Association or the Jjajja Ndawula Community, the performers coalesce around a particular spirit and its medium. They can represent a local group of healers in the area, as with the Bugiri District Healers' Association or many of the groups that Barz mentions.[56] PROMETRA Uganda stands out among these on the strength of its comprehensive, respectful approach to mobilizing healers, training, treatment, and research.

On the surface, PROMETRA Uganda resembles some other NGOs in at least one way: it has a music, dance, and drama (MDD) troupe that performs didactic skits to entertain and inform audiences on a range of health and wellness issues. As with their peer groups, many members of the troupe are living with AIDS. They openly disclose their status in service of edutainment, which the organization uses as one of several HOPE activities. However, these didactic performance activities differ significantly from those of their Ugandan peer groups. As Barz has shown, the usual contexts for these performances include regular organizational meetings and events, annual events focused on particular challenges like HIV/AIDS, and grassroots efforts to reach local communities via schools and public gatherings. This last, highly localized type of performance might well be closest to its *kusamira* and *nswezi* roots, but again, PROMETRA Uganda staff take a different approach. For example, staff member Kasirye "Moto Man" Ahmed produces music videos with this kind of material. One distinctive video features images of healers clad in traditional garb as Moto Man sings about "my shield," a coded multiple entendre referring to prophylactics, antiretroviral drugs, and plant-based therapies.[57] More overtly, the video addresses a lack of investment in traditional ways and encourages the protection of Kiganda culture.

Even when PROMETRA Uganda's performances do resemble grassroots efforts by other organizations and *kusamira* rituals of old, they carry new significance in the training-site context. Their MDD troupe composes songs and creates performances not only to educate community audiences, but also to advocate for sustainable conservation practices and respectful incorpora-

Ritual Work in Uganda 55

tion of traditional medicine into clinical health care. In these performances (as in Moto Man's video imagery), sound, clothing, and gesture become emblematic of *kusamira* tradition; these indices encourage respect for indigenous repertories of medicinal and therapeutic practice.

Membership in the MDD troupe includes many diviners and other spiritualists of PROMETRA Uganda. These groups spend more time at the field training site than any of their peers. The *basamize* spiritualists frequently meet in the evenings prior to peer training days to perform *kusamira* rituals and to serve the needs of the local community. Nearly every week, the MDD troupe stays to rehearse after everyone else has gone for evening tea. On several occasions, its members stayed so long to rehearse that they nearly missed their ride from the institute: I ran with the troupe, instruments in tow, to catch up with the lorry that transports healers back to the taxi stages where they hail public transport back home. Their Tuesday evening gatherings frequently involve opening an *okwaza* (spiritual inquiry) into physiological or psychological problems. One of the most common types of *kusamira* ritual, *okwaza*, serves as an important way to train people who come to the organization as novice and intermediate spiritualists. I will return to a specific diagnostic inquiry of the ritual in chapter 3.

The focus for the moment remains on a song that those same elders sang frequently at PROMETRA and that other healers sang frequently elsewhere: "Nsula-nkola" (I spend the nights working). Common to Kiganda and Kisoga healing repertories, the song celebrates the pursuit of well-being and the good life through ritual work, broadly construed. "I spend the night working; I work with spirits," goes the chorus. At one of PROMETRA's Tuesday night gatherings, this chorus of ritual determination accompanied one medium's closest moment to the desired outcome: her first possession experience. Among the many forms of ritual labor, this too is work. The spirit Magobwe meanwhile shifted shape by slithering around on the floor as the animal in which he often moves, a python. This action assumed the appearance of his medium, Nalugya Hellen, wriggling around on the floor on her stomach with arms at her sides. Like other demands of mediumship, her embodiment of Magobwe constituted a rather demanding and exhausting kind of ritual work.

On another occasion, some 250 km (155 mi.) away in a place in Busoga called Munamaizi, mediums and other ritual specialists sang this very same song—"I spend the night working; I work with spirits"—in reference to a protracted, multiday series of rituals surrounding the dwellings they were building for spirits who had been either lost or too-long neglected by the community (see figure 7). In that context, the work mentioned in the song

FIGURE 7. Small houses under construction for spirits at Munamaizi. Photograph by the author.

likewise referred to a broad range of ritual tasks from calling and appeasing spirits to building them houses. The juxtaposition of these two performances joins disparate forms of ritual work in useful ways. At Munamaizi, a team built new homes for a variety of spirits and planted barkcloth and banana trees in front of those houses just as traditionalists across Buganda and Busoga do for newly wed or housed humans (see figure 8). The intention here is that barkcloth clothes the inhabitants of the dwelling and the *matooke* bananas feed them. The same cloth clad Magobwe when he occupied his medium at PROMETRA Uganda's Institute of Traditional Medicine, just as it does spirits and mediums across both regions for a wide variety of ritual work.

These two performances of a song built around the phrase "I spend the night working" (*nsula-nkola*) offer audiovisual indices for the many and widely varied things implied by musical references to ritual work. It is a category of labor that ranges from the particulars of performing ritual to complex navigations of ex-colonial discourse. It also encompasses social action that will shape the next generation of healers and their organizations, of clans and their patron spirits, of people and their communities. The tune's insistent, duple meter and repetitive chorus also highlight the perpetual na-

FIGURE 8. Newly constructed houses for spirits at Munamaizi with barkcloth and banana trees planted nearby. Photograph by the author.

ture of said work: it goes on day and night, never finished, constantly adapting to new dynamics.

Conclusion

This chapter has begun to show how people in southern Uganda perform music as a form of ritual work. It has argued that music operates within broader repertoires of well-being that exhibit sophisticated ways of thinking about illness and wellness. Beginning with the wide range of activities that constitute ritual work, I have outlined how such work engages with both traditional points of reference that practitioners regard as stable and new cultural demands wrought by a prevailing developmentalist politics of the Ugandan ex-colony. That analysis demands consideration of the defining affliction of the late twentieth and early twenty-first centuries: HIV/AIDS. The traditional healers who offer palliative care to people "living positively" distill with urgency the same issues that these repertoires raise through their intersections with a much broader range of physiological, psychological, social, and spiritual challenges.

The dynamics of interaction among patients and healers in the twenty-first century motivate forms of ritual work that are simultaneously consistent with a long tradition of mutual aid, aligned with accessible, local, popular health care in the region, and mutable when necessary to suit immediate priorities. The song "Nsula-nkola" highlights the perpetual character of *kusamira* and *nswezi* traditions as both ever present and constantly adaptable. The song evokes a sense of just how tenacious their associated repertories have been and continue to be. Later chapters will return to flesh out this theme and the multiple resonances of ritual work. The next chapter deals with a complex ecology of well-being that informs and motivates various kinds of ritual work, while chapter 3 describes the venues for ritual work, as well as its personnel and its products. In short, the work of the spirits and the things of tradition permeate virtually every part of this study. They point up human actions that produce repertories of well-being at the nexus of human agency and contextual circumstance.

2. Ecologies of Well-Being

Hearing the World through Ritual Repertories

The preceding chapter shows how healers in southern Uganda work at the intersection of several domains to address spiritual and physiological well-being through music, plant medicine, and propitious relationships with patron spirits. This chapter examines how the repertories they use for this work help *basamize* and *baswezi* manage ecologies of well-being. Healing repertories, used interchangeably here with repertories of well-being, include all the behaviors involved in fostering and maintaining well-being, including musical behaviors. These Ugandan repertories of both practice and song help define such ecologies more expansively than ecologists might, including not only physical domains of flora and fauna, but also their underlying and closely linked spiritual features. Healers' efforts to bind and unbind, to contain and distribute resources according to their clients' needs, reflect ecologies inextricable from the plants, animals, and spiritual influences that surround their homes, shrines, compounds, and communities. Anthropologist Marilyn Strathern has articulated an "implicit analogy between an individual's relationship to society on the one hand and an organism's relationship to its environment on the other."[1] Kiganda and Kisoga repertories of well-being merge these domains to elucidate how *basamize* and *baswezi* understand the world around them and their place in it. Ontologies of ritual healing—like the repertories they inform—link people with other people, with powerful plant medicines, with equally powerful animal and spiritual forces, and with the places where these powers dwell. Repertories of well-being across both regions invite the influence of these powers, attempting to manipulate them, to incorporate them into human bodily and spiritual substance, and to negotiate their influence on human life.

60   CHAPTER 2

As Henny Blokland has observed, studies of *ŋoma* traditions should be wary of exchanging a preoccupation with trance and possession for an equally arbitrary preoccupation with healing and therapeutics. She argues that the all-encompassing symbol of *ŋoma* traditions is neither the medium nor the song, but rather the drum. Blokland hastens to add that while the drum holds potential for overcoming adversity, it remains flexible enough to accommodate other purposes. This chapter and this book align with Blokland in proposing that it is "the drum around which people unite and which proclaims their unity to the world around them."[2] This analytic turn supports a broadening of prior concerns with healing toward understanding how healing repertories participate in larger projects of well-being. Here the drum, personified, serves as a womb that gestates and reproduces society, as a container of powerful medicines to overcome adversity and reproduce knowledge about well-being. As we will see, it is also homologous to the ceramic vase that holds the fermentation starter for home brew and to the cooking pot used to prepare the sustaining food of ritual. Above all, the drum is an ontological tool to make sense of a complex world.

Situating what might otherwise be characterized as ontological or epistemological matters in the domain of ecology challenges ex-colonial norms in Uganda and elsewhere in Africa. These models too easily collapse the rich diversity of healing repertories into a single, convenient container: if critics, champions, and casual observers of traditional medicine can all agree on the value of their expertise as herbalists, somehow their practices seem to find broader legitimacy with all. As in the previous chapter on healers' work, I have lamented elsewhere that this conflation of discrete domains within repertories of healing has a flattening impact.[3] What of the value of bonesetting or pain relief? Of time-honored birthing practices that have long supported Uganda's high live birth rate, often far from the reach of clinicians and hospitalists? How about the counseling or pastoral care so often lauded by communities who depend on their priests, imams, and rabbis? Colonial and ex-colonial habits taught too many people to ignore the similar work that public healers were performing and to deny that it sometimes holds even greater potential social value because it affects more people. Repertories of well-being are not some kind of panacea, but they do offer a remarkably flexible suite of expertise that Ugandan specialists combine and use to extraordinary effect. Part of that value emerges through the capacity of the repertories to weave meaning, reciprocity, and catharsis from seemingly disparate, sometimes chaotically interacting domains.

Demonstrating this impact demands a consideration of two things: the context in which healers bind bad things and unbind blessings, and the

Ecologies of Well-Being   61

stakes of their work. Because these bad things can cause everything from minor physical irritations and social problems to major, disruptive, even widespread catastrophic afflictions, the stakes range from quality of life to no less than life and death. The context that accounts for this range broadens from a single organism to the world of variables that affect its life, creating a thorny analytic problem: where does it make sense to begin accounting for something so expansive as an ecology of well-being? One of the most common songs and several excerpts from others across both Kiganda *kusamira* and Kisoga *nswezi* repertories show how performances situate humans and other-than-human animal and spirit familiars in an ecology of well-being. The songs demonstrate healers' efforts to bind bad things and unbind blessings, all while consciously linking interdependent domains:

- people with other people
- people with the land and plants that feed and heal them
- people with animals
- people with spirits, who interact with people through animals, plants, and other people

The result is a snapshot of repertories that manipulate environments of risk and abundance, danger and trust, dearth and wealth, drought and rain, and hunger and feasting. These circumstances abound in localized Kiganda and Kisoga ecologies of well-being.

Invoking the Twins

Kiganda notions of twinship distill the ever-present duality of abundance and risk that energizes these ecologies. The ubiquity of twin songs offers a frame for how twins link to clanship and totem, for how kinship domains link to the ecological homes of animal familiars, and for how plant medicines come from those places. One ubiquitous twin song articulates that frame and its terms, but it does so in somewhat opaque language that begs analysis. It indexes the ecological context in focus here, connecting it directly to the Kiganda kingship via the *lubiri* (royal enclosure) and therefore to a royalist construction of ethnicity.

In Buganda, twin songs often begin by invoking the royal twins, a multivalent reference to the following twin pairs:

- *lubaale* spirits named Kiwanuka and Musoke, who are associated with lightning/thunderstorms and rainbows, respectively
- *misambwa* spirits Mayanja and Magobwe, who move through leopard and python animal familiars, respectively

- human twin births
- spiritual twins of humans

The first song examined here, "Ssewasswa," hits the last three of these four marks, and in some performances it names Kiwanuka and Musoke in the solo verse motifs as well.

The importance of twins derives from a belief in Kiganda ontology that all human beings come into the world with physical evidence of their attachment to a spiritual twin: it is inscribed on human infants via umbilical attachment to the placenta. People understand that the umbilical cord has a physiological purpose during human gestation, but *basamize* imbue it with another meaning: it offers a physical manifestation for an overlapping spiritual attachment. Twins complicate this ontology of twoness because instead of a person and a spirit—or a person and an other-than-human wraith, much like what Djibril Tamsir Niane describes in his retelling of the West African *Sundiata* epic—the parents produce two physical human persons.[4] When human twins are born, each comes into the world with its own umbilicus, but traditionally, Kiganda families treat this situation as both special and potentially dangerous. The parents and the children receive special names, which elders typically bestow on them through a ritual called *okuzina abalongo* (dancing the twins) or *okusiba abalongo* (tying the twins), which involves binding and mitigating their potential for danger (see table 1 for a list of the twin-related names).

The term *balongo* (twin) could have been a reference to a husband's sexual prowess. Author and folklorist Waalabyeki Magoba explains:

> Of all wild animals, that which the Baganda fear most is a leopard, *engo* in Luganda. In olden days the birth of twins was a very rare occurrence (in fact this was true up to the '60s; when my parents introduced twins it was a very big deal in and around the entire Kakiri subcounty and in our extended family). A father of twins was therefore likened to *engo* in his sexual "fierceness." The mother of twins' friends teased her husband like this: "O! O! Balo ngo!" [i.e.] "O my Lord, your husband is but a leopard!" From *balo ngo* we derived the word *balongo*. Then the father of twins was referred to as Ssaalongo and their mother Nnaalongo.[5]

This explanation is consistent with the song's reference to Mayanja, a spirit whose animal familiar is a leopard. Magoba adds that *ssa* and *nna* are male and female gender indicators, respectively, though they can also be deployed as monikers of respect. As the infinitive verb *okusiba* suggests, the purpose of twin tying is to bind the negative potential caused by the physical birth of two human beings; the ritual produces a power object from the twins' umbilical cords that becomes the physical locus of a family's power to restrict such potential (see figure 9).

Ecologies of Well-Being

FIGURE 9. The *balongo* power object, containing umbilical cords from the twins, encircles offerings of medicinal plants and money. Photograph by the author.

Ritual actions of binding almost always open other possibilities. Twin tying and twin naming celebrate the procreative power of their parents and acknowledges the children as manifestations of that power. While the ritual restricts the spiritual danger inherent in the birth of twins, it also initiates the twins and their parents into a powerful category of people, opening their pathways to the spiritual blessings associated with the careful handling of twinship.[6]

Because twin songs invoke the power of twins and their families, and by extension the power of archetypical twin spirits like Mayanja and Magobwe or Kiwanuka and Musoke, *basamize* sing them in pairs to begin virtually every Kiganda *kusamira* event. *Basamize* and other Baganda likewise use them to begin some other high-profile public events. For example, an April 2009 village meeting at Kookola involving village, subcounty, and county chiefs and the minister of culture for Buganda Kingdom began with the widely celebrated traditional musician Nakayima singing four twin songs. The songs index not only prominent features of the traditional spirit pantheon, but also the immediate geographic environment and the broader Kiganda ontology. Ideas about the efficacy of healing practices draw explanatory power from all three of these categories. The songs therefore establish the symbolic

64　　　　　　　　　CHAPTER 2

TABLE 1. Kiganda Twin, Sibling, and Parent Names

Male	Female
Ssaalongo: father of twins	Nnaalongo: mother of twins
Kigongo: immediate elder sibling of twins[1]	Kigongo: immediate elder sibling of twins[1]
Wasswa: firstborn twin	Babirye: firstborn twin[2]
Kato: second-born twin	Nakato: second-born twin
Kizza: immediate younger sibling of twins	Kizza: immediate younger sibling of twins
Kamya: immediate younger brother of Kizza	Nakamya: immediate younger sister of Kizza
Kaggwa: immediate younger brother of Kamya/Nakamya	Nakaggwa: immediate younger sister of Kamya/Nakamya
Kityo: immediate younger brother of Kaggwa/Nakaggwa	Nakityo: immediate younger sister of Kaggwa/Nakaggwa
Kitooke: immediate younger brother of Kityo/Nakityo	Kiteerera or Nansukusa: immediate younger sister of Kityo/Nakityo[3]

Note: This table was developed in consultation with Waalabyeki Magoba.

1. Literally "big back," from the Luganda noun *omugongo* (back), as in the sibling who carries the twins on his/her back. So goes the Luganda proverb *Kigongo kirungi ekiweeka abalongo* (the big back is good/strong/blessed that carries the twins).

2. This word resembles the term for two people, *babiri*, as if to denote in literal terms that she is not one, but two, and thus the first of two.

3. According to Magoba, some families prefer Nansukusa because Kiteerera refers to a peripheral part of the banana grove where parents and caretakers dump the twins' feces. He adds that Kitooke can also be construed as a euphemism for Kiteerera.

atmosphere within which Baganda articulate and understand so many of their cultural categories for spiritual life and well-being.

The selections that follow here represent only a small portion of a repertory that encompasses ideas about twinship in particular, human reproduction more generally, and the social reproduction of well-being writ large. Baganda specialists performed some of the most common twin songs often enough for me to generate more than ten recordings of each. Basoga have their own twinship repertory, but they also sing the Luganda twin songs regularly. This observation reveals two important features of twinship songs in southern Uganda. First, the vast repertory and its expansive contours continue to shift both within Buganda and in its neighboring regions. Second, because twinship in both Buganda and Busoga exists as part of a larger cultural logic surrounding social reproduction, its discrete formations nevertheless overlap and interact, just as these regions' languages and their speakers do.

Ssewasswa: Performing Idioms of Risk and Abundance

The term "Ssewasswa" distills a vast cultural index into a single praise epithet for virtually all twins, human and spiritual. It parses as follows:

Sse-	a prefix for something powerfully male or socially elevated; sometimes articulated in gendered opposition to *nna-*, though both prefixes carry connotations of respect
Wasswa	the Kiganda name for the firstborn twin if male

The epithet's primary meaning in this song is an honorific reference to the father of twins, but as with so many praise names and other song lyrics, its additional associations are myriad. Its direct translation above reveals a reference to the firstborn child of twins if that child is male. One possibility for the use of a male-gendered name here rather than a female firstborn twin name could be that more male babies than female babies die in the womb.[7] An alternative explanation could be that *sse* here aligns with a cultural habit of using male-gendered prefixes and pronouns as honorific attachments to otherwise female words and people, suggesting that any reference to the firstborn twin, regardless of the firstborn twin's biological sex, deserves this epithet. One way to think about justifying that form of respect is that a healthy, head-first delivery of the first twin is critically important, even more so than for the second. If any firstborn twin is born breech (feet first), the birthing process might not place enough pressure on the cervix to promote its effacement and dilation, processes that permit babies' passage into the birth canal. This is only one among several possible problems with a breech presentation; others include umbilical cord prolapse and even uterine rupture. The former can stress the umbilicus, deprive the fetus of oxygen, and possibly result in stillbirth. The latter can result in a range of catastrophic maternal and fetal consequences. Particularly in any environment where cesarean section and other obstetric surgical techniques might be too risky, or where traditional birth attendants lack the expertise to perform them, breech presentation of the first twin could be quite dangerous for both babies and potentially the mother.

As indicated in this song's later reference to the (royal) enclosure, neither this song nor the wider twinship repertory restricts the focus to male reproductive power. On the contrary, songs from twin-tying rites lay out in explicit detail the spectacular physical and spiritual power of the mother and father of twins (Nnaalongo and Ssaalongo, respectively), sometimes remarking specifically on their genitals. When tying or "dancing" the twins, singers shift from praise epithets for both male and female roles in twin-making to the kind of

66 CHAPTER 2

direct *okuwemula* ("big words" or vulgar language) that most Baganda find obscene in polite company.[8] A mild example is *okuzina* (the Luganda term for dancing), which can be a euphemism for sexual intercourse, but which also operates in *okuzina abalongo* (the name of the ritual) to refer to how people literally dance with the power object that the ritual produces. The songs sung at that ritual do frequently play on the other meaning of the word *okuzina*, lending to the name of the ritual and the lyrics of its most emblematic song a double entendre. Performances of *okuzina abalongo* (or *okusiba abalongo*) produce ritual spaces that lift sociolinguistic taboos. While male symbols and phonemes indicate reproductive power, terms like Nnaalongo connote femininity, and still other terms like *nannyinimu* (landlord or landlady) indicate potentially gender-ambiguous power. This last epithet, often shortened to *nnyinimu* (owner of land) or *nnyinimuno* (owner of this land or owner of land here), offers a particularly flexible category in which the "land" could also be construed as the body of a medium, as a marriage bed, as the body of a spousal participant in that space, or as a fertile parent of children. Lyrical interpretation does not mean necessarily settling on one meaning, but rather appreciating a singer's suggestion of multiple meanings surrounding the agency of the owner.

This kind of cleverly coded index enables singers across many genres—not only *kusamira*—to invoke the categories of gender, sex, and human reproduction in terms appropriate for a wide variety of contexts. In this way, musical performance articulates and transcends maleness and femaleness through patterns of language enculturation that create a boundary between juvenile vulgarities and the thoroughly adult linguistic codes for sexual intercourse, labor and childbirth, postpartum physical and spiritual phenomena, and initiation into parenthood, particularly parenthood of twins. For children who accompany their elders to various rituals throughout early childhood, lifted taboos teach the difference between obscene language and acceptable speech about reproduction. The reenactment of taboos reminds adults of their responsibility to maintain the sacred and the profane as discrete (if ultimately inextricable) sociolinguistic categories.

The tune for "Ssewasswa" is short, consisting of only four compound duple cycles (see musical example 6). After a standard initiating caller motif, a soloist asserts idiomatic textual variations, layering them into the most spacious areas of the repetitive choral response. Two alternating choruses of similar length respond to the soloist's *bisoko* (idiomatic motifs). A specific performance of this tune from February 2010 in Kirowooza village bears out the driving rhythmic and textual consistency of these choruses, offering an opportunity to examine some of this tune's relatively short, simple solo variations.

MUSICAL EXAMPLE 6. Tune for "Ssewasswa."

MUSICAL EXAMPLE 6. Continued.

MUSICAL EXAMPLE 6. Continued.

MUSICAL EXAMPLE 6. Continued.

MUSICAL EXAMPLE 6. Continued.

MUSICAL EXAMPLE 6. Continued.

MUSICAL EXAMPLE 6. Continued.

MUSICAL EXAMPLE 6. Continued.

MUSICAL EXAMPLE 6. Continued.

76 CHAPTER 2

The singer, Ssematimba Frank Sibyangu, first encouraged the drummers to answer by sounding the drums. This call, "sound the drums," is the standard opening *kisoko* (motif) for the tune. Throughout the first three stanzas, he used typical *bisoko* for this tune, which is often the first tune to arise from the room after people have shared coffee berries, had their tea, or finished an evening meal. Ssematimba's performance reflected a typical way to rouse a crowd for ritual responsibilities. The opening *bisoko* not only call drummers to beat the drums, but also call people to respond and call spirits into the space.

Soloist: Waalaalaala kuba eŋŋoma ewuune!	Waalaalaala sound the drums!
Chorus: Ssewasswa kazaala baana	Ssewasswa, father to the children
S: kuba eŋŋoma, taata	sound the drum, daddy
Ch: Ssewasswa kazaala balongo	Ssewasswa, father to the twins

Even the first iteration of the chorus could be heard in the context of this ritual's tendency toward *kuwemula*, the coded and potentially vulgar language. The translation above shows a kind of appositive: Ssewasswa, father to the children (i.e., the twins). However, if the phrase is heard as a proper noun followed by a verb, the diminutive prefix *ka-* could stand in as a pronoun for his phallus, the physical reality of his bodily seed-planting, which leads to the birth of his twins. Of course, the miracle of this physical reality cannot happen without his female counterpart, as later *bisoko* demonstrate. But this is not simply a crass penile reference; rather, it constitutes the third layer of meaning for just one word, Ssewasswa, which is also the father of twins and the mighty firstborn. It speaks clearly of a Kiganda fascination with highly lauded progenitors and, by extension, of their respect for their ancestors and their history.

The next two *bisoko* acknowledge specific types of spirits, the *mayembe* and the *misambwa*, willing their arrival as if it had already happened.

S: amayembe gatuuse	the *mayembe* have arrived
Ch: Ssewasswa kazaala baana	Ssewasswa, father to the children
S: emisambwa gy'atuuse	the *misambwa* have arrived
Ch: Ssewasswa kazaala balongo	Ssewasswa, father to the twins

Then, in the third set of *bisoko*, we see a reference to *abalongo b'embuga* (the twins of the shrine). This line indexes the laudable female capacity for containing these tremendous physical and spiritual powers, the womb, but according to Ssematimba, it also refers specifically to Mayanja and Magobwe, spirits associated with a leopard and a python, respectively. Ssematimba's

Ecologies of Well-Being

assertion about this begins to show how closely linked every shrine is to the Kabaka's royal shrine, the *lubiri* or enclosure.[9] Since *basamize* often perform this song immediately preceding another twin song, "Abalongo twabazaala" (the twins we gave birth), this reference is embedded in a lengthy series of other references that index a close relationship among royal twins, other kinds of twins, human fruition more generally, the spirit world, and the animals and spirit mediums that mediate between humans and spirits.[10]

S: abalongo b'embuga	the twins of the shrine
Ch: Ssewasswa kazaala baana	Ssewasswa, father to the children
S: mukama wange	my lord
Ch: Ssewasswa kazaala balongo	Ssewasswa, father to the twins

The interdependence of these domains emerges in part through the phrase "mukama wange" (my lord), which is not a prayerful reference to a deity, but rather an idiomatic phrase used to show respect. In daily life, a person might use it as an alternative to *ssebo* (sir) for an elder or even for an equal who has said or done something laudable. It can also be used when agreeing with someone or asking them for something. In this case, Ssewasswa has done the laudable thing, complete with his associations with human twin parenthood, spiritual power, and animal familiars.

In the fourth stanza, Ssematimba made a double (or possibly multiple) entendre about a mother of twins, Nnaalongo, referring to both the sexual experience that conceived the twins and the pause between their births. He followed with a sequence in the fifth stanza that is open to several interpretive possibilities. The translation offered here attempts to capture the poetic idioms.

S: Nnaalongo yasooka n'agaana	Nnaalongo refused at first
Ch: Ssewasswa kazaala baana	Ssewasswa, father to the children
S: mukama wange	my lord
Ch: Ssewasswa kazaala balongo	Ssewasswa, father to the twins
S: olwamala n'asaawo	but later she gave in
Ch: Ssewasswa kazaala baana	Ssewasswa, father to the children
S: mukama wange	my lord
Ch: Ssewasswa kazaala balongo	Ssewasswa, father to the twins

The lines "Nnaalongo refused at first, . . . but later she gave in" could be more literally translated as "Nnaalongo began by refusing" or "Nnaalongo began to refuse," and "when he finished, he instituted." As complex as the relational dynamics between any couple, this pair of phrases lauds Nnaalongo for accepting the blessings of twin motherhood even as it acknowledges Ssaalongo for his role.

78   CHAPTER 2

This performance did not precede a twin-tying ritual, which would have lifted many taboos, giving Ssematimba much broader latitude for vulgarities, but the references here suggest some similar possibilities. This passage could be consistent with his performances of other songs, which often refer to a refusal of sex for one reason or another. In all likelihood, however, this *kisoko* functions a bit differently. At this performance in 2010, the group had just finished tying *engole*, small crowns fashioned out of a medicinal creeper vine called *bombo*. During these twin songs, candidates for initiation into mediumship wore the crowns. They resembled those that brides wear because *basamize* construe mediums, whether male or female, as *bagole* (spouses or intended spouses) of their patron spirits. An initiated medium of Magobwe, for example, might even be called Muka Magobwe (spouse of Magobwe). Hearing his suggestive nod to the twin-tying ritual as she fashioned these items, an elder mother of twins present at this 2010 performance indulged Ssematimba's double entendres briefly, but she admonished him not to go any further. As was his habit, Ssematimba incorporated the elder woman's warning into his *bisoko*, subtly but defiantly indexing both the twin-tying ritual and the sexual dynamics that such rituals frequently call to the foreground.[11]

Songs about *bagole* (spouses) among *basamize* articulate some core symbols of Kiganda identity. This phenomenon of gender interdependence is common to many traditions in the kingdom, from ideas about kinship to personified aspects of musical instruments. Ethnomusicologist Sylvia A. Nannyonga-Tamusuza has discussed the gendered aspects of drums and their roles, as well as other aspects of gender in the ubiquitous Kiganda dance form called *baakisimba*. Likewise, Damascus Kafumbe's more recent work examines aspects of gender complementarity in royal Kawuugulu performances.[12] Ssematimba's early allusion in the song to Magobwe, a spirit associated with a python, is far from arbitrary; in a later *kisoko* in this performance, Ssematimba sang "you snake give birth to children."[13] Again, this could be heard as a double entendre referring to both male genitalia and the powerful symbolic category of archetypical twin spirits. Alternatively, as others have suggested, this kind of *kisoko* aligns with gender ambiguities surrounding python-associated spirits capable of giving birth.[14]

S: owange weebale	my dear thank you
Ch: Sewasswa kazaala baana	Sewasswa, father to the children
S: ndigenda n'ani nze?	with whom shall I go?
Ch: Sewasswa kazaala balongo	Sewasswa, father to the twins
S: yaguggyayo n'agukuba emeeza	he drew it out and hit the table with his phallus

Ch: Ssewasswa kazaala baana	Ssewasswa, father to the children
S: abaaliwo ne beebuuza	those present wondered
Ch: Ssewasswa kazaala balongo	Ssewasswa, father to the twins
S: omusajja aggyeeyo ki ekyo?	what is that the man has taken out?
Ch: Ssewasswa kazaala baana	Ssewasswa, father to the children
S: mukama wange	my lord
Ch: Ssewasswa kazaala balongo	Ssewasswa, father to the twins
S: ggwe musota kazaala baana	you are the snake [hero] that fathered the children
Ch: Ssewasswa kazaala baana	Ssewasswa, father to the children
S: mukama wange	my lord
Ch: Ssewasswa kazaala balongo	Ssewasswa, father to the twins

This formulation displays thematic unity with the earlier *kisoko* about *abalongo b'embuga* (the twins of the royal enclosure, i.e., Mayanja and Magobwe).[15] While these praise epithets certainly recall the joking relations and venerations of sexual "fierceness" that Waalabyeki Magoba noted, this index of the royal twins and the *kisoko* about the snake take that thread even further. Taken together, they scale up individual human births, especially twin births, from family to clan to kingdom to a part of the spirit pantheon foundational to Kiganda identity, the twin spirits Mayanja and Magobwe.

Moreover, as a standard idiomatic motif for this tune, the phrase *abalongo b'embuga* is further multivalent: it indexes female reproductive power by reference to three linked sign domains: the *lubiri* (royal enclosure), similar enclosures called *biggwa* and *massabo* (shrines) at every level of the Kiganda kinship/clanship hierarchy, and the womb, the physiological enclosure that carries the twins. The relationship between each index and the next in this group demonstrates a phenomenon akin to something in semiotic analysis called a dicent index. Following Charles Sanders Peirce, Thomas Turino has described how a dicent index in musical performance involves an index affected by the thing it references, its object.[16] In the case of this phrase, the motif *abalongo b'embuga* is an index that points to three different reference points or "objects" as noted above, the royal enclosure, the shrines, and the womb, each of which affects the indexing motif. Because they are so closely associated though, these three form a group of indices to one another, each enhancing the symbolic power of its referent and vice versa. Such a complex referential chain suggests a move beyond "dicent," which implies duality. While the motif and initial index, *abalongo b'embuga*, certainly has a dicent relationship with each of its objects, each of those objects can also serve both as an index pointing to an object that links back to it and as an object that points back to a co-occurring index. These points of reference are special

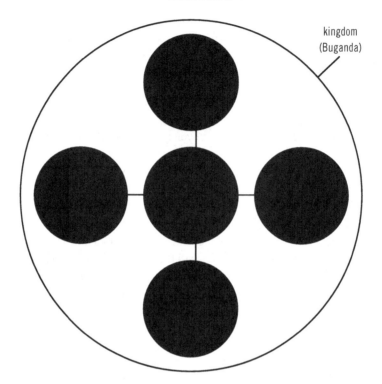

FIGURE 10. Twins of the royal enclosure and their homologous domains. Diagram by author.

because each is linked with the next and therefore with the coherent indexical unity of the group in a related chain. In other words, the phrase *abalongo b'embuga* unifies and empowers these domains, investing them with meaning; their association and alignment with one another contributes to the meaning of the royal enclosure; and all contribute to the linked domains' empowerment as recognizable symbols that often co-occur in ritual song (see figure 10).

This functional level of intertextual complexity in shrine performances surely contributed to the kind of political complexity that Neil Kodesh argues was central to Buganda's functioning as a kingdom.[17] If the leopard and python serve as powerful male symbols at the center of this model, the other symbols enclose and encompass them, articulating male and female as complementary domains. But the possibility of the snake giving birth renders it gender ambiguous, contributing to the complexity of the indexical relation-

Ecologies of Well-Being

ship among the twins and the surrounding domains, the objects of the twins' multiple associations. The interdependence of this whole symbolic system could be usefully enshrined within two analogous symbolic containers:

- the womb that makes the entire kinship system possible; that is, the mother of the *kasolya*/Kabaka (roof apex binding/king) or a more general womb reference
- the drum, a powerful container of cultural and medicinal information that is reproduced through ritual song

After the praise epithet about the snake giving birth, the leader sang "ne bakuba omubala" (then they sound the drum slogan). This translation is shorthand for what Damascus Kafumbe calls a "drum melo-rhythmic pattern with an associated textual phrase."[18] Every clan has at least one slogan, which frequently refers to the clan's totem animal. Such a slogan in this context connects twins—or any children for that matter—directly to the royal system of kinship and kingship that the Kabaka unites as its *kasolya*. Recitation of these *mibala* (drum slogans) at crucial life-cycle events like twin namings, weddings, and last rites called *okwabya olumbe* (chasing death) reinforces the kin/kingdom connection. The remaining motifs in the song alternate between the seriousness of this connection and the importance of vulgar ritual play: the twin "does not mess around with the medium/spirit," and yet the twin must not only beat the drums but also dance suggestively as people do at twin namings/tyings.

S: ne bakuba omubala	then they sounded the drum slogan
Ch: Ssewasswa kazaala baana	Ssewasswa, father to the children
S: aggyeyo ki ekyo?	what is that he has taken out?
Ch: Ssewasswa kazaala balongo	Ssewasswa, father to the twins
S: omulongo Ssewasswa	Ssewasswa the [first born] twin
Ch: Ssewasswa kazaala baana	Ssewasswa, father to the children
S: atazannyisa mandwa	he who does not mess around with the medium/spirit
Ch: Ssewasswa kazaala balongo	Ssewasswa, father to the twins

Phrases admonishing listeners to avoid "playing around" or "messing around" constitute a frequently repeated idiom in the repertory. Taken together with the motif about the python, these *bisoko* link the leopard twin spirit Mayanja and his brother, Magobwe, with this much broader series of references in the *kusamira* repertory, articulating the seriousness of this kind of ritual play and its importance to outlining the definitive relationships of Kiganda familial and sociopolitical life. Here the singer turned that idiom around, praising the one who does not mess around, a reference to Ssewasswa (Ssaalongo) here, but applicable also to Nnaalongo.

A final sequence in this 2010 performance (like most performances of the song) brought back the initiating motif, but that same call to sound the drums took on renewed relevance in the wake of references to twins, human sexual intercourse, animal and spiritual familiars, spirit mediums, and clan-based drum slogans.

S: kuba eŋŋoma tulabe	sound the drum and we see
Ch: Ssewasswa kazaala abaana	Ssewasswa, father to the children
S: kuba eŋŋoma	sound the drum
Ch: Ssewasswa kazaala abalongo	Ssewasswa, father to the twins
S: Nnaalongo waliyoka n'onkoona	mother of twins, it is good you knocked (provoked) me!
Ch: Ssewasswa kazaala abaana	Ssewasswa, father to the children
S: mukama wange	my lord
Ch: Ssewasswa kazaala abalongo	Ssewasswa, father to the twins

Taken as a whole, the sequence scales well-being up from persons to their twins (spiritual or human) to their other-than-human familiars, including the spirits for whom they serve as mediums and the animals through which those spirits move. Linking person to clan to kingdom to ecological surround goes beyond demonstrating Kodesh's argument about how shrines scale public healing from locales far outside the royal enclosure to articulate unity with royalty and to achieve resilient political complexity. From there, having already made some connections to clan via drum slogans and totem animals, songs index other animal and spirit familiars that help flesh out a distinctive ecology in which these entities constantly interact, draw power from physical resources, and affect one another.

Community and Ecology across Two Regions

Baswezi in Busoga also use twin songs to venerate twin spirits. The spirits still dwell in power objects associated with twinship, and those objects closely resemble the items manufactured in Kiganda twin-tying rituals. However, the songs occupy a wholly different and markedly less prominent place in Kisoga *nswezi* ritual life. The presence of an actual power object associated with Kisoga twinship was rare, and *baswezi* certainly did not begin each and every ritual of spiritual healing with twin songs. At a ritual in Munamaizi village to install new spirit mediums for various types of long-neglected

Ecologies of Well-Being

spirits, for example, performers embedded the songs and corresponding veneration of twin spirits within a much broader, multiday event. They did, however, dance with the object when it was present, just as their Kiganda counterparts did at twin-tying rituals.

Scholarship on Buganda offers a coherent rationale for the differing prominence of the twinship trope. Benjamin C. Ray argues that the rituals of royal accession to the throne consolidated the king's temporal and spiritual power by reference to the royal twin. Apolo Kagwa's 1918 record of Kabaka Kimera's accession is one of many narratives about early Kiganda history that places the sounding of a drum at the center of these rites. It is an especially potent narrative that establishes *ttimba*, a drum with a relief of a python carved into its body, as mutually constitutive with Kimera's contested kingship. Citing Kagwa and others, and writing in 1953, Klaus P. Wachsmann described this drum as part of the *mujaguzo* royal set and published a drawing based on a photograph of it.[19] This powerful snake symbolism continues to hold enormous relevance for *basamize* in Buganda. A medium named Nabawanuka (whose name is the female-gendered version of Kiwanuka) explained to me that the python she keeps in her compound had a human twin.[20] As in Nabawanuka's case, it is common for Kiwanuka's mediums to take on the appropriately gendered version of his name. The same is true for Kiwanuka's twin spirit, Musoke (female version: Namusoke), a pattern that replicates the theme of duality between siblings, spirits/mediums, and male/female counterparts.

Oral traditions about spiritual twinship and animal wraiths suggest that the potency of these symbols extends well beyond the royal enclosure. Recent work by Neil Kodesh offers an alternative to Ray's assertion that "the king derived all his powers from the installation ceremonies."[21] Kodesh instead argues that the earlier Kiganda royals achieved political complexity in part through the replication of ideas about embodied political authority in shrines at clan estates all across Buganda. The living tradition recounted by Nabawanuka and the frequent mention of similar symbols in songs strongly suggest that such sociopolitical complexities remain firmly in place today. While Busoga shared similar practical motivations to Buganda for consolidating authority over social well-being in mediums and their shrines, the structural features of their royal system were different, as were the ways that system figured in the emergent politics of independence in the early 1960s.

Neither the varying importance of the twinship trope across the two regions nor the differing cosmologies shaped by discrete systems of political authority prevented Buganda and Busoga from developing quite similar ontologies of collective well-being. Whereas Kiganda twin songs index kinship and kingship through recurring use of terms like owner or landlord

84   CHAPTER 2

(-*nyini*-) and autochthon (-*ŋanda*), Kisoga performances often drop these references while continuing to associate twins with other ecological features common across both regions. For example, the medicinal plants called *bombo* and *lweeza* frequently appear with power objects of twinship across both regions. *Basamize* and *baswezi* both "dance the twins," physically dancing with the power objects fashioned around umbilical cords of human twins, plant medicines, and cowries. Likewise, even when they are not actually dancing with the objects, both groups sing about dancing with twins just as they sing about dancing with other spirits. These song references are part of a much broader conceptualization across both regions of the medium as a wife to a spirit, as a tenant to a spiritual landlord, as a patient to a healer, as a guest to a host (or vice versa), and as a client to a patron. Familiar, idiomatic interdependencies frame the ways that people interact with other people, spirits, flora and fauna, the land, the sea, the sky, and the forest. The framing is especially evident in their interactions with Kiganda and Kisoga spirit pantheons, as subsequent examples demonstrate.

Twins and other themes of human reproduction are just a few ways in which repertories help ritual adepts think through well-being. Humans lead to families, families lead to clans and communities, and communities lead to kingdoms and other larger-order forms of social organization like ethnolinguistic groups. Scaled up to that level, though, some historical, political, and interactional aspects of these healing repertories depend on other neighboring regions, even some beyond Buganda and Busoga, the peoples who occupy them, and elements of their shared histories. Localized understandings of ecology help us parse some of the finer points because people (regardless of affiliation) tend to prioritize features of the places where they reside. For example, Mukasa is a sea spirit who tends to be quite important to both Baganda and Basoga who live along the Nnyanja Nalubaale littoral, and inland populations across both regions likewise situate Nabuzaana within the forest as a locus of medicinal and procreative power.

Other spirits express discrete linkages with geographies, topologies, animals, and plants. General references to spirits, usually to *misambwa*, tend to classify them as somehow associated with nature and to differentiate them from *lubaale* and other classes of spirits.[22] David William Cohen's interpretation of *nkuni* in Busoga offers an important historical interpretation of a class of spirits that remains relevant all over that region.[23] Neil Kodesh's work on both *misambwa* and *nkuni* incorporates these two different types of place-based spirits into an insightful reading of an early historical genre outside the royal enclosure that helped facilitate Kiganda social cohesion.[24] Like Hanson and Cohen, Kodesh analyzes the place of these spirits within specific

Ecologies of Well-Being

historical circumstances that link them to the articulation of sociopolitical authority. Taken together, this body of scholarship elicits several questions: what can musical repertories reveal about how people conceptualize these spirits, especially now that their once place-based associations have shifted? How do the spirits function in living traditions? How might all of that have changed over time?

Frequent invocation of *misambwa* and *nkuni* among Baganda *basamize* and Basoga *baswezi* offers valuable insight, and an important minor estate for the lungfish clan near Nakawuka town serves as a helpful starting point. During large end-of-year celebrations there, singers call *misambwa* in a general way each morning, singing "Come near, come near, come near, *misambwa*."[25] Their songs range from this general call to the naming of specific spirits, as the next example shows.

Mu nkukuulu,	In the *nkukuulu* grass,
Nabuzaana weebale	thank you, Nabuzaana
mu nkuukuulu,	in the *nkukuulu* grass,
kaliba [a]kanyoolagano	it will be a struggle

Ssematimba Frank Sibyangu, a musician and healer familiar with both Nakawuka and this song, explains, "*Mu nkukuulu* means 'in the small negotiation, in the little meeting'; *akanyoolagano* refers to a circus, to social chaos as you have sometimes seen."[26] *Akanyoolagano* translates literally as a struggle, heated exchange, or fight, but here it appears to be a euphemism for the sometimes chaotic struggle of passionate coitus. *Nkukuulu* grass is quite soft and has a pleasing odor that, as with many plants, emerges even more strongly when it is crushed or disturbed somehow. The association of Nabuzaana with this "little meeting" of lovers tempted to do what lovers do has at least two layers: one is the coital act itself; the other is the homologous process of spirit "climbing" or "mounting" its medium. Spirits participate in that process because they enshrine valuable knowledge about childbirth and plant medicine in cultural memory. People discuss the use of plant medicines and the application of other therapeutic techniques at length, both with spirits through their mediums and with one another as professional colleagues invested in common endeavors of health and wellness. Nabuzaana is one of the *misambwa* most commonly associated with that process, earning her the praise name *omunozzi w'eddagala* (gatherer of medicines). Like Ddungu, the hunter, she is closely associated with the forest whence those medicines come, and with children and fertility. She is a patron spirit for all things associated with the birth and care of children. Nabuzaana also holds a prominent place in one of Buganda's most frequently performed twin songs.[27]

86   CHAPTER 2

The history of *misambwa*, together with Kisoga invocations of *nkuni*, offers a few important points of conceptual contrast between Kiganda and Kisoga spiritual traditions, despite some similarities. Like the Kiganda conception of *misambwa*, *nkuni* often reside in various elements of the natural environment, but while *misambwa* often "move in animals," *nkuni* reside in the stones, rivers, or trees of specific places. Also unlike *misambwa*, they have attachments to totem animals of Kisoga clans.[28] They function differently, too. *Misambwa* were initially linked with specific places but then moved beyond those locales, a phenomenon that Kodesh calls "portability."[29] Cohen's work shows that *nkuni* were also associated with locales, but in an even more specific way: not just representative of the natural environment, they were spirits of firstcomers from each Kisoga clan to those places.[30] These are two contrasting ways of expressing human and other-than-human connectedness by linking spiritual autochthons to specific features of ecology.

Evidence for this phenomenon can be found, for example, in a song about barrenness that binds the members of a clan with a bird totem to one of the group's historical settlements. The song was part of a much larger, multiday attempt to re-connect the community with its patron spirits.

Kasinga ngalagira;	Let me direct you;
otanvumye bugumba	don't abuse me about barrenness
munnange Namunobe	my dear Namunobe [unwanted one]
eibale ery'eBuwongo	the stories of Buwongo

The song admonishes members of the community who had ridiculed a woman of this clan for her inability to conceive. The woman's peers explained that the "stories of Buwongo" (a place) included cases in which a spirit, one of the *nkuni* for the clan, had helped women previously considered to be barren to conceive and give birth to healthy children.[31] Buwongo, they explained, was the main *nkuni* for this clan, and Namunobe, the unwanted one, was his wife.

Understanding Namunobe requires examining her complex cultural, historical, and ecological context. The various associations of people, animals, plants, spirits, and possibly even historical natural catastrophes with her husband's clan are myriad. The name of the clan, Namusisi Waititi (Buutu), references both an earthquake and a bird, and the patriline or common ancestor affiliated with this group is Mukose (sesame seed). Extant sources are silent on the *musisi* (earthquake) component, so it could refer either to a historical seismic event or, more metaphorically, to something else. The full clan name, the sesame seed patriline, and the bird totem offer a few clues. Cornelius Wambi Gulere writes, "the sesame seed, like the small ant, [is] tiny, but they could be killers. This is compared to the totem of the huge

Ecologies of Well-Being   87

black bird, which is believed to be full of charms. A small glance at its behind could cause death." In contrast to Cohen's assertion that this totem is a shrike, Gulere identifies the bird Waititi Buutu as a ground hornbill.[32] Whether the bird is interpreted as the small shrike with a vicious method of rapidly killing its prey or as the large ground hornbill full of harmful potential, the bird's effect on its surroundings clearly has seismic consequences. The performers' interpretation recalled how the place called Buwongo became associated with the spirit of the first people of this clan to arrive in that place, an explanation that resonates somewhat with Cohen's understanding. Cohen also interprets the place, Buwongo, as being related to the Lusoga verb *kuwonga*, which he translates as "to sacrifice," but which more precisely means "to pray." His oral source explained that this is a reference to Buwongo as an important site for the Mukose patriline to participate in prayer and the sacrifice of animals.[33] Both translations affirm that the same kinds of clan-based spiritual leadership that helped shape Buganda, in which an innovative person or influential people became associated with specific geographic locations and movements, were also important in Busoga. According to Gulere's table of totems, places of origin, patrilines, and other data of kin and clan from Busoga, Buwongo is only one among several *nkuni* for the clan associated with both the bird and the Mukose patriline.[34] The performers identified Buwongo as the clan's main *nkuni*, however, and Gulere also lists it first among the others. The other names on Gulere's list, considered alongside Cohen's quote from an oral source about the dispersal of Mukose affiliates throughout Busoga, help establish this group's primacy in this bird clan. These sources also help explain why people I met at Munamaizi, so far north of the historical Buwongo settlement (120 km; 75 mi.), would be concerned with reconnecting their clanmates with a distant but important *nkuni* site/personage as part of their effort to promote human and plant fertility. Just as the firstcomers of this Kisoga clan affiliated with a *nkuni* called Buwongo that also became the name of an important site for prayer and sacrifice, the barren among them likewise got attached to the moniker Namunobe.

This case is instructive on several levels. It offers insight on Kisoga clanship; on conceptualizations of barrenness as a specific affliction that calls for specific interventions; on the history of the Basiki, a subgroup of the Basoga who speak a Lusoga dialect called Lusiki; on the geographic spread of Abaise Mukose (the Mukose or sesame seed patriline) of the Waititi Buutu (ground hornbill) clan across Busoga; and more generally on the ways that Kisoga spirituality links all these domains through the performance of songs. These dynamics underscore local understandings of the song as an efficacious intervention amid difficult physiological and social circumstances. The

88   CHAPTER 2

audience for this song understood it against the backdrop of a common clan heritage. Elders in the group understood the precise location of Buwongo and the relevance of its history to the situation of barrenness. Their communal embrace of a woman who was frustrated with her fertility situation simultaneously reassured this young kinswoman and censured her critics by recalling a lengthy and specific history of their people and their movement through Busoga. The work they did with these young counterparts at Munamaizi during the week of this performance not only installed a physical place for Buwongo and other *nkuni* in the family compound, it also established a similar space for Lukowe, a more general (not clan-affiliated) patron spirit for fertility, childbirth, and women's health. Lukowe is an archetype of the female Kisoga healer, and her name serves as a title for initiated women who hold and share this kind of knowledge according to their communities' needs. Many women with this title were present, all helping lead the ritual activities at Munamaizi. At this and other gatherings, people invariably consulted this spirit and her mediums on matters of fertility and childbirth. This performance enriched an understanding of how Basoga *baswezi* healers understand fertility-related challenges, like other afflictions, as directly influenced by the dynamics of the clan, its spirits, the patriline, and the eco-cultural context. They hold this in common with *basamize* in Buganda.

Mayembe: Binding Spiritual Work and Ecology into Concentrated Space

The notion of a working spirit or *jjembe* (pl. *mayembe*) is unlike any other type of spirit in Buganda or Busoga, but the idea is similar in concept and use across both regions. If someone has a specific challenge to address in life, they might enlist a *jjembe* and "feed" it with sacrifices to overcome the challenge. Examples include:

- helping children do well in school
- addressing the underlying spiritual cause of a condition (often while concurrently seeking biomedical attention)
- soliciting spiritual assistance in returning to solvency after some devastating economic misfortune
- restoring a suffering relationship, often a romantic situation

Another layer of possibility exists, too: if someone's deceased ancestor had a *jjembe* while living, and that person died and became a *muzimu* (ghost), the same ancestor could well choose a living heir to both their own spiritual legacy and to the care of the working spirit they employed while living.

Ecologies of Well-Being   89

This peculiar form of inheritance can place considerable demands on the living heir. Whatever work must be done, these *mayembe* require sacrifices commensurate with the magnitude of their spiritual labor. In return, they protect households, compounds, or whole villages from evil or from *ebibi* (bad things).

This wide variety of possibilities for working spirits has often led to two negative perceptions. A colonial and ex-colonial gaze toward practices around working spirits has misunderstood them as witchcraft, while legal, journalistic, or religious venues have deployed a colonial lexicon to lob accusations of abusive or specious healing practices at the manufacture and sale of power objects related to working spirits. Today, a person can certainly commission the manufacture of a new dwelling place for a working spirit, but this ex-colonial atmosphere has fomented broad misunderstanding about the process, often because it involves the blood of sacrificial animals.[35]

Many songs across the diagnostic and therapeutic spectrum name these spirits, both by type (*jjembe, mayembe*) and by name. The creation of power objects in which they dwell goes well beyond musical repertories into a category of ritual practice that deserves deeper study. The narrative below offers an entry point to frame working spirits as a discrete conceptual category with fascinating ecological elements situated in a regional ontology. Chapter 3 will return to a different part of the same narrative to examine performances involving both the objects and the working spirits' mediums.

Working spirits frequently motivate building projects embedded in multiday ritual events like the one at Munamaizi. Singers call on *mayembe* to make themselves known during diagnostic phases of ritual, and other healers in both Buganda and Busoga have helped communities erect tiny buildings for particular working spirits. Before people know anything specific about the *mayembe*—whether they might need one, or whether neglected intergenerational *jjembe* associated with a deceased ancestor might be causing problems—they name this entire class of spirits in song in hopes that the spirits will make themselves known in ritual. If a previously unknown *jjembe* does arrive through a medium, it can then also make its provenance, its associations, and its desires known. Both *basamize* and *baswezi* use the following song to invoke *mayembe*:

Ejjembe ly'ekika lyagwa	The clan *jjembe* landed
lyagwa nga ndaba	it landed before my sight
ejjembe lyekika lyagwa	the clan *jjembe* landed

The idea of a spirit landing in this song carries at least two meanings. It could mean that the *jjembe* "landed" on a medium, either living or deceased, en-

90   CHAPTER 2

dowing that medium with the responsibility for its care. It could also mean that the *jjembe* has fallen into a state of neglect, landing in a community where it wreaks havoc until the community members diagnose the spiritual causes of their problems. Either way, these meanings are consistent with the classic ŋoma or "drums of affliction" model discussed in the introduction. In at least two cases, at Wairama and Kyabakaire (both in Busoga), neglect of *mayembe* and other spirits motivated a diagnostic ritual followed by more intensive building rituals in which people gave the spirits physical dwelling spaces in their family compounds. In both cases, the healer Erukaana Waiswa Kabindi (pictured on this book's cover) saw his clients through the building phase to facilitate the work of specific *mayembe* that, at the time of diagnosis, were unknown to the clients who sang with Kabindi to invoke them.

Other cases might well involve a *jjembe* already familiar to a person or community. For example, during a series of building rituals to house spirits in a family compound at Munamaizi, a group of singers and mediums moved out to the periphery of the property, beyond the sweet potato and bean fields, to a bushy area surrounded by trees and underbrush. There they invoked a *jjembe* whose job it was to guard the compound and the fields from misfortune and spiritual attack. The soloist sang:

Ejjembe najjanga	Ejjembe, I used to come
ne nnaku ejjembe	With sorrow, the *jjembe*

A chorus responded:

ejjembe Kalondoozi	the *jjembe* Kalondoozi [the name of the spirit]
wajja olina, ennaku kudaaga!	you came with sorrow, suffering!

For these singers, the urgency of both the text and the insistent duple meter of this song emphasized that such work was long overdue. Once he arrived in his medium, the *jjembe* demanded the sacrifice of a chicken, which the people hastily plucked, sacrificed, roasted, and ate with him right there in the bush. The next several days brought many more interactions with the frustrated Kalondoozi, who eventually accepted more sacrifices and a small house that would serve as both his home and his workplace. The gathered devotees built this outpost somewhat apart from the houses for other spirits and from the main dwelling for the family in this compound. The arrangement bore a close resemblance to the guardhouses at the edges of many compounds in urban and suburban areas of Uganda.

By the time that Kabona Mutale brought me along with him and several colleagues to Makandwa in Wakiso District, these and other songs had be-

Ecologies of Well-Being

come familiar to me as part of a repertory for both *basamize* and *baswezi*. Likewise the practice of searching for working spirits or locating their dwellings at the edges of a compound had proven common across multiple events in different locations, as had some kind of linkage to fields, forests, and the assets they offer. Up to that point, however, the creation and care of various power objects associated with working spirits had remained rather mysterious to me. Healers and others had them, and one even had hundreds of *mayembe*, but either I had previously underestimated their relevance or the right questions simply had not yet led to a clear articulation of their use. Mutale, a colleague, and a small gathering around a family compound at Makandwa spent several days creating two *mayembe* power objects and feeding them sacrifices, a process that elucidated for me just how deeply these spirits are embedded in practices of plant medicine, ritual performance, and sacrifice.

On the night of our arrival, following tea and a meal, they called specific working spirits and *misambwa* in song with the intention of presenting sacrifices to them, but much work would have to precede those sacrifices. The following excerpt from my field notes begins on the morning of the second day.

> *Kabona Mutale and Jjajja Kapere chatted quietly inside the shrine as they chopped, diced, and ground a wide variety of medicinal roots, plants, and animal byproducts: they placed fragrant leafy greens, some dust filed off from the tooth of a wild animal, clarified butter, cowrie shells, and coffee berries all into a new pair of mayembe. Mayembe (sing. jjembe) are power objects that house a class of spirits by the same name. This pair of basamize who brought me here—Mutale and Kapere—mixed these items into a cow horn for the male jjembe and a small drinking gourd for the female jjembe. Their intention was to "install" these spirits in their new dwellings, a process that requires both animal sacrifice and the performance of many other ritual actions, including much singing and dancing. Last night, the healers and other basamize beat the drums, shook the gourd rattles, and aggressively called another spirit who once employed these mayembe into his medium.*

Here it is worth remembering that upon death, a person who has working spirits becomes an ancestral ghost called a *muzimu* who requires offerings and occasional sacrifices from living relatives. Her working spirits, by extension, require similar attention. The gathering at Makandwa, which followed the death of a woman named Namagga, presented just such a case: each *jjembe* got a goat and a chicken to ensure that they could continue

92 CHAPTER 2

their work for their spiritual *nannyinimu* (landlord), Namagga. The onus on the community involved care not only for the ancestor but also for her working spirit.

Mutale and Kapere supervised the process of offering the first fruits of sacrifice to the spirits through their mediums by giving them drinks of the freshest blood directly from the animals' lacerated necks. In order to firmly embed powerful medicines, they "installed" the *mayembe* (working spirits) by pouring the remainder of the blood from their feathery and furry sacrificial victims into the new power objects (also called *mayembe*), where the spirits would dwell. The whole process brought together items and concepts from disparate ecological domains—the forest and the water, plants and animals, and eventually sacrificial animals, spirits, and people—at least in part to remind a community of the crucial linkages animating the interaction of these domains.

The name for this ritual, *okuwanga amayembe*, connotes an installation of the working spirits not only in these power objects, but also within communities that rely on them to do the important spiritual work of guarding against *ebibi* (bad things) and opening the pathways to *emikisa* (blessings), which sustain well-being for human beings, their crops, and their animals, both domestic and sacrificial. Other examples of similar processes would differ from this one in terms of the specific plant medicines and animal by-products embedded in the power objects, the kinds of vessels used as starting points, and the *mayembe* spirits informing the process. In each case, however, *basamize* and *baswezi* alike regard the basic notion of installing physical and spiritual substance in an object as a concentration of power, an investment of energy and resources with potential for manipulative influence over the bad things and blessings in their lives.

Hunting, Gathering, and Joining: Ddungu the Hunter

Another spirit made an appearance at Makandwa, and his capacity for joining forest, animal, and human domains was no coincidence: throughout both Buganda and Busoga, the hunter spirit named Ddungu asserts his relevance and his power for navigating these disparate spaces. When he appears in his mediums, they frequently don a hunting net and grasp a spear. Two rituals in two different places even featured actual "hunts" in which the adepts who had planned to sacrifice a goat for some other spirits placed the animal in a bushy area near the *ssabo* (shrine) in order that Ddungu could throw a net over it, lance it with his spear, and bring it back to the compound for butchering. As he embarked on his task, others would sing a brief tune about

FIGURE 11. Clad in full posthunt, postsacrifice array, the spirit Ddungu receives offerings and prepares to distribute food to his loyal devotees. Photograph by the author.

"Ddungu ng'ayigga" (Ddungu as he hunts). A Luganda song I recorded in Busoga also refers to Ddungu via his dog:

Mbwa yange, mbwa yange	My dog, my dog
leero tekyayigga	today it no longer hunts
eyiggira wala.	it hunts from afar.
Mbwa yange, mbwa yange	My dog, my dog
bw'etannayigga	now that it has not hunted
ebeera y'addalu!	it is wild!

Ddungu appears with all of the fierceness of a warrior, but his sense of responsibility is focused on food security rather than protection. In figure 11, which shows one such ritual hunt at Nampunge, Ddungu not only carries his net and spear, but also wears the skin of the animal he has just slain, as well as a wreath on his head made from *bombo*, a medicinal plant common to both regions.

Ddungu's appearance in this ritual context provides an excellent means of understanding how *basamize*, *baswezi*, and their patron spirits regard spirits, persons, animals, and plants as overlapping entities with porous boundaries. Here the fragrant creeping *bombo* has been twisted into a crown for his medium in much the same way that candidates for initiation or people intending to marry twist it together with *lweeza*.

Pantheons and Litanies, Fauna and Flora: Repertories of Practice

Basamize use *bombo* similarly at twin-tying rituals, as do *baswezi* when they are mourning a deceased colleague. In the twin-tying context, *basamize* sing this song about it:

Akabombo	The *kabombo* [plant]
kaali ka baana	was initially the children's
akabombo	the *kabombo*
nange nkambadde	I am also wearing it

At a funeral for a recently deceased spirit medium in Irondo village, Busoga region, the plant served not only as the common headgear for mourners, but also as a ritual covering for the grave. There it collected and contained spiritual refuse that the ritual facilitators discarded in an elaborate cleansing process before libations were poured and the grave was fully closed. Mourners performed a song about the plant at least twice during these rites.

Chorus: Yebwika mabombo, eee	She covers herself with *mabombo*
omuswezi yafa, babwika mabombo	the *muswezi* died, they covered [with] *mabombo*
Solo: twelile, twelile beene	we mourn for ourselves, we mourn for ourselves—dear ones
(chorus)	
S: nnaagaya ntya nze tabula bw'akola?	how should I explain she can do nothing?
(chorus)	
S: Tulabye, banaife, tulabye	We're mourning, our dear ones, we're mourning

Ecologies of Well-Being

(chorus)

S: nalwegoloile omukono gw'omunafu

straightness—the hand of a lazy person

(chorus)

S: ndi kwogela bingi tyaliile kyaigulo

I'm really telling you she didn't eat supper

(chorus)

S: elikuwaya buwaye wulila bw'eyeta:

[the drum] is just discussing, hear how it calls:

(chorus)

S: nnaayeta ntya nze Mbeedha wabula?

how should I call Princess, you're lost?

(chorus)

S: Ndekela okweta okwelumya omwoyo

Let me cease calling lest I sadden the heart

(chorus)

S: ndekela okweta okwelumya amamilo

let me cease calling lest I sadden the throat

(chorus)

S: nnaayeta ntya nze Kalisa wabula?

how should I call Kalisa [spirit], you're lost?

(chorus)

S: Nnaayeta ntya nze Lukowe wabula?

How should I call Lukowe [spirit], you're lost?

(chorus)

S: Nnaayeta ntya nze Isegya wabula?

How should I call Isegya [spirit], you're lost?

(chorus)

S: Nnaayeta ntya nze enniliengo wabula?

How should I call the gourd rattle, you're lost?

(chorus)

S: Nnaagaya ntya nze abakulu we batyaime?

How should I explain where elders are seated?

(chorus)

S: Nnaagaya ntya nze otatukobela y'olaga?

How can I explain you didn't tell us [where] you're going?

(chorus)

S: Wulila, ennaku bw'on'ofa:

Listen, the day when you die:

(chorus)

S: nnaalila ntya amatembe w'egabuze?

how will I mourn [when] the beads get lost?

(chorus)

S: Nnaalila ntya nze mmindi w'ebula?

How will I mourn [when] the pipe gets lost?

(chorus)
S: Nnaalila ntya nze engaliisi w'ebula? — How will I mourn when the headband is lost!?

(chorus)
S: Nnaalila ntya nze lubaale lw'ewuba? — How will I mourn as the *lubaale* [spirits] swing [possess]?

(chorus)
S: Nnaalila ntya nze lubaale lw'ewumbya? — How will I mourn as the *lubaale* close up [the grave]?

(chorus)
S: Sekula sekula sekula eŋŋoma! — Beat, beat, beat the drums!

(chorus)
S: Akuloga amaiso akuwubisa ngila — The bewitcher of your eyes distorts your way

(chorus)
S: akuloga amaiso akulemesa ngila — the bewitcher of your eyes defeats you on the way

(chorus)
S: tunaalila tutya ife omuswezi waife? — how shall we mourn our *muswezi* [spirit medium]?

(chorus)
S: Tunaalila tutya ife omugaile w'egubuze? — How shall we mourn [when] our barkcloth is lost?

(chorus)
S: Bw'afa omuswezi bwafa — If s/he dies, the *muswezi*, if s/he dies

(chorus)
S: bw'olifa Isegya bw'olifa — when you shall die, Isegya, when you shall die

(chorus)
S: bw'olifa omuswezi bw'olifa — when you shall die, spirit medium, when you shall die

(chorus)
S: bw'olifa, Lukowe, bw'olifa — when you shall die, Lukowe, when you shall die

(chorus)
S: bw'olifa, lubaale, bw'olifa — when you shall die, *lubaale*, when you shall die

(chorus)
S: nnalila ntya nze nga nzila wange!? — how will I mourn when I do not have mine [dear one/friend]?

Ch: Yyebwika mabombo, eee omuswezi yafa, babwika mabombo — She covers herself with *mabombo* the *muswezi* died, they covered [with] *mabombo*[36]

The first time they performed this song, the *baswezi* sat mourning their colleague in song. They sat in the banana grove, beating the drums and singing the version printed here. The second time, though, they began singing the song because it was time to remove the plants from the grave. A leading male elder named Kyambu Ntakabusuni signaled for all to remove their plant-fashioned headbands. His instruction was quickly followed by an admonition from Lukowe Rehema to pull the vines apart, destroying them before placing them on the grave. Another pair of elders, who carried the titles Lukowe and Isegya (the names of two common healer-spirits in the region, to whom *baswezi* look for guidance in matters of healing), then gathered up the grave-topping *mabombo* vines using long sticks. They swept these into a pile and used the sticks to carry them out to the bush and discard them. Then they came back again to repeat the process a second time, ensuring that they had discarded all the remnants.

My main *nswezi* drumming teacher, Andrew Lukungu Mwesige Kyambu, explained that unlike with other uses of *mabombo*, Lukowe and Isegya could not touch these with their hands because it could be spiritually dangerous. He further clarified that one of the chickens sacrificed that day had to be sacrificed over the discarded *mabombo* in order to bind the branches' danger and prevent them from sowing pestilence among the kin of the deceased. Ultimately, even though this was a different physical treatment of the plant than in other contexts, the proceedings clarified for me that the plant's ritual function remains consistent across these domains: where *bombo/mabombo* is involved, it serves as spiritual binding agent. It marks initiates for their patron spirits to be joined in mediumship just as it signals intentions of betrothed to join in marriage; it binds twin umbilical cords into power objects, linking the objects and communities to offerings and sacrifices for twin spirits; and it binds negative potential to protect communities from spiritual contagion.

Twin songs, territorial spirits, and working spirits all illustrate different ways in which repertories of well-being situate humans within complex networks of being and knowledge, glossed here as ecologies of well-being. They also flesh out a few more parts of the sophisticated pantheon of spirits that informs Kiganda *kusamira* and Kisoga *nswezi* practices. The examples below continue along this path with a dual aim. First, they articulate a more complete understanding of spirit types and other nonhuman factors that shape the contours of these ecologies. Second, they reinforce a broader observation of this study that musical repertories are embedded in repertories of ritual practice. Ultimately, what these examples reveal is not that other-than-human factors unilaterally animate human behavior but rather that various human

98   CHAPTER 2

and other-than-human influences within these ecologies all hold agency to affect one another.

Just as the *nkuni* Buwongo is associated with a bird full of potentially dangerous charms, and just as Baganda associate Mayanja with the leopard, some songs invoke similarly powerful animals through which spirits can move. Lusoga *nswezi* songs frequently mention lions, for example. One treats a lion as the physical manifestation of Mukama, a prominent Kisoga spirit and one of two original progenitors of the Basoga.[37]

S: Mmwe wuube Mukama	You [pl.] shake with Mukama [spirit]
Ch: mpologoma yiiyo	the lion is there
S: mmwembeere, mmwembeere Mukama	you [pl.] sing, you sing to Mukama
Ch: bampologoma baabo	the lions are there
S: bakaira Mukama	they have just returned [with] Mukama
Ch: mpologoma yiiyo	the lions are there
S: mmwe wuube Mukama	you shake with Mukama
Ch: mpologoma yiiyo	the lions are there

Here, shaking is one of several euphemisms for the outward physical signs of spirit possession. The *musoga* linguist who translated this text read *mwembeere* as "you sing," but the Lusoga verb *kubeera* can also mean to help or support, a possible reference to the help that a medium provides by hosting a spirit or to the help a spirit provides through its medium.[38] In either case, the association gives rise to *bampologoma* (lion people), a reference to spirit mediums associated with Mukama.

Other songs use the word *kuwuuba* (swinging) as another euphemism for possession.

Ch: Empologoma muwuube,	The lion you swing [possess],
wamuwuuba wamwiza mule	you swing him/her and turn to there.
S: muwuube oyo	he's shaking that one!
Semichorus: Empologoma muwuube	The lion you swing [possess]
S: empologoma muwuube oyo,	the lion you swing that one,
Ch: empologoma muwuube,	the lion you swing [possess],
wamuwuuba wamwiza mule	you swing him/her and turn to there.

Still others use swinging interchangeably with playing or jumping:

S: Mwembele, mwembele Mukama	You [pl.] sing for Mukama
Ch: empologoma egenda	the lion is going

S: (omukazi) abaile ki? abaile ki Mukama?	what's wrong with her, what's wrong, Mukama?
Ch: Empologoma ezaanha	The lion plays
S: Mukama, mukama ali kugya	Mukama, Mukama is going
Ch: empologoma egenda	the lion is going
S: Mukama agiile wa? (chorus)	where has Mukama gone?
S: Agiile wa omunene? (chorus)	Where has the big one gone?
S: Mwewuube, mwewuube Mukama (chorus)	You [pl.] swing, you swing, Mukama
S: agiile wa? agiile wa Mukama? (chorus)	where has s/he gone? where has he gone, Mukama?
S: Empologoma eliwa? (chorus)	Where is the lion?
S: Empologoma etuuma! (chorus)	The lion is jumping!
S: Twembele, twembele Mukama	Let's sing, sing for Mukama
Ch: empologoma egenda	the lion is going

Regardless of how they characterize possession, all these songs associate Mukama with the powerful lion. In some cases, the reference is a bit veiled: songs use the lion as a stand-in for Mukama without directly naming the spirit. And yet, the association is so ubiquitous as to be understood even in those cases.

From Animals Back to Plants Again

Leopards and lions are only two among a wide range of animals associated with spirits, but the forest is rich with other elements that link spirits to the practice of healing. Performed repertories offer an equally rich point of access to these associations. The most esoteric of these emerge through dreams and other exchanges between spirits and humans: a snake or a leopard or a squirrel or a bird leads a person through a forest to a specific medicinal plant, for example. Themes tightly linked with daily life appear in the form of agrarian culture's most pervasive symbols, like iron hoes, bananas, chickens, or cattle. In both cases, songs evoke and elucidate interdependence among spirits, people, plants, and animals.

Perhaps more than any other, one performance in Busoga clarified for me the intimate connection of farmer spirit mediums to their fields via the patron spirit Lukowe and what one participant called an "ancient" hoe.[39] I had arrived at Munamaizi two days earlier with Andrew Lukungu Mwesige Kyambu and his father, a *muswezi* healer named Kyambu Ntakabusuni. Interviews at Munamaizi revealed that the community had experienced a lengthy series of "misfortunes," including several cases of what the community interpreted as acute, spiritually influenced insanity and no fewer than two cases of barrenness as noted above in the song that mentioned Namunobe. We arrived as people were beginning a ritual to reestablish places for several patron spirits within the compound. At one point early in the ritual, after spirits had arrived through mediums both old and new, they crawled on their hands and knees in and around the place where the old, dilapidated dwellings had been. Crying and wailing loudly, they lamented the state of their homes and demanded that the people build new houses. The following field note excerpt, from January 2009, picks up just after the gathered witnesses to this spectacle sang a recurring song of this and other *nswezi* rituals. The chorus of the song stated, "s/he [the spirit] has chosen one, s/he has chosen from among others." It referred to how spirits choose their mediums, but also how some in the village had been singled out for affliction, and how those afflicted had been ridiculed. Their invitation for Kyambu, his son, and other *baswezi* to join them indicated that the people construed these problems as harbingers of broken spiritual relationships. Animals would have to be identified for sacrifice, and some plants would have to be carefully selected to offer along with that sacrifice in exchange for blessings and well-being.

The mediums got up and began marching out to the fields. I followed with camcorder in tow. When we got out past the thatched-roof houses on the southwest corner of the compound, there were open fields of cassava and sweet potatoes, as well as some fields lying empty after harvests. The mediums led the procession over a small hill, where they stopped by a small plant called kasiba nte *in Lusoga.[40] Right behind them, an elder initiated woman named Lukowe Namwase carried a winnowing basket on her head with* mutabaganya *(a mixture of sesame seeds, groundnuts, coffee berries, and small red legumes called* empandi*), a hen, and a hoe called* enkumbi ensoga, *which is a small, traditional hand hoe made from a V-shaped tree limb. A male elder named Isegya Wamunogga followed her with a mortar holding medicinal liquid mixed in water from Nnyanja Nalubaale and a branch of herbs for sprinkling. Another male elder followed with a goat and* enkumbi enzungu, *a modern, long-handled hoe.*

Lukowe Namwase performed kusenga *with the hen: it was a short prayer that introduced sacrifices to the spirits. The mediums possessed by these spirits watched her as they trembled and continued to dance. Nam-*

wase and the other elders repeated the process with the goat. They took the hen around a plant in the ground called kasiba nte *three times and then did the same with the goat. Isegya Wamunogga blessed the animals, all of the others present, and the nearby kinsman using the branch from the mortar, which Lukowe Rehema and Andrew Mwesige informed me had been used to pound and mix a medicinal compound of over fifty different plants. They told me the process is called* kumansira.

The whole group gathered around the mediums, who grasped the traditional hoe together with all of the elders. They raised and lowered it four times, finally breaking ground around the small kasiba nte *plant. Then they repeated the process with the long-handled modern hoe and dug out the plant. They had to use the old version first because "that is what the ancestors used," Mwesige explained. The modern version finished the process in order to simplify the work, as the blade on the old hoe was curled up and it was fairly ineffective with its short handle.*

Lukowe Namwase carefully placed the uprooted plant on the basket along with the hen and the mutabaganya *mixture, covered everything with a white embroidered cloth, and placed it back on top of her head. Then the whole procession, once again led by the mediums, returned to the village compound.*

As this procession returned, all sang a repetitive chorus about the spirit Lukowe refusing to eat greens and demanding meat instead. The sacrificial animals in tow served as reminders of their purpose as offerings to the spirits. They also sang of finding Lukowe in the bush.

Daalima, daalima Lukowe	Meander, meander Lukowe
namwagainc ku italc adaalima	I found her in the hilly place meandering

The entire episode illustrated how, even when people do not make a place for the spirits within the compound, those spirits still dwell in the bushy areas nearby, watching over fields and houses and still wielding enormous potential to affect their lives.

Later in the process, after this group had built new dwellings for a variety of patron spirits within the compound, they sang of their happiness at welcoming these spirits back into a relationship of more positive influence.

S: Oidhanga n'enkata	You come with a pad and
n'akwetwikila Lukowe	I help you carry Lukowe
Ch: tusangaile bana, tusangaile	welcome dear ones we are happy
okubona ku yabula Lukowe	to see you the lost one Lukowe

S: oidhanga n'enkata	you come with a pad and
waaneetwalila Isegya	you shall carry me Isegya
Ch: tusangaile bana, tusangaile	welcome dear ones we are happy
okubona ku yabula Lukowe	to see you the lost one Lukowe
S: oidhanga n'enkata	you come with a pad and
naakwetwalila Walumbe	I shall carry you Walumbe [death]
Ch: tusangaile bana, tusangaile	welcome dear ones, we are happy
okubona ku yabula Lukowe	to see you the lost one Lukowe
S: oidhanga n'enkata	you come with a pad and
waaneetwalila Lubaale	you shall carry me Lubaale
Ch: tusangaile bana, tusangaile	welcome dear ones we are happy
okubona ku yabula Lukowe	to see you the lost one Lukowe
S: ab'e Bulyangada, maama	those of the plant, *maama*
ab'e Bulyangada tuli kubaleetela kasiba nte	those of the plant we are bringing them *kasiba nte*
Ch: tusangaile bana, tusangaile	welcome dear ones we are happy
okubona ku yabula Lukowe	to see you the lost one Lukowe

The soloist, Lukowe Rehema, played beautifully with motifs of mutual dependence and support here. Lukowe Namwase had worn an *enkata* (carrying pad) on her head, under the winnowing basket containing sacrificial items for the spirit Lukowe. In the progression of the verses, the singer moved from this theme to carrying Walumbe, a double entendre that signifies both the common notion of a medium carrying a spirit and the human burden that all must carry: Walumbe is the spirit associated most closely with death. From there she shifted again to "you shall carry me Lubaale," an expression of praise for the benevolence of spirits that support human well-being. Finally she returned to the image of carrying *kasiba nte* in the winnowing basket with *mutabaganya*, addressing her ritual comrades and fellow farmers as "those of the plant." The entire assemblage of people, plants, sacrificial animals, and spirits came together in this *kasiba nte* processional as a diverse band of uniformly needy beings making their way in life together through group reliance and mutual aid.

Rivers and Other Waters, Trees and Other Plants

As the intense focus on the *kasiba nte* plant demonstrates, spirits and people alike attribute enormous importance to both plants and places in the natural world. The procession centered a plant used for grazing goats when other sources of sustenance are unavailable. The *kasiba nte* plant served as a symbol of agriculturalist survival, a livestock feeding parallel to the protein-rich *mutabaganya* mixture as something to sustain the community during times

Ecologies of Well-Being 103

of relative scarcity. Throughout the rest of this chapter, songs emphasize the connection of these natural elements with the spirits, highlighting their combined power to influence human well-being. Some of these songs deal with specific plants or spiritual associations, while others bind together a broader cosmological whole through litanies of spirits, places, and plants. For example, another song from the rituals at Munamaizi combined multiple references in a way that articulated the proximity of Kiganda and Kisoga traditions of spirit mediumship:

Ch: Bayita nga kubbalibbali	They call beside/in the river
emitala w'ennyanja	where it meets the sea
bayita nga kulubalama	they call beside the river bank
S: Jajja ndaba ku ki Kifaalu Mumbaale	Grandparent, I'm greeting Kifaalu Mumbaale
(chorus)	
S: ge gali wa mayembe ag'ekika?	where are the *mayembe* of this clan?
(chorus)	
S: Ye wuuyo jajja ow'eboggo	That one is a grand of strong voice
(chorus)	
S: kozine mu amaganda age wala.	he's dancing like Kiganda dances from far
(chorus)	
S: ko mulisse ejjembe ery'omuliro	he's flaring up the *jjembe* of fire
(chorus)	
S: be baabo abasajja be banga	those ones are men of the metal things
(chorus)	
S: abadde atya Kiwanuka omulalu	he's been fearing wild Kiwanuka
(chorus)	
S: nkowoola abukulu ab'ewaffe	I'm calling our ancestors
(chorus)	
S: nkwogereko Namalere atulera	I'm talking about a spirit who sits
(chorus)	
S: nkowoola abalungi ab'ewala	I'm calling the beautiful ones from far
(chorus)	
S: ali waggulu omusajja y'ewanise	he's high, the man is climbing
(chorus)	
S: mbiro, mbiro musajja ow'okumiti	hurry, hurry the man in trees
(chorus)	
S: nkowoola abalungi muggwe yo	I'm calling the beautiful ones from there
(chorus)	
S: gira omwogereko Kiwanuka emmandwa	let's talk about the *mandwa* Kiwanuka

(chorus)

S: yedddira engabi, empologoma girya	he's bushbuck clan, he eats lions
Ch: bayita nga kubbalibbali	they call beside/in the river
emitala w'ennyanja	where it meets the sea
bayita nga kulubalama	they call beside the river bank

Understandably, spirit mediums construe the place where the River Nile emerges from Nnyanja Nalubaale as a locus of enormous power: not only are there large cataracts near this source of the world's longest river, but every spirit medium in the region also knows how many Kisoga *nkuni* and other spirits reside there. The litany that follows that initial chorus testifies to the diversity of those spirits in terms of type and provenance. Although the song is in Luganda, its references to spirits include the Lusoga term *bakulu* (ancestors or "important ones," i.e., patron spirits of all kinds). Meanwhile, it names specific types of Kiganda spirits like *mayembe* and the *lubaale* Kiwanuka, who eats fire, and whom Baganda associate with lightning and thunder. In contrast to these spirits common to both regions, the song calls out a *jjembe* whom I never heard named among Baganda: Kifaalu Mumbaale. This name reads like a mash-up between a Kisoga version of a *jjembe* and the historically important Kiganda spirit Kibuuka Mumbaale. For the performers of this song at Munamaizi (which is located in Busoga), however, this was a highly specific spirit who had arrived in a medium—along with others in other mediums—to demand accommodations within the compound and sacrifices in exchange for blessings on locals' well-being. Moreover, the linkage of *mayembe* to the specific clan and the references to fire and metal things reinforce a Kisoga performance practice that associates ankle bells with *mayembe*. The song locates these spirits in the bush by reference to trees and the bushbuck. One ritual sequence at this gathering saw a spirit climbing a tree in the bush to observe adepts sacrificing and roasting a chicken, which they then offered to him right then and there. His distribution of the meat to those gathered offered a physical logic to the notion that people can derive power from their spiritual interactions in natural places like the forest or the riverbank. In other words, the exchange of sacrifice for blessings not only connected people to a spirit but also linked both to a specific place. Finally, then, this song serves as a reminder of those powers and of their locations all around the people.

Other songs enhance this notion of powers surrounding and supporting human life, locating spirits in the sea and the sky. In fact, *basamize* and *baswezi* often draw on oral traditions that characterize these realms as the origins of the spirits. In the Kiganda creation narrative, for example, a sky dweller named Ggulu (lit. "above") is the authoritative spiritual force. Likewise the traditional name for Lake Victoria, Nnyanja Nalubaale, connotes

Ecologies of Well-Being

a place of the *lubaale* spirits, whose benevolence protects and benefits the people nearby. Its first word, Nnyanja, also connotes fish and, as Jennifer L. Johnson has observed, "is a term that references the uncontainable material and metaphoric qualities of impressively large bodies of water."[41] Numerous songs praise spirits while locating their power in these domains. One chorus in particular combines them in a celebration of the Kiganda spirit Kiwanuka.

Sserubwatuka, wansi wali ennyanja,	Sserubwatuka, down [on Earth] there is a sea
Sserubwatuka wanuka waggulu eriyo omuliro!	Sserubwatuka, descend, there is fire above!

Sserubwatuka is a praise name for Kiwanuka that refers to *bwatuka* (the sound of thunder). Some verses of this song name Kiwanuka specifically, rather than using this praise name:

Yanguwangako, Jjajja Kiwanuka Omulalu,	Hurry, wild grandparent Kiwanuka,
yanguwangako, Jjajja, wa ggulu wali omuliro!	hurry, grandparent, there is fire above!

The chorus locates Kiwanuka in Nnyanja Nalubaale with the other *lubaale*, but also in the realm above, where he shows his presence through "fire" (lightning). This not only demonstrates a local understanding of the ecosystem and its meteorological principles, but also weaves them into a cosmological understanding that attributes these powers to spiritual forces. The second part of the verse refers to Kiwanuka eating fire because, as several people explained to me when I saw his spirit mediums munching on coals or burning logs, that is Kiwanuka's food. His presence in his mediums endows them with almost superhuman strength: they eat fire and hot coals, and in many cases they use them to "bathe" as well, spreading burning logs all around their bodies as if they were scrubbing themselves. So the power of the spirits, for *basamize* and *baswezi*, is everywhere. It begins in the sky and in the sea. They experience it in their dreams, where ancestors direct them to medicinal plants. They direct that power through the use of those plant medicines, so their patients find it in the plants themselves. Singers and dancers locate it in the bodies of animals. Virtually all *basamize* and *baswezi* at some stage also locate it in the bodies of the mediums, whose initiation empowers them to serve as hosts for these spirits.

The ubiquity of spiritual and medicinal power is a common theme in *nswezi* ritual and in traditional healing more broadly. One local study lists 220 plants and their uses as mere samples of a broader healing repertory, and

PROMETRA Uganda teaches nearly four hundred medicinal plants to first-year participants in its three-year program.[42] This training regimen reflects the same ecological and cosmological complexity evident in the manufacture and maintenance of *mayembe* (power objects). Healers making these objects often use dozens of plants, sometimes claiming the use of over one hundred for an individual object.[43] Mediums expressed the constancy of these useful plants, the work they require, and the spirits that direct people to them in a song that they performed at Munamaizi and have performed elsewhere in Busoga, as well as in Buganda.

Nsula-nkola,	I spend the night working
nkolera mayembe	working for the *mayembe*
nkola-nkola, nsula-nkola	I work and work, I spend the night working

This chorus alternates with a litany of spirits that, depending on the location, often includes other types in addition to *mayembe*. The middle line of the chorus could thus be changed to *nkolera lubaale* or *nkolera misambwa*, as soloists identify spirits in each category.

Conclusion

This chapter has examined ecologies of well-being via the repertories of ritual practice in which specialists embed and perform songs. The final example returns to the theme of ritual work, hopefully further clarifying the many meanings of such work. These repertories—of both practice and song—grapple with the contexts, challenges, and opportunities surrounding Baganda *basamize* and Basoga *baswezi*. Kiganda twinship repertories reflect a cultural logic of risk and abundance. Kisoga agrarian themes and an archetypical midwife spirit coalesce, linking metaphors of abundance together. *Misambwa* and *nkuni* help people navigate their histories, their familial and clan dynamics, and their deep connections to the places they associate with their ancestors. Songs across both regions about the working spirits called *mayembe* bind seemingly disparate ecological elements together to help people cope with various forms of danger, trust, boundaries, and frontiers. Through the wide variety of ecological elements examined only in part here, these repertories of well-being begin to define some elements of ontology, some regionally specific and others shared more broadly.

The hypothesis driving this chapter—that repertories of ritual and musical practice elucidate Kiganda and Kisoga ecologies of well-being—follows a progressive chain of logical elements. First, an attempt to hear and understand these repertories at least somewhat like the specialists who perform them offers pathways to understanding internal variabilities as part of the richness of traditions. In other words, understanding requires listening to the constant and simultaneous recollection and revision of the concepts, entities, and practices that these specialists and their ancestors hold dear. Second, interregional commonalities indicate shared histories and ethno-linguistic practices that have long connected Baganda and Basoga across a large swath of southern Uganda. Third, the attempt to grasp these elements of specificity and commonality helps transcend the erroneous notion that such specialists' only legitimacy consists in their plant medicine expertise. This narrative has too often dominated attempts at professionalizing, regulating, and controlling healers, ultimately stifling their considerably more varied contributions. Fourth, an understanding of the repertories' power to link social and ecological domains offers a move beyond a "cults of affliction" approach—focused primarily on reactive capacities of ritualists—toward a deeper look at their proactive capabilities and those of their allied colleagues. All four logical features support the central aims of this study, especially in their emphasis on deeper listening to what constitutes efficacy for patients and healers in Uganda.

In many ways, this chapter frames the three that follow it. The next chapter, on gathering medicine, builds from the foundational notion that humans and other-than-human entities interact within these ecologies precisely because their various features are interdependent. The chapter that follows, which looks at sacrifice, outlines movement across, exchange between, and manipulation of those features. An understanding of boundaries between the ecological features motivates the celebration of successful, productive interactions among them. These are the subject of chapter 5, which returns to themes of hospitality to discuss how feasting shapes repertories of well-being. Meanwhile, the stakes of these repertories—shaped as they are by dualities of potential risk and abundance, danger and trust, barrenness and fecundity, dearth and wealth, drought and rain, hunger and feasting—constantly remind professional healers, other specialists, regular clients, and novices alike that ecologies and repertories of well-being help them in many ways to navigate the complexities of experience between life and death.

3. Possessing Sound Medicine

Gathering Resources, Strengthening Networks, Composing Knowledge

Performing repertories of well-being gathers people and resources together. *Basamize* and *baswezi* gather to assess needs and to actively develop available resources to meet those needs. Ultimately, they compose and refine knowledge to meet challenges both esoteric and practical. To explicate that iterative knowledge-making process, this chapter examines three aspects of ritual practice and performance. First, a consideration of the venues in which specialists perform repertories of well-being situates the gathering process vis-à-vis established discourses about ritual symbolism and public healing networks. Second, responding to a well-researched Africanist discourse on spirit mediumship and possession, Kiganda and Kisoga ideas about carrying, dancing with, and conversing with spirits inform an examination of spirits and people—especially spirit mediums—as resources for confronting challenges. Third, a return to power objects created at Makandwa reveals that they, like other resources, serve both symbolic and utilitarian purposes.

Anthropologist Paul Stoller asserts that ethnographers must attend to both shifting spaces and their effect on multiple senses.[1] Venues, people, and power objects are just three of many dynamic aspects that shape intense sensory experiences, and those experiences become a standard part of any ritual adept's understanding of *ebintu eby'obuwangwa* (the things of tradition). This part of the ethnographic encounter with *kusamira* and *nswezi* continues to unpack and clarify what it means for healers and musicians to produce, refine, and reproduce medicinal knowledge through performance. They use music as one tool to produce and shape resources for the express purpose of relating to various entities within ecologies of well-being, including their patron spirits, additional other-than-human familiars, and one another. To consider sonic elements apart from the multisensory reality of ritual would be to artificially separate domains, and yet because musical sound is such a ubiquitous presence in ritual, it remains the primary conduit in this chapter for understanding the relationship between resources, networks, and knowledge. Following a general look at shrines that serve as venues for ritual performance, the chapter offers ethnographic evidence from two performances in order to elucidate the roles of musical performance and spirit mediumship in repertories of well-being. These representative examples demonstrate how *basamize* and *baswezi* gather to assess and develop their resources, strengthen their networks, and generate valuable knowledge. These are social processes of creative thought and action about the resources and relationships that affect illness and wellness.

Sanctuaries of Tradition

The vast majority of the field sites that inform this book feature either a shrine called a *ssabo* (pl. *massabo*) or a shrine associated with Kiganda clan spirits called a *kiggwa* (pl. *biggwa*). They range from small, conical structures—constructed according to local conventions—to much larger structures that are sometimes conical, sometimes built on triangular or square footprints, and often roofed with corrugated tin. In Buganda, the more traditional grass thatching on the roof of such dwellings links them symbolically to similar structures that still house many rural families and those that shelter the remains of Bassekabaka, the kings of Buganda's past. Baganda conceptualize their king or Kabaka as the apex of the kingdom, the one thing that binds it all together. In Luganda, the term *akasolya* serves as both the noun for this physical binding at the roof apex and part of an honorific title for leaders: *Ow'akasolya k'ekika* refers to the head of a clan, but the Kasolya refers to the apical leader of all clans. A full accounting of the other links between household symbols, clanship, and kinship in Buganda lies beyond this book, but the visual and symbolic alignment is meaningful to *basamize* in Buganda. Clan linkage appears to be the only distinguishing feature between *massabo* and *biggwa*, and in many places in Buganda people use the two terms interchangeably. They nevertheless understand that one is more specific than the other. Shrines as defined here are among the main venues for performing repertories of well-being, and they are important nodal points in the articulation of ethnicity via *ebintu eby'obuwangwa* (the things of tradition).

As physical spaces, *massabo* and *biggwa* can overwhelm the senses. Full of fascinating objects, sounds, smells, and tastes, they are undoubtedly special places that attach sensual experience to powerful forms of meaning and

110   CHAPTER 3

signification. Entrants remove their shoes, and at some sites they wash their hands, faces, and feet with water from Nnyanja Nalubaale that has been infused with plant medicines like the fragrant *bombo* and *lweeza*. Many if not most shrines feature a small fireplace where people burn incense and make offerings to various spirits. Most have a designated sitting place for the main spirit medium associated with the site. Depending on the mediums who regularly use the space and their other-than-human familiars, the range of associated spears, shields, animal skins, garments, images, baskets, musical instruments, foods, incense, brews, distillates, and plant medicines can vary greatly. Mediums, musicians, and other adepts shape the spaces by anticipating and responding to overlapping, dynamic variables: the clients' physiological and psychological needs, the spirits' needs, and the basic human and logistical needs of ritual events. Invariably, the sounds of instruments and songs form an important part of the atmosphere. They offer a method for gathering people to a common purpose in ritual activity, or often for attracting participants back into the space after they have gone to do some other ritual work. Performing songs in shrines constitutes a compositional method for organizing people, resources, and knowledge.

Smaller structures offer spirits dwelling places, sometimes within the family compound, and at other times embedded in the landscape. In general, Baganda are probably more prone to conceptualize existing features of the landscape as natural dwelling places for specific spirits. This has been the case at numerous historically important shrines, including those I visited at Bakka, Kitala, Kookola, Kungu, Mubende, and Ttanda.[2] Some communities, more commonly in Busoga, anthropomorphize spirits by building and maintaining small houses for them. These houses typically resemble human dwellings, and the miniatures often sit adjacent to or behind the main houses within Kisoga family compounds. These and other ways of associating a spirit with a physical locus differ from the notion of a shrine, which serves as a more flexible space for spirits to inhabit temporarily.

An exhaustive consideration of visual and other sensual variables in shrines across Buganda and Busoga is less useful here than an understanding of how those variables coalesce when *basamize* and *baswezi* perform repertories of well-being. Ritual gatherings constitute the most salient and consistent feature of site-specific social life at shrines across the two regions. When healers, mediums, musicians, and other knowledgeable adepts gather together to perform the repertories, they gather most often in shrines, or at least they begin there before moving to some other part of the nearby compound, forest, or field associated with a specific trajectory of ritual inquiry. When they

Possessing Sound Medicine 111

observe the basics of hospitality for one another and for guests both human and spiritual, they do so most often in shrines.

A return to features of hospitality in chapter 5 will relate such spaces to feasting, but the present focus on gathering invites consideration of *massabo* and *biggwa* as homologous with other tools that *basamize* and *baswezi* use to gather, contain, and distribute resources associated with well-being. One song about a bag and a drinking gourd indicates that while some tools for gathering have changed over time, others remain relevant to healers now.

Soloist: Ensawo, ensawo yange	The bag, my bag
Chorus: Kaamungolo	Kaamungolo
S: nze ndigenda n'ensawo yange	I shall move/go with my bag
Ch: Kaamungolo	Kaamungolo
S: waalaalaala jjajja yaŋŋambanga	waalaalaala, grandparent used to tell me
Ch: Kaamungolo	Kaamungolo
S: nze ndigenda ne ensawo yange	I shall move/go with my bag
Ch: Kaamungolo	Kaamungolo
S: jjajja jjajjange	grandparent, my grandparent
Ch: Kaamungolo	Kaamungolo
S: nze ndigenda ne endeku yange	I shall move/go with my gourd
Ch: Kaamungolo	Kaamungolo
S: jjajja oli	grandparent, that grandparent [of mine]
Ch: Kaamungolo	Kaamungolo
S: nze ndigenda ne ensawo yange	I shall move/go with my bag
Ch: Kaamungolo	Kaamungolo

This song refers to several items used for gathering within and beyond the shrine. The primary focus is an arcane reference to a bag, probably made of barkcloth. It could refer to an item frequently used to symbolize inheritance from known ancestors, a belt called *ekifundikwa*. More likely, though, the bag aligns with what Ugandan musician Herbert Kinobe, in various stories published in connection with his recording of the song, describes as an object invested with the purpose of gathering.

The first of Kinobe's explanations reads as follows:

Kamungolo is a traditional folk song from Buganda. It tells the story of a man named Kamungolo, the model of a generous, strong and successful man. It's said that the composer of this song was Kamungolo's grandson whom he loved dearly, and to whom he gave his carrying bag. The grandson will not leave behind his grandfather's bag, full of Kamungolo's secrets, as he goes from vil-

112 CHAPTER 3

lage to village proclaiming the achievements, goodness and generosity of his Grandfather Kamungolo, encouraging others to work hard and emulate him. The lyrics of the song are personalized and directed to attentive listeners, supposedly Kamungolo's tribesmen and the neighbouring tribes.[3]

Kinobe's other explanation reads as more of a folkloric story:

> Long ago, in the Baganda kingdom [sic], lived an old man. Since he was young he carried a bag called "Kamungolo" in Luganda. In his old age she [sic] walked with a cane and carried his bag. He was not able to feed herself [sic], so people would put food and water in the bag for him. Later, people began calling him by the name of his bag, Kamungolo. This song was composed to refer to his good bag and to the people who were kind enough to put food and water in his bag. The lesson contained in this song is one of kindness and compassion, it teaches us to aid people in need.[4]

The shifting interpretation is consistent with oral traditions more generally: the details might change from one telling to the next, even within the repertory of a single teller, but the essence of a story's lessons remains more or less consistent over time.

For this song, as for shrines, people, and power objects, that essence is both practical and symbolic. As with repertories of song, this feature of oral traditions means that its audiences must listen imaginatively to both kinds of possibilities, a habit easier to develop when they have attended many different kinds of gatherings at shrines. At the practical level, Kinobe's suggestion about carrying "secrets" or gifts in such a bag is consistent with suggestions from other commentators that the bag in the song could mean virtually any bag that someone carries to the forest for collecting medicines or a bag for the kinds of items that people bring when they arrive at shrines for various functions. Barkcloth garments, drinking gourds, rattling gourd idiophones, and tobacco pipes are common things to bring to a shrine. On arrival in their mediums, spirits commonly request these items, so they are as important to the larger project of gathering resources as are the shrines. Healers might add plant medicines in various forms to the mix of items included in such a bag, some as raw materials like medicinal bark, leaves, or roots, others perhaps processed into powder for mixing into tea or compounding for topical use.

At a less tangible level, the possible functions of the bag as a tool for gathering all highlight it as a symbol, a synecdoche, an index of a specific kind of mutual aid that takes place at shrines. These are places and events where people pool their resources, where they need not choose between addressing afflictions and meeting the other, perhaps more basic and constant needs of those gathered. The second of Kinobe's interpretations offers additional motifs in translation that reinforce the theme of mutual aid. These were common across several other performances of the tune, and they characterize Kamungolo as a big man, a tall man, a kind man, and a good man.[5] The motifs champion social largesse, lauding generosity and hospitality as virtues. Perhaps one of the "secrets" that so many healers, musicians, spirit mediums, and those who seek their help carry with them is that their help comes not from the inanimate items contained in a bag or a shrine, but rather from the gathering together of knowledgeable people, spiritual resources, food and drink, and plant medicines. The concentration of resources into space and time carries a strong linkage with shrines as sanctuaries of ritual gathering and cultural tradition, but like the items in them and those in the bag, like the songs and the drums that accompany them, they are means to an end. They cannot directly cause healing—a power uniformly assigned to spiritual influences across Buganda and Busoga—but gathering them and using them can facilitate interactions. These acts can cultivate ecological and social relations to promote well-being and to heal. Shrines are places where people treat these secrets as highly valued resources.

Among the most valuable resources associated with shrines are people, who also emerge in this song as a distinctive, complex pathway to well-being. The person, coextensive with his container of valuable knowledge in this song about Kamungolo, reflects a categorical overlap worth exploring. Every person who enters a shrine space brings along a set of experiences, capabilities, and expertise. The well-being of a given community could be broadly understood in this context as more than the sum of the collective assets that people gather into the shrine, a place where they actively develop resources both tangible and intangible. Many professional healers would hasten to remind their clients and others that this reality is not unique to them or to spirit mediums; they would regard it as a product of spiritual power. All the same, spirit mediums occupy such a powerful space between spiritual power, ecological power (especially from plant medicines and animal familiars of spirits), and human agency that they deserve special attention here.

Spirit Mediums: Flexible Persons, Conduits to Networks, and Bearers of Knowledge

Spirit mediums embody a phenomenon similar to that of shrines and power objects: their capacity to contain and carry spirits facilitates processes through which those spirits meet people's needs. The Luganda term for people capable of embodying spiritual powers, of releasing a usual sense of self to those powers, is instructive here. *Omukongozzi* (pl. *bakongozzi*) means a carrier, from the verb *okukongojja* (to carry). Along with drums, gourd rattles, and singers, these "carriers" of spirits create and shape ritual space for interaction among people and their patron spirits. Well beyond southern Uganda, people working in many traditions place a premium on spirit mediums' capacity for this kind of flexibility, in terms of both ritual dynamics and musical performance.[6]

A number of scholars have offered terms for thinking through practices of personhood that move beyond individuality. The introduction noted how the broad geography of similar practices suggests alignment with Pierre Bourdieu's notion of "transposable dispositions." Marilyn Strathern's notion of "partible persons" could help explain how a single ancestral spirit (*muzimu*) can have several mediums or how the death of one medium often motivates a search for multiple mediums to fulfill that person's ritual workload.[7] Her thinking of such persons as "dividuals" is somewhat aligned with McKim Marriott's work and reminiscent of E. E. Evans-Pritchard's earlier observations about Nuer kinship and spirituality.[8] Along similar lines, Roy Wagner has written eloquently of "the fractal person," an idea that might well apply to the *kifundikwa*, a barkcloth knot, pouch, or belt that binds a deceased person's responsibilities to an heir.[9] Yet some of these ideas characterize the transferable elements of a person across domains in somewhat brittle imagery. Even where those elements take on associations with new people, they do not necessarily lose their prior ties to other people or spirits. Mediums are in this regard flexible persons. Through these repertories, they practice a form of flexible personhood that aligns with the mutability of other-than-human ecological influences, whether those influences are ancestral and other patron spirits, animal familiars, or plants that become medicines.

Comprehending the centrality of musical performance to the ritual dynamics of *kusamira* and *nswezi* involves listening to indigenous terminologies for what spirit mediums do. For example, the notion of carriers depicts the medium as one who has developed a peculiar kind of psychospiritual strength with *omutwe* (the head) to accommodate spirits. But a spirit that "grabs the head" does not simply detach it. The body follows the head, folding the grabbing concept into the person, so people speak of spirits grabbing the head, grabbing the body, and grabbing the person interchangeably and synonymously. Singers gloss that same strength-of-head (or body) in song as a capacity to "dance" the spirits. In both cases, these euphemisms for spirit possession imply a kind of vigorous movement that tends to clear a physical space within the shrine. A spirit once present in its medium might thrash about, jump up and down, gesticulate, or dance, all of which carve out a physical space that marks their arrival in what is otherwise typically a crowded room. When the music stops, people use that same space to greet the spirit, to seek advice, and to negotiate ways of meeting the spirit's needs through offerings of gifts and sacrifices.

Okwaza: Searching for Spirits

Healers share a core concern with the cultivation of flexibilities required to accomplish this work. One common way to open a spiritual inquiry into a set of physiological problems involves *okwaza* (a search). This kind of search— sometimes also glossed as spiritual *kunoonyereza* (research)—requires a communal effort in which groups sing their way to answers from ancestral and patron spirits about how to minimize pestilence or *ebibi* (bad things) and bring forth *emikisa* (blessings). Whether or not illness has known biomedical explanations, and whether or not appropriate pharmaceutical interventions are already underway, *basamize* believe the search to be an important component of medical practice in which they identify underlying spiritual causes for and components of mental and physical afflictions. According to traditional healer Yahaya Sekagya, this kind of spiritual etiological work can significantly improve the quality of life for people living with HIV, AIDS, and other terminal afflictions.[10] The following example illustrates how, in such a case involving terminal illness, *basamize* work together with a client to seek spiritual explanations and develop the capacity to cope with them as a means of addressing health challenges beyond anyone's control.

In this example, a woman named Nakifuba was seeking guidance from the Uganda chapter of the international NGO PROMETRA about how to "live positively" with HIV.[11] Her encounter typifies many people's experiences with the organization's approach: once thoroughly dejected by the specter of life with the virus, she found through PROMETRA a set of approaches to her nutrition, plant medicine to target her symptomatic needs, and spiritual wellness, all of which bolstered her health. She came to rely on PROMETRA to supplement her antiretroviral therapies with plant medicines, addressing specific issues as they arose. Before I met Nakifuba, I had spent several weeks getting acquainted with the PROMETRA staff, the healers who were working and learning at their forest training facility near a trading center town called Buyijja, and the cadre of clients who regularly visited them there. The setup at PROMETRA Buyijja contrasted slightly with the healers' other primary site for client visits, the shrines in their home villages. On the day that I met Nakifuba, a feeling of heaviness in her chest had led her to PROMETRA's group of *basamize*, who recognized her complaint as something that would require spiritual, plant-based medicinal, and physiological understanding and

116 CHAPTER 3

intervention. Already aware of her regimen of antiretroviral medications and the plant-based compounds she was using to supplement them, this group of healers was prepared to assess her spiritual needs through *okwaza*, a search for Nakifuba's unique spiritual challenges and opportunities.

As Nakifuba worked to address this specific physical affliction, the *basamize* used a variety of methods to loosen or open her capacity for blessings.[12] They encouraged Nakifuba to participate—to clap, sing, and eventually dance—in order to accomplish this. They were training her in the way that ritual adepts typically train ill novices to confront the spiritual elements of affliction, encouraging her to see spiritual components as the underlying causes of physiological symptoms. This search began much like any other ritual: *basamize* began to sing, and the gourd rattles and the drums followed shortly thereafter in collective calls for spirits to manifest in their mediums. Their initial call was general in nature, so it included a variety of spirit types announced in song as part of an etiological search. The soloist began with words to sound one such direct call to spirits who might be disturbing Nakifuba. He sang,

Tuyita amayembe, amayembe nga ng'oyo	We invoke the mayembe, the mayembe like those of that one [the ill person]

A chorus responded:

egy'omu nkoola	those in the wilderness[13]

Then the call-and-response continued:

S: Jjajja mmwe nvuge, aa-aaa, n'oggya misambwa egyo	You, grandparent, take charge, aa-aaa, and you draw out those *misambwa*,
Ch: egy'omu nkoola	those in the wilderness
S: nsula ku budde, misambwa gy'ekika gyannondoola	I spend all night, the clan's misambwa pursued me
Ch: egy'omu nkoola	those in the wilderness
S: Jjajja . . . eee	Grandparent [intercessor] . . . yes
Ch: mmanyi w'ekika oyo nnondoola, egy'omu nkoola	I am conversant with the one of the clan, that one I can manage, those of the wilderness

Soon the group was pleased to see one, then two, then a few mediums demonstrate outward physical signs of possession. The singer—a man named Ssemaluulu John—stopped singing just as a spirit arrived in one medium. Knowing that this was among my first encounters with spirits possessing their

Possessing Sound Medicine

mediums, he turned to me, saying, "Ooooh, Kigozi! The grandparent has come!"[14] He and the other adepts greeted the spirit formally, offering warm thanks for its protection with a laudatory greeting: "Thank you for working and keeping [us], grandparent."[15] Then Ssemaluulu and others identified the group's purpose for calling this spirit. Several people repeated the phrase, "there is a sick person here," and at about the same time, Ssemaluulu said, "*Jjajja*, these people have called you, as we want you [to help]."[16] The group offered the spirit his tobacco pipe and a small gourd containing the traditional banana brew called *mwenge muganda*. In observing these and other forms of greeting and hospitable gestures, they actively cultivated a space of welcome for the patron spirit, both in the body of his medium and in the shrine.

Countless later encounters with the same phenomena would clarify for me that these were all standard—if dynamic—elements of a ritual process. The process incorporates musical sound as a core element of socializing with spiritual visitors. Supported by a chorus of other *basamize* and later by other leading singers, Ssemaluulu not only identified possible spiritual causes for Nakifuba's symptoms, he also exemplified to young *bazamize* the musical rhetoric of a diagnostic search, *okwaza*. As this ritual proceeded, it became clear that "calling" spirits was far from the only way that people used music in this and other contexts. A singer named Mpanga John sang another tune:

Akyali wa ddala ng'avugako emmandwa ng'avuga,	She is still real [worthy] when the *mandwa* are upon her, when he is in charge
akyali wa ddala ng'avugako emmandwa, tambula!	she is still worthy when the *mandwa* are upon her, move/walk [trust her]!

Mpanga's song signaled to the spirit that the gathered group acknowledged underlying spiritual causes for Nakifuba's affliction. The spirit responded immediately by calling Nakifuba to come closer. In an empathetic, diagnostic gesture, the spirit Magobwe then placed one hand on Nakifuba's head. The client became physically excited, breathed heavily, and belched. Then one of the adepts nearby came to encourage her to get up and dance to the song. The spirit was assessing Nakifuba's need to develop her own capacity for mediumship. His diagnostic technique was consistent with a widespread belief that locates underlying spiritual causes of virtually all bodily afflictions via potential entry points in the head, on the palms of hands, and on the bottoms of feet.[17] Recognizing the spirit's gesture, the group responded by trying to use the music to promote possession for Nakifuba. An elder then helped her up, inviting her to dance. A staff member would later explain to me that this

118   CHAPTER 3

process is at first physically and psychologically difficult for new mediums, but that music and dance can make it easier.[18] It is a process that aligns with many other forms of *okusumulula* (untying or unbinding) a person's obstacles to holistic well-being, rendering them more open to *emikisa* (the blessings). The performance reinforced the belief among specialists at PROMETRA Uganda that although Nakifuba was getting the physical help she needed through pharmaceuticals and plant medicine, she still had something to gain from spiritual guidance: she could use it to understand the other-than-human components of her affliction and, ultimately, to live better.

These few brief scenes from Nakifuba's protracted therapeutic trajectory depict a woman working to understand her illness in culturally logical, comprehensible terms. She initially came for symptomatic relief, but she began a series of relationships that helped her understand her illness on a deeper level. She lives in a time and place in which—despite the best efforts of many organizations working to combat stigma—people living with HIV and AIDS frequently suffer social consequences in tandem with their physical struggles. She and her spiritual mentors subscribe to a model that actively includes her in social attempts to grapple with her illness. If they, and we, read her belching and heaving as a physical rejection of social alienation, then Nakifuba's dancing means active participation in a fuller, more social acceptance of her illness, her symptoms, and their underlying spiritual causes. Just as they do with other forms of illness, *basamize* associated Nakifuba's affliction with social and spiritual alienation. By contrast, they equated her spiritual connectedness with participation in music and dance, both becoming essential to her reintegration into an atmosphere of social conviviality and a better quality of life.

Nakifuba's encounter with the spirit left her feeling slightly better physically, but when she reflected on it from the cargo bed of a truck on our way to the taxi stage after the ritual, she emphasized her hope that this intervention would help her maintain a link with the spiritual aspects of her illness in the future. She understood that link as one part of a larger therapeutic repertory that would help her pursue and maintain a high quality of life. Her remarks placed a face on something that Dr. Sekagya explained many times about traditional medicine: too often organizations dismiss spiritual pursuits as so much hocus pocus, privileging physiological, often allopathic approaches instead. But this is not an either-or proposition. For Nakifuba, for so many others who work with and seek help from PROMETRA and the Buyijja Traditional Healers' Association, and for those reorienting their failing crops and ailing families to other-than-human influences, the situations demand both spiritual and more tangible practical approaches. Whereas the latter offers important techniques and chemical or plant medicine interventions, the former often enables people to live better through deeper understandings of their afflictions.

Nakifuba's case therefore raises important questions about how the cultural relevance of care affects overall efficacy. Ultimately, the stakes of her well-being and her agency in it go beyond the plant medicines and social or musical activities that make her feel better. At some point in this trajectory, it will also become important for this community and Nakifuba's younger kin to ensure that she finishes her life amid good social relations with both her fellow *basamize* and her patron spirits. A restless spirit, after all, could cause continuing problems for everyone involved. Dr. Sekagya and the healers involved with PROMETRA Uganda take a rather prescriptive approach to this, often inviting allopathic physicians and health workers to their facility in Buyijja, and sending staffers when the Ministry of Health or the Ministry of Culture wants to shape policy around traditional healers. The point here is not to endorse PROMETRA's model or to prescribe any one approach, but rather to draw attention to a pair of daunting realities that swirl around the performance of these repertories. The first is the scale of the challenges: Nakifuba was only one client, and a single NGO can only affect so many healers and patients in any given day, week, month, or year. The second is the complex nature of the challenges: PROMETRA offers one model, but the broader discourses of development, along with the multiple points of intersection and relevance for traditional healers, might suggest the possibility and potential viability of many others.

Spirit mediums respond to those realities, drawing on their flexibilities to extend notions of mutual aid, to expand networks of support, and to integrate ecological and spiritual resources. In the search described here, as in other contexts that encourage spiritual intervention, repertories of well-being enable spirit mediums to gather spiritual power into specific moments, spaces, and bodies, often for consultation on particular challenges. Through ever-shifting networks of healers and fellow mediums, they constantly develop and revise their flexibilities, building their repertories of songs, their capabilities for other kinds of ritual work, and their networks of social support. In these ways, they also become bearers of specialized knowledge to one another, to novices, and to client patients at varying levels of experience.

Mayembe: The Musical Socialization of Spiritual Power

So far, this chapter has considered shrines and spirit mediums in processes of gathering resources, strengthening resource networks, and composing

120   CHAPTER 3

medicinal knowledge. Turning now to a specific kind of physical object that
contributes to the same processes, this section examines the use of objects
called *mayembe* (sing. *jjembe*). Chapter 2, on ecology, gave an overview of the
working spirits that share this moniker and people's motivations for consult-
ing them, as well as the array of materials used in the objects' creation and
the associated repertory that indexes those materials, especially flora and
fauna. Because *basamize* believe that spirits directly affect the well-being of
their families, clients, communities, domestic animals, and crops, they take
seriously the social responsibility to create and maintain spaces for spiritual
devotion and dwelling, including these power objects that *mayembe* inhabit.
A return to the same research site at Makandwa will demonstrate how Kabona Mutale and the others who gathered there used newly created power
objects—along with songs, garments, and musical instruments—to perform
a social mediation of conflict with a nearby church community.

I first met Kabona Mutale in May 2009 through a mutual friend whose
reputation for singing was—and remains—sterling throughout Buganda.
Mutale's gregarious nature and his generosity in teaching that singer and
other acolytes about ritual praxis in this region had made him one of my
most reliable sources. I visited him one rainy Friday in 2010 after nearly a year
away from the hospitality of his compound near Joggo in Mukono District.
Having seen him only seldom in the interim, I arrived with a housewarming
gift of *mwenge*, the mild traditional banana and millet beer that holds such a
prominent place in local rituals of all kinds. When I arrived, Kabona Mutale
and a small entourage were preparing to leave for a ritual in Makandwa to
create and install *mayembe*. It would take some time to iron out the details,
but when I asked to join them, Mutale readily agreed. He instructed me to
offer *ekigali* (a gift of special significance) to ask Jjajja Muwanga's permission.
Mutale explained that this gift would preclude anyone at Makandwa from
taking issue with my presence. They might take issue with him or with me,
he explained, but they would not trifle with the spirits. As the song goes,

Ozannyisa kirala,	You play with something else,
naye tozannyisanga jjembe;	but you do not play with a *jjembe*;
wankwata ndi muto	you [the spirit] grabbed [possessed]
	me when I was young;
sigenda [ku]kwerabira!	I shall not forget!

His impulse reflected a common pattern of granting access to ritual spaces
and events, but in this case it also foreshadowed something new: Mutale
was preparing to use a similar form of spiritual authority to navigate a tricky
social dynamic between some of the *basamize* living at Makandwa and their
fellow parishioners in their Christian church communities.

Gimme Shelter: Meeting Spirits' Demands for Places to Call Their Own

The community gathering to install *mayembe* at Makandwa helps illuminate some widespread motivations among *basamize* for promoting forms of ecumenical pluralism. Kabona Mutale's presence at Makandwa followed on dozens of stories about people being involuntarily possessed in church and at other inconvenient or dangerous times. The potential for danger arises because people can be shunned from their religious communities, sometimes violently, or their homes or shrines could come under scrutiny or physical attack from people who perceive their traditional practices as evil. The main spirit mediums in this narrative had personal experience with this phenomenon. For them, as for so many others, involuntary possession during church services had raised a graver set of concerns. Many Pentecostal and nondenominational holiness churches in Uganda regularly cast out spirits that they believe to be evil. Should people who maintain commitments to both church and shrine—as was the case at Makandwa—be exposed in their church communities, their actions could be construed as disloyal or even sinful, and reactionary measures could easily be drastic. Religious fervor has driven people to destroy many shrines, including at least one *kiggwa* at a lungfish clan estate. The shrine in Mutale's compound at Joggo has also been damaged in the past, but it remains unclear whether the culprits were rival healers or religiously motivated vandals.

Patron spirits have as many reasons to prevent these violations of sacred space as do their mediums and other devotees. As noted above, a major purpose of *kusamira* ritual across southern Uganda is to create and maintain physical spaces in which ancestral and other patron spirits can dwell. While the gourd rattle, the drum, and various offerings can make a spirit feel more welcome in a shrine or spirit mediums, a small house or a power object offers a stable, physical space of honor for a spirit in a family compound. Spirits demand regular upkeep and sacrifice, which become occasions for human gathering and interaction with patron spirits. Unlike the small houses that people build in their compounds for other kinds of spirits, though, a *jjembe* or power object for a spirit by the same name is almost as physically portable as its associated spirit, even if many people still store them in shrines or in their homes.

Basamize use materials and music together in these efforts. Prior to Makandwa, I had only limited experience with these power objects, having witnessed *okusalira amayembe* (a "feeding" of *mayembe* spirits via an offering of sacrificial blood through mediums and power objects). At Makandwa, in contrast,

122   CHAPTER 3

I witnessed as Mutale and Kapere worked together with the community to create new power objects for existing *mayembe*, and installed those specific spirits—Jjajja Gaboggola and Jjajja Nakavuma—in their new dwellings. The stated purpose of making such an offering was for the community to manage a negotiation between their patron spirits' demands and their simultaneous Christian loyalties. Neglect one, and they risked the health of the community; neglect the other, and they could incur both unwelcome scrutiny from the local Christian congregations and other potential consequences for their *emyoyo* (souls) as conceptualized by their Christian counterparts.

The Ritual Seriousness of Play

The gathering to install *mayembe* at Makandwa offers evidence of Mutale's lofty motivations and of the community's commitment to peaceful pluralism. Of particular interest here are questions about how and why the community assembled these materials and repertories to reproduce useful, propitious social and spiritual relations. Once the spirits were present in their mediums, Mutale and the other *basamize* introduced them to a range of objects: a razor used to cut a bit of hair, fingernail clippers, a mirror, a comb, a watch, skin-care products, a radio, a phone, a hymnal, a Bible, pen and paper, and lye-based soap. He placed these alongside the medicinal herbs typically used for ritual bathing. Demonstrating their use to the spirits, he claimed that these items were "not bad," and he asked that the grandchildren (i.e., their gathered devotees) be permitted to use them.

Kabona Mutale gave particular attention to the sounds of Christian hymnody and prayer. *Basamize* surrounded the medium to sing a song that named a *jjembe*, Nakavuma. In a typical arrival scene for a female spirit, that spirit then mounted her medium. The other *basamize* clothed Nakavuma in barkcloth according to appropriate traditional gender norms: a skirt with a belt around the waist rather than the male-coded over-one-shoulder technique. Mutale shifted his focus to sound: first he used his phone to play a Christian hymn for a ringtone, and then he used a radio to pick up a signal from the local Catholic station, Radio Maria. Regarding each of these technologies, he asked the spirit, "have you heard this other *jjembe*?"[19] In so doing, he momentarily elevated the radio and the other objects to equal footing with the spiritual technology of the power objects. He created a kind of equivalency in the capacity of phones, Bibles, and hymnals to house spiritual powers and facilitate human communication with other-than-human powers. Mutale then opened a Bible to perform Christianity for the spirit. He lined out a Catholic hymn, a process that involved chanting its opening stanza, and he

Possessing Sound Medicine 123

encouraged the group to respond by singing along so that the spirit could see and hear what this might look like in a church service. They responded, playing along with his strategy.

Once Nakavuma nodded her agreement that these physical and sonic emblems of modernity did not threaten her important role in the community, the group went through a similar process with the male *jjembe* Gaboggola. As described in chapter 2, they sacrificed animals, feeding the *mayembe* some of the blood and pouring the rest into the power objects that would house them. They also made a sacrifice for Namagga, the "landlord" *muzimu* who once employed these *mayembe*. The process demonstrated to Namagga and to the *mayembe* that the community remained committed to them, that neither their changing lives nor their religious habits threatened their maintenance of that commitment. Once finished, the power objects (also called *mayembe*) occupied a place of honor within the compound's shrine. The community has no doubt used those objects to feed the *mayembe* again in later offerings of gratitude and continuing hope for their spiritual protection. In this sense, the objects now serve as microcosmic physical indices of the rituals that local *basamize* once performed to create them and of songs and sacrifices they will continually repeat to maintain them. Ultimately, this capacity to index a specific interaction and to offer a tangible presence for the relationship it fostered endows *mayembe* with enormous power. They become physical manifestations and dwellings for the spirits that inhabit them. They become a physical locus for plant medicine, sacrifice, song, and other ritual actions all directed toward the eradication of illness, misfortune, and conflict, and ultimately, the distillation of positive intentions for the good of the group.

During the installation of *mayembe*, Mutale fostered a jovial atmosphere of ritual play that served a serious purpose: the *basamize* showed the spirit Nakavuma that like other emblems of modern living, Christian ritual and hymnody constituted innocuous unfamiliarities. This assemblage of ritual materialities and repertories generated a signifying technology of spiritual safety and well-being (i.e., the physical power object) for the people of Makandwa. Although the personal stakes for the spirit mediums were certainly high, the process of creating power objects superseded any individual affliction. Their manufacture and the installation of *mayembe* spirits in them offered Makandwa village a broad sense of spiritual protection by situating Namagga's working spirits—Gaboggola and Nakavuma—in places of honor. The reassurance that neither spiritual nor technological modernities would displace Namagga and her *mayembe* generated a more specific form of protection for the spirit medium, whom Kabona Mutale asked the spirits not to disturb during Christian church services. The community's investments in

124 CHAPTER 3

sacrificial animals, in time spent with the spirits, and in cultural commitment amid social change expressed hopeful anticipation of their patron spirits' blessings.

Kabona Mutale's motivations as an interreligious peacemaker appear to emerge from related concerns. A series of interviews with him and one of his spiritual protégés depicted the shrine as a space that has long been associated with "cooling down" spirits, easing the process of possession for new mediums, and fostering propitious relationships among humans and patron spirits.[20] Although *mayembe* can be, in the words of several specialists, "fierce" or "hard" on both their mediums and bystanders, Mutale shares an awareness with many other *basamize* that when properly maintained, they have enormous capacity for ritual play and spiritual protection. Again, the ubiquitous *mayembe* song comes to mind, but this time with its reference to play enriched by Mutale's ritual performance:

Ozannyisa kirala,	You play with something else,
naye tozannyisanga jjembe;	but you do not play with a *jjembe*;
wankwata ndi muto	you [the spirit] grabbed [possessed] me when I was young;
sigenda kwerabira!	I shall not forget!

More than a ritual facilitator, Mutale is also a spirit medium, *omukongozzi* (one who "carries" spirits), and he takes this responsibility just as seriously. When, on a regular basis, he offers his body as a vessel for a patron spirit, his personal investments of time, energy, and resources promote well-being. For him, as for other mediums, the material concerns of spiritual embodiment could not be more constant. Meeting spiritual needs and negotiating spiritual priorities requires a total devotion of their creative resources.

Ritual Innovation: High-Tech(nē) Hymnody

Facilitated by Kabona Mutale and Jjajja Kapere, the gathering at Makandwa creatively integrated a Christian written tradition and the accoutrements of modern life into the complex materialities and spiritual infrastructures of a *kusamira* oral tradition. This ontological shift produced an ecumenical technology of ritual innovation, which constitutes a peculiar kind of technology. In his ethnography about the performance of Tumbuka healing, Steven Friedson invokes philosopher Martin Heidegger's phenomenological treatment of technē (technology as art), a move that invites comparisons to other ethnographic theorists.[21] Among them, Claude Lévi-Strauss's notion of bricolage presents an interesting set of possibilities.[22] A generous reading of

Possessing Sound Medicine 125

the concept sees the bricoleur not as a purveyor of haphazard improvisations, but rather as an arbiter of creative prowess. In Friedson's use of the technē formulation, he writes of the Tumbuka in Malawi that, "medical technology is part of musical experience, and musical experience [is] a mode of being-in-the-world for both spirit and human."[23] Following this thread demonstrates how the power objects and the process of creating them at Makandwa, like the musical instruments and the process of performing songs with them, became social technologies of well-being. By using the power objects in a ritual sequence that stimulated and enhanced favorable local social relations, *basamize* manufactured them as a durable physical locus of intentionality and consciously imbued them with power.

Having earned the honorific title *kabona* as a long-time practitioner of *kusamira*, Mutale was thoroughly accustomed to integrations of ritual technē—musical and otherwise—in what anthropologist Charles Piot calls "village modernity."[24] Mutale's ritual innovations mix diverse approaches, philosophies, technologies, and traditions in order to cultivate spaces in which he and others can relate to patron spirits and deities associated with those traditions. A devout Muslim, he frequently enters the shrines in his own compound by either greeting spirits by their praise names and or blaring sonorously, "*Allahu akbar!*" Once, when he served as the best man to a mutual friend named Kabona Jjumba, he arrived at the wedding with the groom and his bride in a helicopter (the DVD was quite a spectacle). He brought me along with his small group to Makandwa in his own car, a rare luxury even for many middle-class Ugandans at the time, to create power objects. His methods testify both to his creative influence and to the strength of this community's commitment to a sense of convivial, ecumenical post-modernity. The popular healer has made a name for himself—and no small number of rivals from various camps—by reinforcing the notion that traditional medicine and its associated rituals should create inclusive spaces for the propagation of both well-being and civic virtue. He has meanwhile overtly rejected the notion that this process is in any way at odds with the distinctive simultaneities of ex-colonial postmodernity, whether religious, technological, social, or some combination of all these domains.

Conclusion

The cases presented in this chapter point to a pervasive concern among ritual specialists in southern Uganda with gathering ecological, human, and other-than-human resources. The examples have demonstrated how *basamize* and *baswezi* assess, develop, and deploy those resources. These examples happen

126   CHAPTER 3

to emerge primarily from Kiganda contexts, but the tendencies to gather
and distribute, to bind and unbind, prove just as pervasive in Busoga. The
concerns in chapter 2 with gathering spiritual influences into new dwellings at Munamaizi, for example, echoed these themes. In that context, *ba-*
swezi gathered resources that constituted the inheritance of the surrounding
landscape and its spiritual patrons. Other rituals, like the creation of power
objects at Makandwa, gathered plant medicines and sacrifices into physical
objects that *basamize* shaped and empowered by association with working
spirits. Together, the prior chapter on ecology and this chapter describe how
Jjajja Mutale and the community at Munamaizi have used those new power
objects as part of an innovative effort to mediate conflict with an overlapping
Christian population. *Basamize* at Buyijja working with PROMETRA foster
yet another kind of gathering to help novices understand the demands and
techniques of mediumship. As in so many communities, PROMETRA Buyijja
offers examples of mediumship as an embodied practice of gathering and
distributing, of binding bad things and unbinding blessings.

All these efforts pursue the same flexibility that has been the hallmark of
the region's indigenous healing traditions for hundreds of years: they cultivate ritual gatherings or "functions"—as *basamize* and *baswezi* so often
call them in English—in which patients and healers come to seek mutual
understandings of illness, and to hone expressive tools and habitual practices
of wellness. For people like Nakifuba and others whose access to health care
mostly engages local healers, these efforts and the flexibilities they actively
develop constitute enormous assets to well-being. The flexibility of the shrine
space and the mediums who operate within it aligns with the most prominent
aesthetic ideals that shape *kusamira* musical performance. A good singer,
for example, is not only someone who sings with a clear tone or who can be
heard above the drums. As noted in the introduction, a good singer is also
someone who sings inventively, imaginatively, who "has many motifs" (or
verses or variations). The same could be said of a drummer, especially one
who plays the main *mbuutu* drum or the flashy variations on the *ngalabi*.
When a person plays or sings with all these qualities, that person can earn
other accolades: *mukugu* (master), *muyonza* (one who moves people), or
even *kaffulu* (a master across several domains like someone who can sing
and play several instruments quite well). In all these cases, healers, mediums,
and musicians champion flexibility and creativity—a fecund imagination
for playing with motifs and their meanings—as their most highly valued
aesthetic qualities.

Basamize and *baswezi* manipulate musical instruments, ritual power objects, and human spirit mediums to carry out their work, which involves the

Possessing Sound Medicine

containment and release of powerful knowledge, medicinal substance, and performative signification. Just as they shape objects and develop people's capacity for spirit mediumship, *basamize* also sculpt sound in the interest of constantly reproducing propitious relations with patron spirits. These parallel flexibilities within musical and therapeutic social spaces suggest a broader conceptual homology between musical and medicinal repertories. Both of these are repertories of practice. They are constellations of human action and means of human/spiritual interaction. Just as a good musician must contain and deploy many idiomatic rhythmic and poetic motifs, a healer must also learn, collect, know, and appropriately dispense a complex range of medicinal knowledge. Both repertories emphasize the ability of their practitioners to contain and share their expertise with good judgment, timing, discretion, and political and social sensitivity. Both domains place a premium on the willingness of practitioners to experiment. Among *basamize* and *baswezi*, healing repertories catalog a cultural logic of physiological and spiritual well-being that connects each person to the social group, patron spirits, other-than-human familiars, and the land.

Whether deployed in shrines or at other spiritual dwellings, musical instruments, songs, power objects, and human bodies all serve to gather, contain, and deploy the powerful impact of *kusamira* and *nswezi*. People use each of these tools in its own way to cultivate meaningful and mutually rewarding relationships with their patron spirits. Two analogies can help clarify these entanglements of space and substance:

- musical instruments are to sound as songs are to words
- power objects are to plants, other medicines, and sacrificial blood as bodies of mediums are to spirits

Each of these entities operates on the capacity to gather and contain one or more form(s) of healing power for distribution or release at a time and in a manner negotiated among ritual specialists and their patron spirits. In this regard, repertories of healing necessarily imply a process that is mutually beneficial to humans and spirits. As with so many other forms of performance, the negotiated mutual benefit ensures that these repertories remain broadly unified in purpose across a sizeable geography, even when they can never be the same twice across variable times, places, and resources.

4. Sacrifice and Song
Ritual Exchange and the Production of Relational Ideals

At the heart of *kusamira* and *nswezi* ritual practices, the relationships between humans and other-than-human entities constantly reproduce resilient ideas about what it means to live well. Sacrificial exchanges in ritual constitute and foster these relationships, and ritual music reveals much about how both the relationships and the transactions generate meaning. This chapter examines practices and songs surrounding the ritual exchange of various sacrifices, invariably for blessings that contribute to well-being. By engaging throughout their lives in a series of sacrificial transactions with other-than-human familiars that share a common ecology, *basamize* and *baswezi* learn what it means to live well with one another, with the spirits, and with the animals and plants that sustain them. Each category of beings acts on a variety of motivations both physiological and social in order to articulate and shape their respective places in the relational sphere, their shared ecology of well-being. In other words, they learn to meaningfully engage with what they regard as the good life. An examination of music and meaning in these exchanges helps elucidate the significant commitments of time and resources allocated to them. In that regard, this chapter pulls together the themes of ritual work, ecology, and relational space into an investigation of song and sacrifice. Ultimately, repertories for sacrifice and celebration discussed in this chapter and the next lead back to some enduring questions about the cultural logic of efficacy.

Throughout this book, the themes of binding and unbinding have already surfaced frequently. Sacrifice focuses on the eradication of illness, pestilence, and other forms of negativity, as well as the opening of pathways for blessings, good health, and convivial social relations, or, in other words, the binding of bad things and the unbinding of blessings. Sacrifices designed to bind and unbind take many forms. The typical slaughter of a live animal (or several) is certainly a central emphasis of many rituals, but this is only one form of exchange situated within a protracted series of transactions in which humans offer something in trade for blessings. Every offering—coffee berries, beer, tobacco, money, barkcloth, *matooke* roasted in the peel, sesame seeds, fruit, and other foodstuffs—demonstrates the seriousness with which specialists approach a relationship with a given spirit. They locate a sense of commitment in tangible offerings that require, first and foremost, sacrifices of time and resources from those who offer them. Ultimately, it is the commitment to these relationships, not the things themselves, that opens the pathways for blessings. After all, the specific offerings often turn out to be negotiable.

The process of negotiating a sacrifice with the spirits that demand it is important, as it parallels the system of flexible fees for service that has rendered traditional healing so consistently accessible to Ugandans. People gather, they sound the drums and sing, and they call the spirits. When their visitors arrive, those spirits invariably make demands, but people's relative ability to meet their demands varies greatly. A spirit might request a cow, for example, but then accept a goat or several chickens in its stead. In fact, spirits do often request cows, but the actual sacrifice and slaughter of an animal that large is rare, and usually accompanied by large gatherings of many people who contribute to procuring the animal. In virtually every other case, a smaller, more affordable sacrifice stands in for the spirit's initial request. Likewise a healer might diagnose someone and begin negotiations with a list of demands that seems unreasonable to some clients. A client's response can demonstrate her seriousness about the transaction, which is often much more important than whether the demands are met in full.

Research participants had several names for these negotiations: they referred to *kuteesa* or *kutanya*, both verbs for negotiation, but also to *okutta omukago* (cutting a pact). *Omukago* refers to a kind of blood pact in which two participants split a coffee berry into its two halves, cut their own bellies near the navel, dip the halves in blood, and exchange them, rubbing them into the cuts or eating them to create a specific form of consanguinity. The reference reminds participants that every offering of coffee berries and every ritual negotiation over sacrifice is also a kind of blood pact in which the blood of the sacrificial animal cements an agreement. *Basamize* and *baswezi* "tie" such agreements with spirits when they commit to specific ritual work like the brewing of some banana beer or the slaughter of an animal. As with other rites, the language of tying or binding is important here: healers explain that

130　　　　　　　　　　　　　CHAPTER 4

such agreements bind people to spiritual power and simultaneously unbind blessings or clear pathways to blessings.[1]

Throughout these processes, spirit mediums act as important bearers of exchange communications and responsibilities. Specialists refer to mediums as carriers of spirits (see chapter 3), but their work also mediates a great deal of crucial information. If the commitment is large, the mediums and their comrades may need to organize resources for the purchase of items for sacrifice. It is not enough to locate these items; people must prove the fulfillment of their commitments to the spirits by showing them the intended sacrifices, an act accomplished through the embodiment of the spirit in a human medium. Giving or furnishing intended sacrifices to the spirits also reinforces the mediums' important role by locating the crux of a transactional relationship in the bodies of those who host their patron spirits.[2] At these moments, *basamize* and *baswezi* offer prayers as they show sacrificial animals and foodstuffs to the spirits. Like singers renowned for knowing many idiomatic motifs, some experienced elders have attained notoriety through these exchanges. They not only say appropriate prayers, but also offer many widely varied prayers, lauding the patron spirits for their positive influence on well-being.

The Cultural Logic of Sacrifice:
Singing and Praying, Blessing and Feeding

If song reveals a great deal about what motivates *kusamira* and *nswezi* ritual practices in general, the songs embedded in processes of sacrifice go even further toward illuminating the cultural logic of transactional relationships between humans and their patron spirits. A series of sacrifices near Nakawuka offers contextualized case studies for understanding how song performances and the idiomatic recitation of prayers demonstrate this kind of logic.

Many prayers display a poetic character that parallels ritual songs, and some ritual adepts acquire special positions or titles through their ability to recite prayers within this quasi-improvisatory idiom. One example is a *musiige* (caretaker for a shrine). A *musiige* named Ronald Bwette cares for the sacred sites and manages sacrifices at a place called Kisuze. The name of the place comes from the Luganda verb *kusula* (to spend the night) because a branch of the lungfish clan claims this as an early site where ancestors arrived, resided, and established a clan estate. The clan's historical tradition holds that the main patron spirit is an ancestor whose people had been in the region for some time when Tonda (the Creator) inquired with him about how he (the ancestor) would move around the place. The head of the lungfish clan at the time gestured to the largest feature of the locale, a large boat that now

Sacrifice and Song

appears as a boulder some 3.5–4.5 m (12–15') high and roughly 15 m (50') long. Tonda was impressed with how the people had organized their transport, so he called the place Katwe Kagezi, which means "the clever head."[3]

Now a minor estate for the lungfish clan on the largest hill overlooking Nakawuka town, this place maintains close links with a borough of Kampala that bears a shortened version of the same name, Katwe. The latter is home to many panel beaters, welders, and automotive mechanics, as well as the chess champion who was the subject of the *Queen of Katwe* story.[4] When I inquired with Bwette about a possible connection between the two places, he confirmed that many people from Katwe in Kampala go to Kisuze/Katwe Kagezi for year-end celebrations that often last from December 31 well into the second week of the new year and sometimes beyond. Whereas Americans and Europeans typically characterize this time of year as "new," people in this part of Uganda celebrate the completion of the year gone by.[5] Bwette also informed me that a venerable elder of Buganda's musical community named Ssaalongo Deziderio Matovu Kiwanuka was married to the main spirit medium at this place, the late Jjajja Byuma, so named after the main patron spirit. At the time, Deziderio's Kampala office for his performing ensemble sat nestled among the varied creative industries of Katwe in Kampala. Therein lies the most potent symbolic link between these two places: the word *ebyuma* refers to metal things of all kinds, but often to items that people use in creative and innovative processes. Historically, the term was used to refer to metal bells and tools of an earlier era, but today it can also refer to an iron hoe, a toaster, a microwave, an oven, a welding torch, or even car parts. I had seen Deziderio perform, and I knew him to be among Buganda's most innovative living *badingidi* (single-string fiddlers) and singers. Bwette's stories asserted that Jjajja Byuma, the patron spirit of these and other creative capacities, provided the symbolic binding to link these two creative centers. The prayers, performances, and rituals at Kisuze/Katwe Kagezi not only reinforced that link, but also typified the kind of internally logical symbolism common across *kusamira* and *nswezi* traditions.[6]

Bwette offered numerous examples of this creative logic. For example, he prayed over a goat about to be sacrificed:

Jjajjange mukama wange	My grandparent, my lord
embuzi eno embulize bwe bibi byonna.	may this goat take all the misfortunes.

The euphony of this phrase comes from the word *embuzi* (goat) and the word *embulize* (a conjugated version of *kubula*, losing things). Bwette prayed likewise over a basket of beef being offered to the same spirit:

Jjajjange mukama wange Byuma	My grandparent, my lord Byuma
kino kye kibbo eky'ennyama y'ente	this is the basket of cow's meat
ne nsaba enteele buli kimu kyonna.	and I pray it opens up everything.[7]

Here, *nte* (cow) resonates in a shortened form of the word *kutereera* (settling something or getting something straightened out). The ability to improvise poetic prayers like these comes with experience, and it is as widely valued by ritual specialists as is the singer's ability to improvise idiomatic motifs in ritual song.

What people ask for in prayers reveals a great deal about the central focus of these and other *kusamira* rituals. Some standard prayers—used by people whether they are offering sacrifices before spirits possessing their mediums, kneeling at shrines without mediums present, or offering prayers elsewhere— focus on the same kinds of things. One version commonly recited at shrines simply lists the various components of a full life:

Jjajjange mukama wange	My grandparent, my lord
tukusabire kutuwannula,	we pray you free us [ransom us]
otuwe ku mulimu,	you give us work,
n'azadde,	and fertility,
abaana n'amaka amalungi,	children and beautiful homes,
obulamu obulungi,	a good life,
obuwangaazi,	long life,
okumanya n'okutegeera.	knowledge and understanding.
Tukwebaza . . .	We thank you . . .

In particular, prayers for fertility, quality of life, knowledge, and understanding are quite common.[8] Virtually all healing rituals are directed toward cultivating relationships that sustain the good life.

It is not enough for a given spirit to grant these blessings. Ritual actions, prayers, and songs clarify that the blessings must be distributed equitably throughout the community, among humans and spirits alike. Along with a rather large cadre of adepts who return to Kisuze at the end of each year, Bwette devotes considerable time and resources to ensuring a grateful offering to many spirits for their blessings. Jjajja Byuma appears on the first of these nights, December 31, and occupies his medium frequently throughout the subsequent days of the celebration. Meanwhile, though, people offer sacrifices to many other spirits and observe rituals peculiar to each. When Jjajja Byuma comes on the first night, people spend most of the night greeting him and coming to make offerings. Some bring food to be cooked and served to spirits and adepts alike, others bring barkcloths to cover the boulder that

Sacrifice and Song 133

resembles a large boat, others bring goats and chickens to sacrifice for other spirits, and the collective offering always includes one or two cows for Byuma. I attended these year-end rituals for a second consecutive year at the end of 2009 with the intention of staying at Kisuze long enough to experience the entire range of year-end celebrations and sacrifices. Although space will not permit an examination of all the songs performed there, I describe here a series of representative rituals that illustrate the practices around sacrifice in this annual tradition.

At this second year's celebrations, the person who had brought me to Nakawuka the previous year, a healer and former PROMETRA staffer named Umar Ndiwalana, explained the first of these offerings to me as it happened: "They reveal/introduce the cow of Byuma, and Byuma is going to give us the cow," he explained, summarizing the basic model of sacrifice, feeding, and distribution to come. He continued, "They introduce the containers of banana beer and milk, along with all of the other gifts that people have brought to Byuma and those they have brought to the other ancestors."[9] Slaughtering began immediately, beginning with the cow to be offered to Byuma.

Those uninvolved with the slaughtering took to singing, drumming, and dancing as they continued the celebration. The first of these choruses remarked on the division of labor: the phrase *Tamanyi kusamba lulege* (he does not know how to kick [dance with] a pellet bell) has a dual meaning here. The bell could be a synecdoche for drums and other instruments, an assertion that those doing the slaughtering did so because they did not have expertise in music and dance. However, the opposite is also true, as drummers and dancers singing this chorus knew nothing about how to silence the cow's bells (i.e., how to slaughter it for distribution). By extension, everyone had his role, whether drummer or butcher, human or spirit, presenter or recipient of sacrifice, distributor or recipient of blessings.

When the butchering and at least some of the cooking were complete, Jjajja Byuma returned, along with several other spirits who occupied their mediums. Some of these shifted shape to their animal forms, a transition signaled through movement: the mediums crawled around as lions and leopards would. They received their offerings of meat like this before gesturing to the butchers and cooks that the others present—those whom Byuma called *bazzukulu* (grandchildren) regardless of their ages—should be given some food as well. Cooks offered elders food stewed inside banana-leaf packages, while others received plates with cassava and liver followed by additional plates of rice with meat. Such an inclusive feast at the command of ancestral spirits demonstrated how children learn from a young age that their ancestors sustain them and vice versa. Songs and drumming continued throughout the day and into the night. One song toward the end of the day looked ahead to the veneration of other spirits:

Soloist: Saamulaba	I never saw him
Chorus: yali yekwese	he was in hiding
S: saamulaba	I never saw him
Ch: anzaalira ddala saamulaba,	I never saw my biological parent
yali yekwese	he was in hiding

The day's events fed everyone physically, but this song expressed a longing on behalf of those who had yet to greet their patron spirits and offer them sacrifices.

The next day brought similar opportunities: it was not my first encounter with the hunter spirit Ddungu, but it was certainly among the most intense. The first sounds of the morning echoed the calls from the day before: *Sembeza, sembeza emisambwa!* (Come near, come near, *misambwa!*). Bwette beat loudly on the drums, a rhythmic symbol of the phrase.[10] Some people consulted with Jjajja Byuma already in this early part of the day, suggesting that perhaps he had been busy doing the same throughout the night. Another song seemed to confirm this:

| Jjajja akeera, akeera | Grandparent wakes up early, wakes up early |
| Jjajja akeera mu nkoko emberyemberye! | Grandparent wakes up to the crowing of the early morning cock! |

I could not have known when I heard this song that it foreshadowed a spirit moving through the animal behaviors of its medium. Once the whole camp was stirring, however, it was not long before we all made our way out to the bushy area behind the enormous boatlike boulder for a ritual and sacrifice devoted to Ddungu the hunter.

Hunting Productive Power: Sacrifice, Sexuality, and the Contours of Liminality

This moment in the broader progression of rituals devoted to various spirits presented a fascinating opportunity to examine the contours of a liminal phase, in which suspended taboos rendered several boundaries porous. A possessed medium who behaved like a leopard, a group of overtly vulgar songs, and an argument about those songs—all during a rich sensory experience of ritual—worked together to depict complex notions of human productivity and well-being inextricable from the wild energy of the bush. Like

Sacrifice and Song 135

other rituals devoted to Ddungu, this one took place in the bush. However, embedded as it was in an annual series of rites that looked back over the previous year's triumphs and anticipated the coming year's possibilities, this sacrifice was bound up with a focus on human productivity that embraces reproduction as its core essence. Equal parts sacrifice, liminal vulgarity, ritual performance, and meal, the ritual demonstrated how each of these things related here to the others even though in other contexts, *basamize* more typically separate them.

The entourage sang as we hiked out to the forest, about a quarter mile from the huge boulder atop Kisuze's main hill. They stopped only momentarily to get situated once we reached the trees at the base of a steep rock formation. Having long since heard the first songs of the day, including the twin songs that begin nearly all rituals, I was surprised to hear the group begin to sing "*Ssewasswa kazaala abaana*" (Ssewasswa, father to the children). Twin songs do occasionally recur throughout rituals, but the singers had, up to this point, proven so fertile of imagination that I had scarcely heard them repeat any songs, much less these common tunes. The song that followed pushed this trend in a different direction, though. It featured a vulgar reference to one of the most verbally uninhibited of rituals, the twin-tying ceremony. In fact, that was the only other context in which I ever heard this song:

Ziizi awunya, awunyira mu nju yange,	The *ziizi* grass smells, smells in my house
waalaala awunya, nga waliwo amukoonyeko	waalaala it smells, when someone tampers with it

The final word here comes from the verb *okukoona* (to knock or thump). Like other herbs (think cilantro), the scent of this *ziizi* emerges more strongly when it is disturbed, purposely or not. Knocking, in this sense, can refer to dancers bumping hips, but here it is a sexual reference, as is the euphemism for the pubis (*ziizi* or grass) that begins the chorus.

A nearby companion, Arafat, pointed out some of the many spirits who occupied their mediums during this song: Mayanja, who moves through a leopard; Ddungu the hunter; and Kasajja, a working guard or soldier. A new song began:

S: Maama, kalanga	*Maama, kalanga* [an invasive plant]
Ch: kalanga omuti ogumu ogwako mu gy'ekibira, kalanga	*kalanga*, its only tree in the forest, *kalanga*

Arafat explained to me that these words were also veiled sexual references. He translated loosely: "one tree can make a forest. A man and wife, they can produce a family." This comparison of human fecundity to a rapidly prolif-

136   CHAPTER 4

erating invasive plant species was no mere sophomoric wordplay: Bwette had earlier shown me a tree that had split into two trunks except for one part that his predecessors at Kisuze had anthropomorphized as male and female sex organs. They so closely resembled those organs that Bwette had been instructed to keep them covered. So this conceptual overlap between the productivity of a single "tree" and human fecundity—signified audibly here by a single *kalanga* plant and elsewhere by the phallic tree entering its female counterpart—holds a prominent position within the compound at Kisuze. The actual lyrics offer something of a triple entendre: they refer to a tree falling in the woods, a man planting seeds with his "tree," and an ancestor dying. This last reference likens an ancestor to a great tree falling, an idiom common across many African cultures. The expression has special significance in Buganda and Busoga, where people bury their dead near the banana grove and those ancestors then become part of the earth and "feed" the living.

Just as Arafat was explaining the song to me, the sacrificial goat met its inevitable end: someone cut its throat, and I looked over to see Ddungu drinking blood directly from its severed neck. When he finished, he climbed a tall tree nearby much like a leopard would. He walked around on the branches on four limbs and even jumped from one tree to another. "He can even jump from there down!" claimed Arafat. Shifting shape again, he then danced in the second tree as people beat the drums, ululated, and sang this song:

S: Nti waalaalaala weekebere	Waalaalaala, inspect yourself
Ch: awo wa manga waliwa kawojjolo	there is a little butterfly down there
S: weekebere, weekebere	inspect yourself, inspect yourself
Ch: awo wa manga waliwa kawojjolo	there is a little butterfly down there

Again, the singers continued the pattern of sexual references, this time through the use of *kawojjolo* (butterfly), a euphemism for the vagina and, according to Arafat, a possible reference to sexually transmitted infections or problems.

Jjajja Ddungu shifted back as the drumming ended, finding a spot on the very branch where he had just danced to lie down and nap with one hand hanging off the branch, swinging like a leopard's paw. Ddungu's shifts, followed by his resting, signaled to those below that it was time to butcher and roast this goat. As a few young men did that, they and others continued to sing with lyrics not only about sex organs, but also about the sexual act itself, using words that would be taboo under most other circumstances. At one point, the *musiige*, Bwette, protested. He instructed people not to use "abusive" language in their songs because children and visitors were present.

A spirited debate ensued, and in the end, the rowdy crowd won the day by calming things for a moment only to return to loud, unabashed vulgarities in subsequent songs.

Their insistence on these songs and their themes structured this as a liminal moment at the threshold between the old year and the new. It also marked the transition between sacrifices for Byuma and sacrifices for other spirits whose shrines are scattered across the large compound at Kisuze. Victor Turner's important work on liminality has situated it as a structural phase in rites of passage.[11] The ethnographic evidence presented here suggests that such rites are not confined to life-cycle events or social installations for individuals or groups of age-mates. In this case, a heterogeneous group encompassing the entire age and gender spectrum offered sacrifices and songs to mark the passage between years. In this rite, though, the signs characterizing this liminal period resembled those of any other, and in fact indexed the liminal phase of the *kusiba abalongo* (twin-tying) ritual, which is a rite of passage for both twin children and their parents. In the ritual at Kisuze, the recitation of sexual vulgarities in song performed an audible suspension of taboo, while the shape-shifting spirit possession episode with Ddungu and the leopard contributed strongly to what Turner calls the "topsy-turvy" atmosphere of the liminal phase.[12] As the rest of this progression of sacrifices will show, fire consumption, fresh fruit, passage through a doorway, and birth—in that order—confirmed the liminal features of this initial sacrifice. Even its location in the bush—a place that is physically in between the compound, the town of Nakawuka, and the steep rock formation nearby—reinforced the liminality of this episode.

Having consumed his first portion of the sacrifice, Ddungu entrusted the roasting of the goat to those near the fire below. They finished butchering quickly, proceeding to roast the meat over the large fire. Ddungu descended the tree to partake of the liver and to distribute portions of it to others. Then he invited all to partake of some sacrificial meat. People ate hastily. Rain had begun to fall, and it fell harder with each passing moment. They quickly put out the fire and returned to the compound to seek shelter in the *ssabo*. Their willingness to endure the rain until completing the distribution and consumption process highlighted the importance of these activities at the nexus of physical and spiritual sustenance. The sacrifice accomplished additional purposes: Ddungu's "hunt" and distribution of meat gave a physical component to the distribution of blessings returned to the people in exchange for the sacrifice, and the rite launched a series of other sacrifices. These began back inside the shrine with other spirits associated with the bush: the *misambwa* and a guardian *jjembe* named Kasagga.

138   CHAPTER 4

Omukolo gw'Emisambwa: The Rite of the Misambwa

A handful of spirits elongated the liminal phase, continuing to suspend taboos and to enact lewd behaviors, especially suggestive dance. Arafat and
others in the *ssabo* called them "the wild *misambwa*," and they included:
Nakayaga, wife to Kiwanuka; her brother, Bamweyana; Nambaga, the wife
of a *jjembe* named Lubowa; and their guard, a *jjembe* called Kasagga. This
group of spirits demonstrated how people at Kisuze had come to understand
the various types of spirits, in this case *lubaale, misambwa*, and *mayembe*,
as interrelated at a level resembling human marriage affinities. These spirits
were entertaining in their behaviors. Nakayaga made one joke after another,
danced with everyone, and drank a local distillate called *waragi* to excess.
Nambaga uttered complete nonsense almost constantly, and in a cartoon-
ishly high voice. Bamweyana also spoke in a high vocal range and smoked
a marijuana-tobacco mix, constantly offering it to others.[13] Their *jjembe*, the
guard named Kasagga, did not seem to actually guard anything because he
was too busy laughing at the other *balalu* (wild ones). One singer, a spirit
medium for Nakayaga, later claimed that because of their antics, they would
typically come out in the small hours of the morning, usually between two
and four.[14]

Omukolo gwa Kiwanuka: The Rite of Kiwanuka

The *balalu* high jinks during this liminal phase gave way to an important
sacrifice for a spirit who looms much larger in the Ganda pantheon: the
lubaale Kiwanuka, often dubbed Kiwanuka Omulalu (Kiwanuka the wild
one). Although his marriage alliance links him to Nakayaga, his moniker
does not derive from the *balalu* described above. As noted in chapter 2,
Kiwanuka's praise names reflect his enormous power, his association with
lightning and thunder, and his penchant for eating fire.

The next morning, the crowd followed Bwette from the main rock in the
compound, atop of which the *ssabo* sits, west about 120 m (394') to a place
they call *entebe* (the chair). It is so named for the cone-shaped hill there,
where Kiwanuka's medium sat as people consulted the spirit. Bwette got some
help to build a large fire at the base of this chairlike rock formation, where
the group offered a special sacrifice for Kiwanuka. They first offered prayers
over the sacrifice: Bwette and his companion, Harunah Mbogga, pulled out
some incense called *kabanni* and distributed it to everyone. Each person
broke a small piece of this wax incense into two pieces and placed it on the
fire, praying the usual prayers for work, fertility, children, good homes, good/

Sacrifice and Song 139

long life, knowledge, and understanding. Then they led a red sheep to the top of the rock, slit its throat, and drained its blood into a natural bowllike rock formation near Kiwanuka's seat. Bwette mixed the blood with water from Nnyanja Nalubaale as the assistants carried the sheep back down to place it on the fire they had built. As the sheep burned whole atop the fire, everyone present climbed to the top of the rock to receive an anointing from Bwette, who used the sacrificial blood to mark people on the forehead, chest, and feet. As he began this process, the musicians beat drums vigorously and sang:

Nannyinimu agambye	The landlord [or household head] has spoken
waggulu waladde	above is peaceful
waliba emirembe	there shall be peace

Soon, Kiwanuka possessed his medium, and he danced around the fire where the sheep continued to burn as his sacrifice.

Kiwanuka's sacrifice was among the last of the rites focused on closure of the year gone by. Mbogga explained that with this sheep sacrifice for Kiwanuka, they burned up all their bad luck, all the negative things they had brought with them, and they threw the ashes in a bushy place beyond the banana grove intended for rubbish both physical and spiritual. When they rekindled the fire anew, he said, they did so to light their way home and to illuminate their lives in the coming year.[15] Later it became apparent that among his many responsibilities as the caretaker of this place, Bwette continues to keep its embers burning all year. This helps explain an idiomatic exchange of greetings between people and patron spirits: on many occasions, often just after a spirit arrives in its medium, Bwette and others say to the spirit, "Weebale kukola n'o[kutu]kuuma, Jjajja" (thank you for working and keeping [us]), to which the spirit replies, "Nammwe mmwebale okutukuuma" (thank you all as well for keeping us). This simple, eloquent greeting expresses the mutual need among humans and spirits that multiple interviewees emphasized as a central feature of *kusamira* and *nswezi*.[16]

Rituals of New Life, Open Doors, and Fertility

The next ritual in the sequence at Kisuze reiterated this expression of mutual need among humans and spirits. The spirit in focus was Ndawula, whom *basamize* associate with diseases of the skin. People offer him sacrifices in exchange for blessings to address these afflictions and to make sense of them. The medium donned a cloak of yellow and green, he said, because those are the colors of the fruits and vegetables that people offer as Ndawula's sacrifice.[17]

140 CHAPTER 4

Whether because of his association with healing and nutrition, his proximity in the pantheon to the twin *lubaale* spirits Kiwanuka and Musoke, or simply as a matter of habit, this rite began with twin songs. The singers continued with songs focused specifically on Ndawula:

S: Kale sirina ngabo etabaala	So I don't have a fighting shield
Ch: Ndawula, jangu e Buyego ngabo etabaala	Ndawula, come to Buyego, the shield is fighting [the battle is on]

This song outlined two core features of Ndawula as a spirit: his status as a fighter, and his association with Kawumpuli, who resides in Buyego. Both spirits are princes, and many *basamize* associate them both with smallpox, chicken pox, and other skin afflictions.[18] Some also associate Kawumpuli with varying levels of physical ability. Some of his afflictions appear consistent with polio, others with the bodily impacts of violence and war. These two spirits are not twins per se, but their quasi-militaristic alliance against skin diseases and debilitating affliction places them in association with each other.[19]

As the singers continued, some songs and dances in this moment retained the character of twin songs in their focus on procreation. In fact, a *jjembe* guarding Ndawula when he first arrived in his medium danced around with a spear substituting for a thrusting phallus. There was a clear link here (as there was above in the song's mention of the invasive plant species *kalanga*) between fruits of fertile plants and human fruition: when a basket of cut-up mangoes and pineapple circulating the room reached Jjajja Byuma's medium, she exclaimed to Bwette, who handed it to her, "Aaa, Bwette is going to father twins! Blessings!"[20] Her fellow adepts nearby answered, "bwa Mukasa" (of Mukasa). She was only half joking about the twins. Hers was a common response to receiving blessings of many kinds. The expression invokes Mukasa as an archetypical parent of the twins Kiwanuka and Musoke, and therefore iconic of all twins and parents of twins. The crowd also addressed Ndawula as Ssaalongo (father of twins), as is common custom for many spirits. When the basket had made its way around the room and back to Ndawula, his receipt of it met with ululations and multiple interjections of "Bweeza [blessings], Ssaalongo!"

A song quickly followed:

S: Abaana bange	My children
Ch: mujjanga ne mulya	you [pl.] should always come and eat
S: bwe ndi vaawo	when I am gone
Ch: mulirya endagala	you will eat leaves [feed on leftovers]

Here the spirit and the singers expressed the theme of human dependence on spiritual blessings in strong parent/child terms. An alternative lyric for *endagala* here is *ebitobo* (emptiness, as in an empty plate or a breast that no longer makes milk). The song spoke with the voice of the spirit, urging his *bazzukulu* (grandchildren) to receive his blessings and to consume them or use them well while they could. Leaves in this context would be most likely interpreted by most listeners as banana leaves, which helps explain the idiomatic translation that connotes leftovers: people cook and mash the staple banana called *matooke* in banana leaves, and they also use the leaves to serve food or wrap it for short-term preservation.

A woman soon brought a large winnowing basket lined with banana leaves and full of fruits and nuts, sacrifices that the spirit depends on. She presented the cut-up chunks of avocado, pineapple, mango, and jackfruit to Ndawula, whose instructions that she was to distribute them among the people brought signals of mutual dependence full circle. She and a companion distributed a small section of banana leaf with some fruit on it to each person. In other iterations of this offering at other times and places, people offered seeds and nuts like sesame and roasted groundnuts, sometimes supplementing or replacing these with meat. Particularly in the case of seeds and nuts—but also with fruits—these are foods that people associate with good skin health. The logic here establishes a correspondence between Ndawula as the patron spirit for skin afflictions and foods rich in nourishing vitamins and oils. At Kisuze, the people gladly consumed in the moment of distribution from Jjajja Ndawula, as it had been a long day with little to eat.

Omukolo gwa Sserugulamilyango: The Ritual of the One Who Opens Doorways

In the morning came the call: "Wake up, wake up, wake up!" Kiwanuka's medium was cleaning the compound, replacing grasses in some of the small shrines where ancestors reside. Others swept and cleared leaves and debris away from the enormous boulder they call *ekyombo* (the ship). Still others made a small offering for Bulamu, the spirit that has power to give and take life, at his shrine. Many of us went to collect firewood, returning to the mantle of Kiwanuka's sheep sacrifice from the previous day, where Harunah Mbogga produced some wax incense from his bag. Each person took a small piece in each hand, and placed it on the fire, and offered morning prayers. Then they sang:

Mirembe, mirembe	Peace, peace
waliba emirembe	there shall be peace
waggulu waladde	above is peaceful
waliba emirembe	there shall be peace

| Nannyinimu agambye | Landlord [or household head] has spoken |
| waladde emirembe | there is peace |

The song drew attention to the boundary between life and death, between humans and ancestors, just at a moment of transition to a ritual for a spirit named Sserugulamilyango, the one who opens the doorways.

The singers began with the customary twin songs, first "Abalongo twabazaala," then a chorus less common elsewhere but recurrent here at Kisuze. It focused on Namayanja, the female counterpart to Mayanja, twin brother of Magobwe.[21]

S: Mu nkuukuulu	In the *nkuukulu* grasses
Ch: Namayanja weebale	thank you, Namayanja
S: bannange	my dear ones
Ch: kaliba kanyoolagano	it will be a struggle

According to *musamize* and traditional healer Umar Ndiwalana, the term *kanyoolagano* (a struggle) refers to something good, momentous, but a little bit frightening. The lyric could also be heard as *kayogaano* (chaos), but would carry the same connotation. When I probed a bit, comparing it to a human birth, he replied "exactly."[22] Such an event aligned with the themes of fruition and the life/death boundary repeated throughout these rituals. The singers then turned their efforts to the arrival of Sserugulamilyango, singing:

S: Gulawo jjajja, eee, gulawo oluggi	Open, grandparent, yes, open the door
Ch: ggw'oyagala ggwe onoonkwata	you will settle on your own chosen
S: gulawo, ssebo	open, sir
Ch: eee	yes
S: gulawo oluggi	open the door [clear the way]

Many songs invoke spirits, encouraging them to possess their mediums, but few songs focus so specifically on the conceptual portals between human and spirit. At the outset of this ritual for Sserugulamilyango, this song highlighted what both Steven Friedson and Daniel Reed have called the "translucent boundary" between the domains of humans and spirits.[23] The theme emerges in two meanings of the line, "you will settle on your own chosen": one implies a fearless confrontation with death as a transition from human to ancestor, and the other directly encourages the spirit to take hold of its medium. Perhaps frequent engagement with the latter meaning (the moment of possession) helps explain the fact-of-life approach to the former (death).

Responding to the call, Sserugulamilyango occupied his medium. When the song ended, people greeted him. They made offerings of coffee berries,

Sacrifice and Song

reinforcing the symbolism of twinship and blood pact alliance. In this instance, though, the spirit distributed blessings differently: Bwette brought a container of ghee (clarified butter), which the spirit then spread on the faces of all present. Each recipient responded, "blessings, Grandparent!"[24] The sung response offered yet another form of thanks:

S: Omugabi agaba	The [generous] giver gives
Ch: yangabira	he gave me
S: amazima agaba	truly he gives
Ch: yangabira ng'agabira owuwe	he gave me as he gives his own

Another singer chimed in with a tune that equated this process of giving and receiving—and mediumship possession—with peace among humans and spirits.

The singer who joined the festivities, Lisa Nakawuka, requires some introduction. She features prominently as a singer and spirit medium in many rituals near the town that shares her namesake. She arrived at Kisuze well after most of the year-end crowd, and yet they knew her well as the granddaughter of Jjajja Byuma's medium. There were thus four personages between the two people:

- Byuma's medium, a woman who refused any other names apart from Muka Byuma or Jjajja despite my many questions about her given clan-associated name or any other names
- Jjajja Byuma, the ambiguously gendered spirit associated with all things creative and metal
- Lisa Nakawuka, a gifted young singer and the granddaughter to Muka Byuma
- Jjajja Nambaga, the female spirit (and wife of the *jjembe* Lubowa) who most frequently possessed Lisa

Lisa Nakawuka had evidently earned or grown into her latter name as a young culture bearer of the Kisuze *kusamira* tradition, whose gifts for singing, mediumship, and knowledge of the spirits vastly outpaced those of her age-mates and some of her elders. She did not reside at Kisuze, but the place and the people there served as a touchstone for her identity just as they did for so many members of the lungfish clan and their kin from Katwe in Kampala.

During a lengthy string of songs, one of the first of many she led featured a litany of spirits and celebrated their capacity to "enter" their mediums.

S: Ggwe w'atali, jjajja, watalise ennyimba	In his/her absence, grandparent, while you are roaming, I sing
Ch: omugenyi akyala waladde	a visitor comes where there is peace

144 CHAPTER 4

S: ggwe w'atali, jjajja, watalise   In his/her absence, grandparent, while
   ayingirawo   you are roaming, I sing
Ch: omugenyi akyala waladde   the visitor comes where there is peace

The song lauded mediumship as an act that helps the spirits, too. Her wide, infectious smile and her energetic singing of the verses inspired similar energy among the drummers and chorus that sustained this rite even after many days of ritual work and precious little sleep.

Omukolo gw'Abakyala: Rite of the Women

Nakawuka's energy was well timed, as the end of this ritual rolled right into the beginning of one that celebrated the roles of female spirits and mediums, along with the contributions of women more broadly. The *basamize* at Kisuze called it the *mukolo gw'Abakyala* (rite of/for the women). After naming some of the spirits about to be lauded—including Nakayaga, Nakasujja, and Nambaga—she sang playfully, "the women really want the things, woolooloolo!"[25] She referred to the offerings that people would make for these spirits. The crowd responded by starting the ritual with the usual twin songs. From there, they continued with other songs on the theme of fertility, and Lisa Nakawuka continued to lead.

Ch: Laba akyanoonya buyokolo bwa   See, she is still searching for the
    baana, laba akyanoonya   containment of children, see, she
                                     still searches
S: yanguwako, ogabule ezzadde   hurry and serve your offspring
Ch: laba akyanoonya buyokolo bwa   see she is still searching for the
    baana, laba akyanoonya   containment of children, see, she
                                     still searches
S: yanguwako, ogabula abaana   hurry and serve your children
Ch: laba akyanoonya buyokolo bwa   see, she is still searching for the
    baana, laba akyanoonya   containment of children, see, she
                                     still searches

The word *bukyokolo* presents a translation challenge here. Strictly speaking, *akakyokolo* (pl. *obukyokolo*) is a cap, like those on glass or plastic bottles of soda. In this case, it symbolizes the obstacles that might prevent a woman from giving birth, like umbilical cord complications or placenta previa.[26] The connotation of continuity marked by the infix *-kya-* in *akyanoonya* celebrates women's willingness to persist in childbirth despite such complications or to persist in producing more children even after they have already given birth. This retrospective interpretation helps explain the jubilation of mature

Sacrifice and Song 145

women during this song. As a young mother herself, Nakawuka made an excellent vocal motivator for their dancing and joy.

A song in Runyoro about *obukotolo* accompanied the arrival of offerings for the spirits: the term refers to the groundnuts and sesame seeds that had been freshly roasted for this offering. These made their way around to the spirits who had arrived first, who then distributed them to everyone else. Another rendition of "Mujjanga ne mulya" (You should always come and eat) accompanied this distribution, as did several other familiar songs of gratitude. People lounged and ate raw sugarcane along with the groundnuts and sesame. Far from arbitrary additions to the menu, these are typically foods for children waiting as their mothers cook or for travelers undertaking long journeys via public transport. Often women and their young children sell them in taxi parks. They are also foods that women and young girls prepare for men, elders, and guests who await a main course.

A singer returned to "Laba akyanoonya" briefly, but mostly people relaxed and partook in these snacks together. As the drummers did the same, small children experimented with their instruments. Their playful exploration typically only happened during the least formal moments in ritual since the drums were otherwise often in use. The *mukolo gw'Abakyala* ended with this atmosphere of liberal movement and interaction, the kind that mothers allow small children while they accomplish various tasks around a family compound. Just so, the custodians of this ritual, all female elders, ignored these shenanigans as they spread ghee on some rocks at the southern end of the compound, marking the place where women traditionally gave birth.

Interlude: Kalalu (Little Wild One)

After the *mukolo gw'Abakyala*, it was clear that everyone needed a break. It had been a long day with many sacrifices, and yet the last full meal had been too long prior for most people. A ritual for *mayembe* awaited the group's attention that same day. In the shrine, a medium for Mukasa—someone who had been previously unfamiliar to many present at Kisuze—demanded a goat. At this point the demand represented a hardship amid so many other sacrifices already procured, planned, and mostly finished. Outside, the faithful adepts showed their fatigue, some chatting idly, some sleeping. Many staved off hunger by smoking home-cured tobacco. A few stayed alert and curbed their appetites by chewing leaves of a mild stimulant called khat (*Catha edulis*). A *jjembe* (working spirit) showed up before the appointed time to usurp attention. Some youth slipped away to sate their hunger in a nearby mango grove.

146   CHAPTER 4

Back inside the shrine, Mukasa's demand for a goat escalated. A basket circulated to collect funds for its acquisition. There was not enough money. Jjajja Byuma's medium asked how much was in the basket. Someone told her, and then she took out a fifty thousand shilling note to contribute, roughly equivalent to half the cost of a small goat. The people responded with loud cheers and ululations. Then she pulled out another ten thousand, which she said was for Kalalu. Without our knowing it, the spirit whose name means "craziness" or "little wild one" had been slinking around, causing everyone problems. Muka Byuma knew this because she had seen the spirit disguised in her granddaughter, Lisa Nakawuka, many times before. The crowd laughed and cheered again, happy to know that Kalalu would stop pestering everyone and make way for the rituals to proceed. Byuma's action presented an opportunity to see how a classic African trickster persona related to rituals of well-being in Buganda. Most of the chaos subsided. Onlookers had evidently determined that Mukasa's demand for a goat was a bluff by a hungry person or a conspiring group, although they stopped short of calling the medium an impostor. An atmosphere of unrest persisted, however, as is often the case with *amayembe* (the working spirits).

Omukolo gw'Amayembe:
The Rite of the Mayembe *(Working Spirits)*

At the top of the hill, a different live goat stood ready for sacrifice to the working spirits. I volunteered to beat drums this time. In the commotion, a caller began, immediately joined by the others in response:

S: Mbu, jjembe!	I say, *jjembe!*
Ch: ejjembe Kalondoozi	the *jjembe* Kalondoozi
S: ejjembe	the *jjembe*
Ch: wajja alina embuzi	he came having a goat

This gathering's initial foray into *maymebe* songs was short and chaotic, but the mere mention of a goat soon attracted several *mayembe*—Kasajja, Lubowa, Nambaga, Ssemugumbe, and others—who arrived in their mediums to demand sacrifices. These raucous soldiers spoke loudly and talked over one another. Eventually I handed my recording device to Lisa Nakawuka to hold as she sang:

S: Nti ejjembe ly'embogo lyagwa,	That the buffalo's *jjembe* fell,
lyagwa olugendo,	it fell [on] the way,
nti ejjembe Lubowa lyava,	that the *jjembe* Lubowa came from,
ne likutula enkoba	and it broke the strings

Ch: ejjembe ly'embogo lyagwa,	the buffalo's *jjembe* fell,
lyava wala nnyo,	it came from afar,
nti ejjembe Lubowa lyava,	that the *jjembe* Lubowa came from
ne likutula enkoba	and it broke the strings

S: ejjembe ly'embogo lyajja	the buffalo's *jjembe* came,
lyajja olugendo,	it came [on] the journey,
nti ejjembe eryange lyajja,	that my *jjembe* came,
ne likutula enkoba	and it broke the strings

Ch: ejjembe ly'embogo lyagwa,	the buffalo's *jjembe* fell
lyava wala nnyo,	it came from afar,
nti ejjembe Lubowa lyava,	that the *jjembe* Lubowa came from,
ne likutula enkoba	and it broke the strings

S: maama, ejjembe ly'embogo lyava	*maama*, the *jjembe* of the water buffalo was from,
lyava wala nnyo,	it came from very far,
nti ejjembe Kasajja lyajja	that the *jjembe* Kasajja came
ne likutula empale	and it tore the pants

Ch: ejjembe ly'embogo lyagwa,	the buffalo's *jjembe* fell,
lyava wala nnyo,	it came from very far,
nti ejjembe Lubowa lyava	that the *jjembe* Lubowa came from
ne likutula enkoba	and it broke the strings

S: Lubowa ejjembe ly'embogo lyajja,	Lubowa, the buffalo's *jjembe* came
lyava olugendo,	it came from a journey,
nti ejjembe Lubowa lyajja	Lubowa the *jjembe* came
ne likutula empale	and it tore the pants

Ch: ejjembe ly'embogo lyagwa,	the buffalo's *jjembe* fell,
lyava wala nnyo,	it came from very far,
nti ejjembe Lubowa lyava,	Lubowa the *jjembe* came from
ne likutula enkoba	and it broke the strings

The young singer's first offering for this *mayembe* sacrifice set the tone for a lengthy ritual. She sang loudly of the working spirits associated with horns of water buffalo (among other ungulates) who "fell" on their mediums. In turn, she praised the mediums for their sturdiness, as if they were more resilient than wood beneath the axe or pants that wore out and split. These praise motifs spoke volumes about the experience of serving as a medium for a *jjembe*, who as a type are reputed to be rather hard on their carriers.

Led by Lisa Nakawuka, vigorous singing and dancing continued as young men presented the sacrificial goat to the *mayembe*, who were occupying their mediums in increasing numbers. The men quickly slaughtered the beast, and the spirits rushed to drink the blood from its open neck wound before offering the animal back to the men for butchering and distribution to the crowd. As they butchered and roasted meat for the next hour and a half, Lisa bolstered the intensity of the ritual with a song celebrating the chaos of sacrificial exchanges like these.

S: Abange w'alwanidde	My fellows, where he has fought
Ch: wabeerawo	there usually is
S: jjajja w'alwanidde	where the grandparent has fought
Ch: wabeerawo ensiitano	there usually is a struggle
S: jjajja w'aliwanira	where the grandparent fights
Ch: wabeerawo	there usually is
S: amayembe gegayiridde	the *mayembe* undermined themselves
Ch: wabeerawo ensiitano	there usually is a struggle
S: jjajja w'alwanidde	where the grandparent fought
Ch: wabeerawo	there usually is
S: jjajja w'alwanidde	where the grandparent has fought
Ch: wabeerawo ensiitano	there is usually a struggle
S: jjajja we galwanira	where the grandparent fights
Ch: wabeerawo	there usually is
S: jjajja w'alwanidde	where the grandparent has fought
Ch: wabeerawo ensiitano	there is usually a struggle
S: Lubowa w'alilwanira	where Lubowa fights
Ch: wabeerawo	there usually is
S: Lubowa w'alwanidde	where Lubowa has fought
Ch: wabeerawo ensiitano	there is usually a struggle
S: owange w'olwanidde	my dear, where you have fought
Ch: wabeerawo	there usually is
S: Kasajja w'alwanidde	where Kasajja has fought
Ch: wabeerawo ensiitano	there is usually a struggle
S: Nambaga w'alwanidde	Nambaga, where you have fought
Ch: wabeerawo	there usually is
S: Ssekasaka w'alwanidde	where Ssekasaka has fought
Ch: wabeerawo ensiitano	there is usually a struggle
S: mayembe we galwanira	where *mayembe* fought
Ch: wabeerawo	there usually is
S: lubaale w'alwanidde	where *lubaale* have fought
Ch: wabeerawo ensiitano	there is usually a struggle

S: jjajja wemulwanira	grandparent, where you fight
Ch: wabeerawo	there usually is
S: ggwe Kizuuzi w'olwanidde	Kizuuzi, where you have fought
Ch: wabeerawo ensiitano	there is usually a struggle

This was just one among several songs that Lisa performed during that time, but its many motifs are worth including here for two reasons. First, they evoke the chaotic atmosphere of this ritual. Second, though, this was a particular kind of chaos or struggle that both *basamize* in Buganda and *baswezi* in Busoga reflect on in their respective renditions of this tune. A more poetic translation of this text might read something like, "ancestors, wheresoever you fight, you shall leave visible testimonies of chaos as you always have."[27] In her version, Lisa named several specific working spirits: Kasajja, Kizuuzi, Lubowa, and Nambaga. In other versions, though, singers generalize the reflection to sacrificial rituals for all kinds of spirits. The chaotic struggle they mention refers not only to the boisterous beating of drums and to loud, raucous singing, but also to the physical disorder and raggedness that possession leaves behind after feet have danced up so much dust and possessed mediums have rolled around on the ground. It recalls the holes in the ground where poles held up makeshift shelters and where people brewed banana beer. Sacrifices also leave behind the bloodstains of slaughter, animal skins, and the stink of various animals recently sacrificed. They leave an even more indelible mark on the mediums and their communities.

Hungry participants—including me—gobbled freshly roasted goat's meat in comparative quietude. Of all the songs that Lisa Nakawuka sang that day, none evoked the excitement, the sensory overload, and the catharsis of ritual sacrifice quite like her loud celebration of ritual chaos and struggle at the moment of sacrifice. With their hunger calmed but not completely abated, and with no meat left for a larger feast, people dispersed to rest after a long day.

A Contrasting Example of Sacrifice: Irondo

Having examined a series of sacrifices offered regularly at the end of the calendar year to reinforce existing relationships with spiritual and animal familiars, I turn now to a contrasting example. In this scenario, a protracted performance of postmortuary rites culminated in sacrifices focused on a specific ritual task, but the facilitators acted on motivations and accomplished goals similar to those at Kisuze. The task in question was the identification of new spirit mediums to take on some social responsibilities of a recently deceased healer and medium named Lukowe Kotilida Bibireka. It was part

150   CHAPTER 4

of a ritual called, in both Luganda and Lusoga, *okwabya olumbe* ("bursting death" or "chasing away death"). A specialist in women's health, Kotilida was a widely respected elder whose funeral and associated mortuary rites attracted attendees from many neighboring subcounties, counties, and districts. Within the broader sequence of those proceedings, this analysis focuses on the sacrifice of goats for the spirits once familiar to Kotilida. Coming at an important moment of transition at her home in a village called Irondo, the sacrifice helped a community mourn an elder, aided the spirits' transition to new host mediums, and reinforced the continuity of the community's spiritual patronage for the wide range of variables they construed as relevant to well-being.[28]

By the time they reached the sacrifices, mourners including Kotilida's colleagues and family members had been brewing banana beer, sounding drums, singing, and performing a series of rituals for several days. Kotilida had been buried two days prior to the start of those rites, but the group was just finishing the part of the sequence that marked the final time human hands would come into contact with the burial mound. In an action of self-conscious connection with their agrarian ancestors, they used an ancient hoe and a modern hoe to dig a trench in the mound of earth atop Kotilida's grave. Kotilida's family and friends poured libations into the trench, slaking the spirits' thirst in her honor. Then, led by an elder carrying the title Isegya, the Kisoga archetype of a wounded healer, they sang an acknowledgment of their common mortality.

S: Eitaka lino lilindya, maama!	This land will eat me, *maama!*
Ch: Eitaka lino lilindya, maama!	This land will eat me, *maama!*
S: Ni bwe ndisamba	Even if I kick it
Ch: lilindya, maama	it will eat me, *maama*
S: elyalya, dhaadha	it will eat me, grandparent
Ch: lilindya, maama	it will eat me, *maama*
S: lyalya Maama	it ate Mother
Ch: lilindya, maama	it will eat me, *maama*
S: lyalya kojja	it ate uncle [mother's brother]
Ch: lilindya, maama	it will eat me, *maama*
S: lyalya bbaabba	it ate father
Ch: lilindya, maama.	it will eat me, *maama.*
S: Eitaka lino lilindya, maama!	This land will eat me, *maama!*
Ch: Eitaka lino lilindya, maama!	This land will eat me, *maama!*

When they finished singing this song, they closed up the grave in silence. This final gesture bound Kotilida's power into the banana grove as if she—with the other ancestors—would now become directly responsible for its fertility

Sacrifice and Song

and that of the household. It expressed a powerful form of reciprocity common to *kusamira* and *nswezi* traditions: humans offered gifts of hospitality and sacrifice to spirits to meet their needs, and other-than-human familiars offered their distinctive gifts to meet human needs. Just as Kotilida had interceded for her community as a medium during her life, the transition saw her into the next phase of a supportive role.

Although that process and its symbols offered some comfort to her survivors, Kotilida's absence in the world of the living still left a potentially dangerous chasm between the bereft and their patron spirits. Those survivors expressed the danger by reference to vermin that disturb improperly buried corpses.

Ch: Nsolimo, nsolimo dhili ndya	Rats, rats will eat me
S: nze mbula omwana	me who has no child
obwange	my dear little ones
Semichorus: nsolimo	rats
S: nze mbula bbaabba/maama	me who has no father/mother
Ch: nsolimo, nsolimo dhili ndya	rats, rats will eat me
S: nze mbula koiza	me who has no uncle [mother's brother]
Semich: nsolimo	rats
S: nze mbula senga	me who has no auntie [father's sister]
Ch: nsolimo, nsolimo dhili ndya	rats, rats will eat me

For the next several days, then, the potential for bad things and a yearning for human-spiritual reciprocity motivated the identification and initiation of new spirit mediums to begin fulfilling some of Kotilida's former duties in the community.

The group made sacrifices—one goat for each new medium—and spilled their blood at the head and the foot of the grave. They purified Kotilida's ritual tools with blood from the same sacrifices: they washed her pipe, gourd rattles, beads, and other items in the blood, and then rinsed these items in water from Nnyanja Nalubaale. Although Lukowe Kotilida did not immediately return as an ancestral spirit, the new mediums for the spirits she had carried inherited these items to signify their new responsibilities to the community.[29] After offering these sacrifices to the spirits, the gathered mourners shared a meal of the sacrificed animals' meat and roasted bananas together. These foods indexed their shared substance in the spiritual life of the deceased medium, in the spirits they venerated together, and in the new mediums they had initiated. The ritual work of the rites and preparation of the sacrifice indexed their agrarian and ritual labor shared across generations within the banana grove and beyond. It bears noting that families constantly maintain the bio-

152   CHAPTER 4

diversity of their banana groves by digging up and sharing plants between and among family and friends.[30] In this sense, all who cultivate *matooke* share a larger, unified grove that feeds their communities. The practice contributes to a sense of shared substance among the living and the dead, whom survivors bury in or near their banana groves.

Other features of Kotilida's postmortuary rites, those focused on hospitality and celebration, will be discussed in the next chapter, but this sacrifice offers a glimpse of one way in which *baswezi*, like their *basamize* counterparts in Buganda, exchange sacrifices for blessings. The act of washing Kotilida's ritual accoutrements in sacrificial blood aligned with the broader themes of the events: *basamize* sought to bind the negative potential of Kotilida's death and keep open their pathways to blessings from spirits. A return trip to Irondo during summer 2015 confirmed their perceived success of their efforts. Abundant rains had made the crops flourish that year, and in the intervening years, the elder mediums had successfully brought younger women into their ranks. Not only was Kotilida's widower still alive at an advanced age, but these women and their age-mates had also given birth and begun to raise the next generation of their community.[31] It would be an exaggeration to trace all of these successes back to this one sacrifice; no doubt many have taken place since 2009. Those present in 2015 emphasized the important contribution that this sacrifice made to the spiritual blessings that sustain the community.

Conclusion

The sequence of sacrifices at Kisuze and the postmortuary sacrifices at Irondo concentrated many different offerings to a variety of spirits into relatively brief time lines (about a week each) that invite comparison. Their value as diachronic examinations of ritual events lies in their capacity to illuminate the exchange of sacrifices for blessings via the parameters and vocabulary of limited geographic and cultural spaces. Sacrificial exchanges throughout the year at other sites across southern Uganda follow a similar conceptual framework, but they often focus on their own circumstances. Examples appear throughout this book:

- builders of houses for spirits at Munamaizi in Busoga were concerned with the fertility of some young women in their community and the productivity of their fields
- creators of power objects at Makandwa focused their efforts on alleviating a potentially dangerous situation with a nearby Christian community that included some of their mediums

Sacrifice and Song 153

- elder mediums at PROMETRA Uganda in Buyijja helped a young woman living with HIV/AIDS enhance her capacity for quality of life, a process that initially demanded not raucous, expensive animal sacrifices but rather smaller sacrifices of time and resources.

Like other forms of ritual work, sacrifice reveals complex ways of producing and preserving repertories of well-being and the things of Kiganda and Kisoga culture.

Ever present as a motivation for sacrifice are the dual potentials of abundance and risk discussed at length in chapter 2. These categories have analogues in community and isolation, in blessings and bad things, in well-being and illness. Sacrifice, for *basamize* and *baswezi*, operates on both functional and symbolic planes. It meets the physical needs of those gathered, sometimes drawing large crowds as at Kisuze, other times feeding existing large crowds, as at the major life-cycle event at Irondo. It also meets the needs of ancestors, sometimes with the hospitality of banana beer, other times with the immediacy of blood, and often with the satisfaction of resource distribution to grandchildren. Both the functional and symbolic aspects of sacrifice articulate human and other-than-human places in regionally specific ecologies of well-being. They demonstrate a strong emphasis on the relational aspects of those systems through their transactional nature and through lively performances of songs.

Almost invariably, sacrifices lead to distribution, as the examples here have shown. The next chapter takes up that theme at the level of hospitality and feasting. As with other stages in virtually any given ritual, specialists in Buganda and Busoga integrate songs into their efforts in these areas. The feasting repertory carries themes of sacrifice forth through their logical next phases: these songs shape transcendent occasions in which ritual adepts and spiritual familiars celebrate successful exchanges and the powerful sense of reciprocity those exchanges reproduce.

5. From Tea and Coffee Berries to Beer and Meat

Sound, Hospitality, and Feasting in Repertories of Well-Being

Across the spectrum of ritual healing events and practices, hospitality and celebration constitute major themes. The title of this chapter gives a sense of the broad range of foodways and other practices that animate these themes. One participant went so far as to remark that without food and drink, there would be no such events. His reflection endured throughout the fieldwork for this study as a constant reminder that the pursuit of well-being is as much about offering mutual aid and meeting daily needs as it is about addressing any particular affliction. The remark also emphasizes that a person is not so much an individual as a dividual, an entity inextricable from the other people, circumstances, and other-than-human relational context in which that person exists.[1] Dividuals, especially mediums who perform flexible personhood within a human and other-than-human surround, are not strictly bounded entities but rather mutually constitutive members of a dynamic social collective, which often links with other collectives. That process of mutual constitution is likewise dynamic, full of human agency to shape it, and nowhere more apparent than in the exchange of hospitable contributions to loud, raucous celebrations. We begin, then, with small, customary gestures embedded in daily life—coffee berries, groundnuts, and tea—and move to larger social gestures that require more resources. The whole spectrum shows how sound is embedded in the performance of constant, sustaining reproduction of community and well-being. In combination with the sharing of food, drink, and hospitality, musicking is an important part of the production and celebration of social relations and spaces, shared substance, and ideals around well-being.

Coffee Berries, Groundnuts, and Banana Beer

Many if not most rituals begin with an exchange of coffee berries or groundnuts that indexes multiple interactions in Kiganda and Kisoga social life. Larger events in both Buganda and Busoga commonly proceed with brewing or purchasing banana beer as an offering to the spirits. These are two in a series of ritual actions homologous with mutually sustaining exchanges among people and their other-than-human familiars. Others include elements of daily life long common in the region, like sharing and smoking home-cured pipe tobacco, as well as daily regimens adopted from the British, like drinking tea. The oldest of these exchanges have developed meanings deeply embedded in social life. For example, coffee berries grown ubiquitously in the southern central region of Buganda offer a physical index of the pervasive dualities in Kiganda ontology:

- each human is born with a physical body and a spiritual twin
- like their ancient royalist predecessors, *basamize* venerate twin spirits, especially those associated with Nnyanja Nalubaale, the sons of Mukasa ow'Ennyanja (Mukasa of the Sea), Kiwanuka and Musoke
- the exchange of coffee berries also recalls their use in *omukago* (the blood pact)[2]

Hosts sometimes even refer to serving groundnuts to houseguests as giving them *mmwanyi* (coffee berries), another reference to the *mukago*. The same could possibly be claimed of groundnuts in Busoga, but the Basoga do not tend to ritualize twinship with the same intensity or invest it with as much significance as do the Baganda. In many homes in both Buganda and Busoga, people simply prefer roasted groundnuts to the more bitter coffee berries as a matter of taste. They nevertheless frequently refer to them as *mmwanyi* because they stand in for coffee berries and because the physical structures of both food crops serve the same symbolic purpose: they reinforce the pervasive trope of duality. Taken together, these small, hospitable gestures are crucial components of what it means to gather, *okuŋŋana*.

In both regions, brewing has multiple symbolic resonances both ritual and ethnographic. In *kusamira* and *nswezi* ritual, banana beer is an important gift for human and other-than-human guests. Its brewing processes offer theoretical inspiration for thinking about novices and adepts, the integration of diverse social spheres, the production of knowledge, and the reproduction of social relations to support well-being. The brewing process begins with small, ripe bananas. *Basamize* harvest them and then dig a shallow earthen

156   CHAPTER 5

trough. Collaborators prepare banana leaves to place in the trough as a lin-
ing. The brewers peel and place the bananas in the leaf-lined trough with
long grasses called *ssubi*. When they squeeze the juice from the bananas, the
fibrous banana waste sticks to these grasses, leaving the sweet juice behind
in the trough. Brewers then strain this juice into a container where they mix
it with *marwa* (a fermented liquid starter made from millet), and then they
place the mixture in the ground for two to three days. They remove it after
the *marwa* has promoted fermentation in the *mubissi* (fresh juice), at which
time they test it to ensure its readiness for offering to the spirits.[3]

Glossed in the *ffumbe* (civet cat) clan drum slogan with the verb *okusen-
gejja* (to strain something through a filter or sieve), brewing offers a point
of entry for understanding the homologies generated through repertories of
well-being.

Galinnya, galinnya e Bakka;	They are climbing, climbing [the hill] at Bakka;
basengejja, banywa omwenge;	they are straining, they are drinking the banana beer;
kaakozaakoza:	the one who dips everywhere:
tolikoza mu lw'Effumbe!	let him never end up dipping in the civet cat's sauce!

This slogan tersely encapsulates how activities like brewing and singing scale
up well-being from the person to the clan to the kingdom. People climb
the hill at Bakka, the traditional locus of Walusimbi, the highest authority
figure in the civet cat clan.[4] They bind and restrict more than just banana
waste in their brewing there: both this and their stated prohibition against
eating their totem animal articulate exogamy (i.e., an avoidance of marrying
those who share this totem). The consumption of refined beer rather than
brewing waste, and of other foods rather than the totem civet cat, reminds
clanspeople to be patient, to let relationships mature like fermenting beer,
and to choose their marriage alliances carefully from outside the confines
of kin and clan. It is precisely these alliances that maintain the well-being of
both the clan and the kingdom. This kind of totemic exogamy is consistent
across the entire Kiganda clan system, and similar prohibitions abide among
the Basoga. As with other culturally embedded forms of well-being, these
sophisticated features of music and culture undergird the biological reality:
were people to marry and produce children within too small a gene pool,
biocultural catastrophe could ensue.

The linkages between brewing, binding, and unbinding did not emerge in
this study until early 2009, with the postmortuary *okwabya olumbe* (bursting

Sound, Hospitality, and Feasting 157

death) ritual at Irondo discussed in the previous chapter. The unification in grief and "bursting" death reproduced—as all *kusamira* and *nswezi* gatherings do—many ritual actions of binding evil and unbinding blessings. To welcome the spirits who would initiate new mediums, mourners at Irondo brewed banana beer. Whereas their earlier actions from arrival to that point had been carried out separately, with family on one side of the compound and the late Lukowe Kotilida Bibireka's fellow mediums and musicians on the other, they joined in cooperation for this task. It was part of a progression of actions they took to bind and restrict evil as they opened and encouraged blessings. Having first gathered in mourning and sung lamentations, they strained the waste from the beer, leaving the pure banana juice to ferment with the "mature" *marwa*. The process resembled the way that the ancestors and elders train initiates and adepts to become mature in *nswezi* tradition: just as the "mature" *marwa* encourages fermentation in the "young" banana beer, so elders encourage initiates, promising to train them in *nswezi* traditions.[5] The process bound the initiated elders to their responsibilities as mediums, positioning them socially as a sieve woven into one another and their communities to strain out "bad things" (pestilence in all its various forms). They became like the grasses that stuck to the fibrous banana waste, binding it up and leaving behind sweet juice. Similarly, having covered the grave with *mabombo* grasses and crowned their heads with twisted rings of the same, they proceeded to destroy these symbols of mourning, casting them on the grave. The *mabombo* bound up spiritual waste much like the *ssubi* grasses in the brewing process had bound up physical waste. The mourners gathered these castaway grasses, discarding them in the bush. The process purified the mourners, binding their evil for banishment to the bush and gathering them into the banana grove for social renewal and new growth.

Ultimately, these parallels constitute dynamic process of knowledge production about illness and well-being. As I noted in the introduction, *basamize* and *baswezi* consistently organize the production of such knowledge around two interdependent notions:

- *okusiba ebibi*: binding "bad things," often construed as misfortunes, bad potential, or evil, in order to truncate, restrict, diminish, or banish their power
- *okusumulula emikisa* and *okusumulula amakubo*: unbinding blessings or pathways, respectively, to blessings associated with wellness and fruition writ large

Basamize and *baswezi* recognize a common necessity for well-being and fruition to encompass plants, including crops, medicinal plants, and other

158   CHAPTER 5

flora; animals both domestic and wild that sustain human life either as food sources or spiritual dwellings; human clients who seek their guidance as much for fertility and preventative measures as for illness and misfortune; and spirits who guide, aid, and bless these processes in exchange for sacrifices. Brewing renders the containment of fibrous waste and the release of useful material both tangible and conceptually legible as a process that accomplishes binding and blessing to energize broader processes that also bind and bless.

These are some of the specific activities of ritual work embedded in the performance of ritual healing repertories. The songs in those repertories index the activities, and each song and activity in the repertory resonates sympathetically and conceptually with the next. The exchange of coffee berries promotes friendship: offering them to guests invites the guests' blessings into the house or shrine, and encouraging shrine guests to offer gifts to spirits promotes openness to blessings from spiritual visitors. Throwing two in front and two behind before eating them two at a time indexes the duality of *omukago* (the blood pact). Destroying the banana fibers that carried the coffee berries, as two *basamize* explained, unbinds the pathways to blessings.[6] Brewing produces banana beer. Offering it to a bride's family opens the door for the groom to negotiate a dowry. As the Luganda proverb says, "Ekitta ky'omwenge kisumulula oluggi" (the gourd of beer opens the door). The dowry exchange binds alliances and produces children, whom people count among their most precious blessings. Offering the same kind of beer to spirits likewise opens the pathways for blessings. In these ways, coffee berries and banana beer connote exchanges that foster positive social relationships, open doors, unbind multiple pathways, and ultimately sustain well-being at every level from the person to the family and clan to wider social circles to the kingdom. They often initiate a series of small reciprocal gestures, moving from the distribution of rather mundane resources toward progressively larger, more complex distributions, sometimes culminating in extravagant feasts. The song examples below typically continue from themes of sacrifice and exchange in the previous chapter toward activities and themes of cleansing and gratitude that accompany feasting.

Cleansing and Gratitude

The process of sacrifice, and particularly the subsequent distribution of food and drink, emphasizes the importance of exchange. *Basamize* and *baswezi* make sacrifices in many different ways: the spirit Kiwanuka requires that an animal be burned whole, for example, as opposed to being slaughtered and cooked, which is a more common method. Perhaps the clearest expression

Sound, Hospitality, and Feasting

of sacrificial exchange takes place when people offer an animal, the spirit accepts, people slaughter and cook the animal, the spirit eats, and then the spirit finally places some of the cooked meat in each participant's hands or mouth. I saw these actions a number of times, including at Kisuze near Nakawuka, but a ritual at Kotwe venerating a *jjembe* named Kasajja stood out as well. The spirit supervised the thorough roasting of *ekibumba* (a cow liver). When it was finished, he partook of a small portion before turning to beckon all those gathered. As the *bazzukulu* (grandchildren, what most spirits call ritual attendees) came forward, he fed each person two pieces of the liver with both of his hands at the same time. Then he gave each person two additional pieces, one in each hand.

As I moved away from the spirit/medium to watch how others consumed their small gifts and to follow suit, I contemplated something the same spirit had told me earlier in the ritual. We had piled into a car to take some of the uncooked butchered meat to a neighbor. Kasajja still occupied his female medium in the car, so it became an occasion for an informal interview of the spirit himself. Having witnessed many other rituals in which *basamize* assigned special importance to the cooking and consumption of liver, I asked him what made the organ so important. Jjajja Kasajja responded, "Now then, when I finish with drinking the blood [from a sacrificed animal], it organizes my grandchild, do you hear, brother?"[7] He emphasized that both actions are important: the spirit must feed on the blood of the sacrifice, and the "grandchild" (a reference to an adept of any kind) must "lick" (consume) some of the liver. He used the verb *kuwumbirawumbira* to capture the essence of the process, which others in the car translated as a reassembly of things once lost, missing, or disorganized about one's life. The sharing of a physical component of the sacrifice reinforced notions of *okuŋŋana* (gathering) and *okuwumba* (organization).

Once a person had undergone such a process, often glossed by mediums and other specialists as *kulongoosa* (a cleansing), it was quite common for adepts to observe taboos. In the case of Kasajja's feeding and distribution at Kotwe, the main singer at the ritual warned me not to bathe for the rest of the day. I was to reach home, she instructed, and sleep as I was, only to bathe in the morning. At Kisuze, the taboo was similar: after receiving a smearing of clarified butter on the face from a spirit through its medium, a person could neither leave the site that day nor bathe until the next day. In this case at Kotwe, however, she granted that I could make an exception if I bathed with *lweeza*, the medicinal plant so often used for ritual cleansing. Having slept in the shrine without bathing for a few days already, I was pleasantly surprised to return to my residence in Kampala to find that the staff there

160 CHAPTER 5

knew just where to find it, a testament to the ubiquity of the plant, the bathing traditions that surround it, and the linkages of both to ritual purity and healthy living.

Like the convivial atmosphere that people enjoyed when they received food from Kasajja, many rituals ended with elaborate celebrations of successful sacrificial exchanges. Prohibitive taboos accompanied the experiential understandings with which participants left ritual sites, all shaped by lingering scents, tastes, and other sensations. People call this kind of meal *ekijjulo* (a feast), which comes from the verb *okujjula* (to uncover food, to inaugurate or culminate something). *Basamize* and *baswezi* alike sang songs of celebration for this moment in a given ritual. The songs ranged from simple offerings of thanks to specific mentions of meat to lengthy verses of praise. One example of a simple tune for thanksgiving used the same chorus each time with solo verses that deviated only slightly:

Soloist: Weebale weebale naye munnange weebale,	Thank you, thank you, but my dear thank you,
weebale weebale ogabudde nnyo weebale	thank you, thank you, you have served much, thank you
Chorus: weebale weebale ssebo Jjajja weebale,	thank you, thank you, sir grandparent, thank you,
weebale weebale akwagalanga omwebazanga	thank you, thank you, always thank whoever loves you
S: waalaalaala naye munnange mmwebaza,	waalaalaala but I thank my dear,
weebale weebale ogabudde nnyo weebale	thank you, thank you, you have served much, thank you
(chorus)	
S: weebale weebale naye munnange weebale,	thank you, thank you, but my dear thank you,
weebale weebale ogabudde nnyo nkwebaza	thank you, thank you, you have served much, I thank you
(chorus)	

Songs of thanksgiving can also double as litanies for the spirits who have received sacrifices during the ritual, as in this tune:

Ch: Tweyanzizza, tweyanzeege	We are grateful, we are very grateful
S: tweyanze Kibuuka tweyanze	we are grateful, Kibuuka, we are grateful
(chorus)	
S: tweyanze mayembe tweyanze	we are grateful, *mayembe*, we are grateful

Sound, Hospitality, and Feasting 161

(chorus)	
S: tweyanze Kibuuka Omumbaale	we are grateful, Kibuuka Omumbaale
(chorus)	
S: tweyanze lubaale tweyanze	we are grateful, *lubaale*, we are grateful
(chorus)	

As in the first of these two tunes, many thanking songs play on the term *kugabula*, which literally means to serve a feast, but which derives from the verb *kugaba* (to give, to distribute). When a person enjoys a meal as a guest in someone's home, custom dictates that he should thank those who cooked the meal, particularly the elder matriarch of the household, saying, *ofumbye nnyo, nnyabo* (you have really cooked, madam). The same custom obliges the guest to use a form of the verb *kugabula* to thank the host for providing the feast, saying, *ogabudde nnyo, ssebo* (you have really served a feast, sir). At a ritual in Kirowooza village entirely devoted to Muwanga, one song focused this kind of gendered customary attention on the spirit as a host for the feast.

S: Yangabula, Muwanga agaba, yangabula	He served me, Muwanga gives, he served me
Ch: yangabula ng'agabula owuwe	he served me like his own
S: Muwanga agaba	Muwanga gives
Ch: yangabula	he served me
S: Muwanga agaba	Muwanga gives
Ch: yangabula ng'agabula owuwe	he served me like his own
S: agaba ku nnyama	he serves/shares meat
Ch: yangabula	he served me
S: aaa	aaa
Ch: yangabula ng'agabula owuwe	he served me like his own
S: Muwanga agaba	Muwanga gives
Ch: yangabula	he served me
S: misambwa gy'ab'edda	the ancestral *misambwa*
Ch: yangabula ng'agabula owuwe	he served me like his own

The song thus reversed the typical order of things as sung in the early stages of ritual, in which the spirits are cast as visitors and the adepts—especially mediums or candidates for mediumship—are cast as their hosts. Once the people gathered had provided the sacrifice to the spirits and either distributed it or facilitated its distribution via the spirits, it was the spirits as providers of food and blessings—specifically meat—who became hosts to those who ate it.

S: Siraba nga agaba ki?	I have never seen one who gives what?
Ch: omugabi	the giver
S: siraba nga agaba ki?	I have never seen one who gives what?
Ch: omugabi agabye ennyama	the giver has served meat

162   CHAPTER 5

S: Jjajja ng'omuwadde	Grandparent, you have given
Ch: omugabi	the giver
S: munnange omuwadde	my dear, you have given him/her
Ch: omugabi agabye ennyama	the giver has served meat
S: emisambwa ogiwadde	you have given the *misambwa*
Ch: omugabi	the giver
S: n'abalongo abawadde	s/he has also given the twins
Ch: omugabi agabye ennyama	the giver has served meat
S: n'amayembe gawadde	s/he has also given the *mayembe*
Ch: omugabi	the giver
S: Jjajja ng'ogabudde	Grandparent you have [really] served
Ch: omugabi agabye ennyama	the giver has served meat

Again, as in earlier examples, the song became a litany for all the spirits who had arrived in their mediums, received sacrifices, and distributed blessings.

Dancing with the Spirits: Well-Being beyond Therapeutics

These songs of celebration and thanksgiving serve as important reminders: whereas overcoming multiple forms of adversity is a major focus of *kusamira* and *nswezi* rituals, it is not their sole purpose. Many rituals determine underlying spiritual components of common health ailments like malaria, eczema, syphilis, or symptoms of HIV/AIDS. However, several rituals I attended had the sole purpose of calling spirits to celebrate propitious, ongoing relationships with the communities who called them. In this regard, *kusamira* and *nswezi* demonstrate broad coherence with other regional *ŋoma* traditions, which consistently have medical, religious, and sociopolitical overtones.[8] The celebratory and feasting songs in repertories of well-being therefore provide a basis for examining relational ideals.

Whether a given feast celebrates a successful exchange with a single spirit, a brief litany, or a broader pantheon, those moments in ritual in which spirits dance through their mediums with their devotees or "grandchildren" emerge as valuable opportunities to understand who those spirits are and what they gain from these relationships. Some examples have already surfaced, like the mediums at Buyijja and Kisuze whose movements constituted shifts in shape toward the animal familiars of their patron spirits. But spirits need not climb a tree like a leopard or slither on the ground like a snake to participate physically in ritual beyond the movements that accompany the onset of possession. At Kisuze, spirits regularly danced with *basamize* through their mediums. The *balalu* spirits at the same site routinely pushed Kiganda hip-centered dances in a vulgar direction, an impulse consistent with their breach of multiple

Sound, Hospitality, and Feasting   163

taboos. Ddungu the hunter spirit's mannerisms at Makandwa (see chapter 2) were remarkably consistent with another ritual at Bombo the previous year involving a different medium and a different community. Ddungu's dancing with spear and shield, his tendency to don a fishing net and disguise himself with leaves and branches for the hunt, and his crouching movements were all consistent between the two mediums at these two rituals, and at others where he figured prominently. Whether through their animal familiars or through their specific personae, spirits' interactions, negotiations, and movements with ritual adepts shape their identities and, by extension, the contours of Kiganda and Kisoga spirit pantheons.

The same is true for spirits associated with bodily afflictions. *Basamize* associate Ndawula, a spirit with a long history linking southern Uganda with its northern neighbors in the Bunyoro region, with skin diseases. The association has changed through the region's encounters with measles, mumps, smallpox, and now various HIV-related cancers, but the result has been an association with skin problems sufficiently consistent to have fostered the development of a specific tobacco pipe and beer gourd for Ndawula, both of which feature raised bumps.[9] When he arrives in his medium, the initiated know to offer him these items to meet his basic hospitality standard. Adepts recognize spirit Kawumpuli, a warrior, by his limp or through some other indication that they characterize as his "lameness," the results of his exploits in battle. These are just two among many examples of spirits distinguishable by bodily characteristics, accoutrements, and songs. When they dance and sing with *basamize* and *baswezi*, these actions invariably follow from a warm welcome in which people met their hospitality preferences, offered them appropriate sacrifices, and sought these interactions as indicators of the spirits' blessings.

A strong current of social diversity runs through these streams of hospitality and conviviality. Most readily apparent at events where multiple spirits manifest in their mediums simultaneously, the celebration of multiple overlapping differences often reflects human variety in other-than-human forms. Respect for elders, recognition of a broad ability spectrum, and even skin tone contribute to this feature of ritual life. Kiwanuka, for example, is often discussed and depicted as being white or albino, and some traditionalist families will pass his name along to an albino child in addition to a clan-associated name.

The tendency to celebrate diversity extends to religious variety, too. The creation of power objects at Makandwa to mitigate social conflict with Christians is a prime example, but I have expounded at length elsewhere about the social aesthetics of twenty-first-century Ugandan religious pluralism.[10] Fraught as the politics of religion in Uganda remain, marked as they are by an ex-colonial fervor and even the occasional violent razing of traditional

164   CHAPTER 5

shrines, what began as a reflection of worldly variety in deified forms might now be more important for ritual healing specialists than ever. As is often the case with their repertories of well-being, the stakes of articulating a sociopolitical identity for the things of tradition remain high. *Basamize* and *baswezi* cannot afford so much as the perception that anything about their practices is hostile toward Christians or Muslims, and that situation will likely intensify as proselytizers for both faith traditions continue the work they have long done in Uganda. With traditional practices, at their shrines and among colleagues, people's lives and livelihoods hang in the balance. The public sphere affects their own safety and professional efficacy. For the sake of the spirits and for these reasons, feasting and mutual aid therefore remain major concerns at gatherings of *basamize* and *baswezi* both large and small.

Conclusion

Feasting is ultimately about shared substance. *Okuŋŋana* (gathering) means recognizing common needs and interests. The act of exchanging seemingly quotidian forms of hospitality among those gathered, and extending the same to the spirits, reinforces those interests. The ritual work of *basamize* and *baswezi* revolves around mediums whose flexible personhood binds them to other-than-human familiars and opens spiritual blessings to promote well-being. But the work can be most effective under circumstances in which these entities understand each other and accept that they need each other. At its most socially effervescent, feasting celebrates the mutually reinforcing power of shared substance both physical and metaphysical.[11]

In this regard, feasting and celebratory singing demonstrate an essential component of repertories of well-being: their efficacy simultaneously includes and transcends the physiological plane. It might well be fascinating to have a more thorough understanding of the physical component. Measuring brain waves during mediumship possession, attending to the physical benefits of singing and dance, taking stock of the dietary advantages of gathering regularly for ritual, comparing live birth survival rates or the bonesetting practices of traditional physicians and allopathic clinicians, or closely examining the impact of Ugandan plant medicines on the human body could all make for fascinating perspectives on the physiological efficacy of *kusamira* and *nswezi*. Even then, these would only present a partial understanding of efficacious intervention as *basamize* and *baswezi* understand it. They would not account for the inextricable other-than-human facets of these many variables. As with other elements of these repertories, then, an understanding of how and why people celebrate helps explain the ideals that shape their notions of efficacy.

Conclusion

Listening to *Kusamira*'s Lessons on Well-Being Now

This book has examined musical repertories embedded in broader repertories of action practiced by traditional healing specialists in southern Uganda. This investigation of song as a core habit of traditional medicinal knowledge-making has elucidated how specialists create, manage, and distribute such knowledge. *Basamize* and *baswezi* perform their repertories in deliberate service to the reproduction of the most favorable possible social circumstances, supporting the well-being of people and communities. I have argued that repertories of well-being feature heterophonic and polyrhythmic musical textures, and that these textures offer a convenient frame for thinking about the simultaneities inherent in socially articulating the things of tradition. The invocation of multiple types of spirits, the embodiment of spirits in human bodies, and other manifestations of in-between power likewise place the things of tradition firmly between a process of historically tenacious cultural reproduction and the innovations that practitioners use to grapple with the complexities of postmodern social interaction. I have also argued that this process of social reproduction resembles other ritual processes of binding negative potential or "bad things" and unbinding healing power or "blessings." These interstices and simultaneities are perhaps nowhere more apparent than in the songs that idealize *obulamu obulungi* (the good life) and the prayers that often accompany them.

Examples from the field research have supported the following notions about how and why people perform and experience *kusamira* and *nswezi* repertories:

- to pursue and maintain well-being in the present
- to preserve ideas about illness and wellness for future generations

166   *Conclusion*

- to consider and negotiate the impact of persistent influences on well-being
- to innovate in dynamic sociopolitical circumstances

That four-part argument has asked readers to consider a number of main threads that bind its elements together and link it with a broader literature that spans African studies disciplines. It remains to be considered how these threads might inform further inquiry.

The focus of chapter 1 on the many kinds of work traditional healers do in an African ex-colony replete with development dreams invites both comparison with other contexts and a more practical concern with public policy. The World Health Organization is clearly engaged with both. Meanwhile, the proliferation of health-related NGOs and the anxiety of government ministries that interact with all these entities clarify that the whole discourse repeats a familiar pattern of concern with abundance and risk. Uganda's indigenous medical traditions have socially reproduced their most feasible practices by listening to elders, ancestors, clients, forests, spirits, and the songs that bind them together. The health sector's attempts to engage these communities in some collective listening have so far been modest at best, in part because to do so is logistically challenging, discursively complex, and politically messy. But if it is already clear that a collaborative approach will produce more sustainable results than any heavy-handed top-down directive could hope to, that presents fascinating possibilities for a new medical ethnography of traditional healing. Listening—and yes, listening to expressive culture like songs and other arts—promises important contributions to such a discourse.

Broadening the scale, though, scholars and policy makers alike often do well when they attend to how the masses find practical solutions to their most common health-care challenges. The process of following the behavior of people and the groups that help them make health-care decisions, then developing interventions from that information, has a proven record of success. Uganda's most widely known example of this guiding principle has been the overwhelmingly successful ABC ("Abstinence, Be Faithful, Condom Use") approach to combatting the HIV/AIDS epidemic.[1] Similarly, if government ministries and health-care workers want to understand people's motivations and behaviors to support better health decisions and outcomes, they might have more success by listening and learning than by dismissing esoteric ideas embedded in traditional approaches. Physicians, ministries, and health workers need not accept patient beliefs for themselves, but attempting to listen to them and understand them would be a good start. Traditional practitioners, by contrast, need not eschew the accumulated knowledge of generations in order to attend more carefully to the efforts of population health workers,

Conclusion 167

particularly around formative issues like sanitation, sterile and sanitary working conditions for birthing and health interventions, malaria prevention, and sexual safety. Listening to repertories of well-being is only one path to such an approach, but ethnographic listening more generally portends a multitude of others. Collaboration on these and other matters among traditional practitioners, health workers, and clinicians remains an area of enormous opportunity.

Repertories of song and their performance offer a distinctive contribution to ethnographic listening in discourses of healing: they have been historically tenacious, outliving many other shifts and trends in Ugandan health and well-being. I have highlighted work by anthropologists and historians suggesting that the same is true of other *ŋoma* traditions. This book critically moves away from those proselytizing religious discourses because these tend to actively delegitimize tradition by treating the spiritual aspects of *kusamira* as superstitious. It is a step back from the immediate concerns of health workers, whose definitions of desirable outcomes sometimes intersect with those of *basamize* and *baswezi*, but who too often devalue traditional healers' work as unscientific. It stops just short of stepping into the politicized discourses of the public sector that so often combine the neocolonial tendencies of missionaries and NGOs with administratively hasty tactics.

Part of development discourse articulates shifts in the ways people experience and understand the world, and those shifts have implications for economy, residence, infrastructure, and a host of other domains that affect well-being. Understanding how traditional healing embeds humans and other-than-human influences in an ecological context could usefully inform those shifts. Urbanization and economic change have not somehow magically halted the ecological heritage that people carry with them from their villages into Kampala or Jinja. Banana trees in the backyards of so many suburban houses and the existence of numerous urban shrines offer two indications among many that agrarian life and its attendant ecological and spiritual overtones come into cities along with migrants. Another indication resounds in the constant talk of village connections that seemingly everyone retains, regardless of how many generations deep their urban roots might go. These render the urban-rural dynamic so much more complex than the duality suggests. Only some of the social costs of migration trends toward cities have emerged in the last fifty years; a more thorough accounting of migration's impact on ecologies and on the social reproduction of well-being demands deeper, more sustained attention.

Thinking about sound will continue to generate insight as these other factors keep changing. Human populations, the places and spaces they inhabit, the resources they rely on, and the other-than-human entities with which they interact all portend new opportunities to document and interpret the constant reinvention of *kusamira* and *nswezi* traditions. These repertories have already exerted significant influence on Uganda's popular music (and vice versa). They now resound through speakers on a rapidly expanding variety of technologies seemingly everywhere in Uganda and throughout its global diaspora. While those influences are beyond the purview of this book, they suggest representations of traditional Ugandan cultures well worth consideration. Both the traditional sounds and their more pop-oriented reframing continue to have a stimulating home at Makerere University's Klaus Wachsmann Audio-Visual Archive. The faculty, staff, and students there have already supported accession of some field recordings from this study through collaborations with the communities where the recordings originated. Those and hundreds of other materials at the archive will facilitate new research on *kusamira* and many other forms of music and dance. The continuing development of even more diverse technologies open to near-ubiquitous access ensures a bright future for examining both the sounds and their social implications.

Likewise, perennial anthropological interests in sacrifice, exchange, and social spectacles like rituals and feasts will continue to offer fascinating material for further research. They present ever-changing dynamics for examining the relationship of humans to their social groups and to wider cultural trends. Within these dynamics, the dual potential for abundance and risk promises to continue its central role in twenty-first-century discourses around unequal access to various forms of knowledge and practice that will shape well-being long into the future. *Kusamira* constitutes an ancient, durable, adaptable approach to producing and practicing such knowledge.

Notes

Introduction

1. For a brief review of social reproduction and cultural reproduction literature related to health, see Janzen, "The Social Reproduction of Health," 92. This definition paraphrases and truncates a lengthier version that Janzen cites from Bilton et al., *Introductory Sociology*, 670.

2. WHO, *WHO Traditional Medicine Strategy, 2002–2005*, 1, 9; Chatora, "Traditional Medicine"; see also WHO, *WHO Traditional Medicine Strategy, 2014–2023*, 25–34.

3. For a crystallizing moment in that discourse, see Feierman, "Struggles for Control."

4. Schoenbrun, "Pythons Worked"; Schoenbrun, "Ethnic Formation with Other-Than-Human Beings"; and Schoenbrun and Johnson, introduction.

5. Seeger, "The Musicological Juncture," 47.

6. See, e.g., Doyle, "The Cwezi-Kubandwa Debate"; Cohen, *The Historical Tradition of Busoga*, 19–21, 44–45; Schoenbrun, *The Historial Reconstruction of Great Lakes Bantu Cultural Vocabulary*, 178, 182, 205, 210, 213, 218, 226; Schoenbrun, *A Green Place, a Good Place*, 178, 197–98; Kodesh, *Beyond the Royal Gaze*, 27–66.

7. See Kagwa, *Empisa za Buganda*, for more on Kiganda clans; see also Kafumbe, *Tuning the Kingdom*, 3, for a useful visualization of Buganda's clan administrative structure.

8. For an inclusive, chronologically organized review of this diverse literature, see Hoesing, "*Kusamira* Ritual Music," 42–59. For a more expansive grasp on anglophone and francophone sources, see also Janzen, *Ngoma*, 10–84.

9. Cf. Berliner, *The Soul of Mbira*; Friedson, *Dancing Prophets*; Stoller and Olkes, *In Sorcery's Shadow*; and Hellweg, *Hunting the Ethical State*.

10. Janzen, *Ngoma*; Dijk, Reis, and Spierenburg, *The Quest for Fruition through Ngoma*.

Notes to Introduction

11. Rice, *Ethnomusicology*, 1–10.

12. For a more thorough set of illustrations and descriptions of Kiganda drums and other instruments, see Trowell and Wachsmann, *Tribal Crafts of Uganda*, 369–80.

13. For a good image of *mpuunyi* in the context of the royal Kawuugulu set, see Kafumbe, *Tuning the Kingdom*, 27.

14. See Nannyonga-Tamusuza's definitive study, *Baakisimba*.

15. Feld, "Sound Structure as Social Structure"; see also Feld, *Sound and Sentiment*, 83, 85, 131.

16. Turner, *The Ritual Process*; Kapferer, "Ritual Dynamics and Virtual Practice"; Jankowsky, *Stambeli*, 27–28.

17. Good, *Medicine, Rationality, and Experience*, 37, 48, 240.

18. Turner, *Drums of Affliction*.

19. Schoenbrun, *A Green Place, a Good Place*, 111.

20. Schoenbrun, 111. Schoenbrun's etymology goes well beyond the first-ever monolingual Luganda dictionary (Kiingi's *Enkuluze Ya Oluganda Ey'e Makerere*, first published in 2007), which does not directly associate the verb *okulagula* with the stem *-laga* (Kiingi 446).

21. "Bw'ogenda okusooka okusamira, kati bw'ogenda w'omusajja alagula, n'akuba omweso n'akugamba nti, 'lubaale akuluma, naye lubaale wa kika.' Anti nno lubaale w'ekika, tulina lubaale w'omukago, tulina wa e bukojja, olina balubaale e waffe waawano Buganda." Ssematimba Frank Sibyangu, interview by the author, May 25, 2010.

22. Roscoe, *The Baganda*, 271.

23. Bourdieu, *The Logic of Practice*, 53; Kodesh, *Beyond the Royal Gaze*.

24. Kodesh, *Beyond the Royal Gaze*, 5.

25. Kabona Jjumba and Proskovya "Musomesa" Jjumba, interview with the author, February 2, 2010. The unnamed woman in this interview agreed to participate on condition of anonymity.

26. "Singa okkiriza mu bajjajja n'obawa kye baagala, osobola kukola ki? Kufuna emirembe. Wano e Buganda . . . Naye wo takkiriza mu bajjajja olussi . . . nga balya kasasiro, wali ku dust bin ne balya. Abalalu." Ssematimba Frank Sibyangu, interview by the author, May 25, 2010. I have translated *bajjajja* here as "ancestors" and elsewhere (in its singular form, *jjajja*) as "grandparent." The two are functionally identical, but contextually, the singular *jjajja* often reads or sounds more like a term of endearment, like "granny."

27. Kabona Jjumba and Proskovya "Musomesa" Jjumba, interview with the author, February 2, 2010. The unnamed man in this interview agreed to participate on condition of anonymity.

28. Blacking, "The Context of Venda Possession Music," 67–68.

29. Rouget, *Music and Trance*, xviii, 323; for a similar perspective, see Harris and Norton, "Introduction," 2.

30. Jankowsky, *Stambeli*, 24. Jankowsky's articulation of this notion draws on both his own previous work and that of Michael Herzfeld a decade earlier. See Jankowsky, "Music, Spirit Possession, and the In-Between"; Herzfeld, *Cultural Intimacy*.

Notes to Introduction and Chapter 1

31. Jankowsky, *Stambeli*, 25, 27, 197.

32. Emoff, *Recollecting from the Past*.

33. Kodesh, *Beyond the Royal Gaze*, 5; Stoller, *The Taste of Ethnographic Things*.

34. Jankowsky, *Stambeli*, 24.

35. Marcus and Fischer, *Anthropology as Cultural Critique*.

36. Masquelier, *Prayer Has Spoiled Everything*, 26; see also Herzfeld, *Cultural Intimacy*, 165–74; Jankowsky, "Music, Spirit Possession, and the In-Between"; and Jankowsky, *Stambeli*, 25.

37. Jankowsky, *Stambeli*, 25–26.

38. Janzen, *Ngoma*, 154; Feierman, "Struggles for Control," 74.

39. Janzen, *Ngoma*, 86.

1. Ritual Work in Twenty-First-Century Uganda

1. See, e.g., Janzen, *The Quest for Therapy in Lower Zaire*; Comaroff, *Body of Power, Spirit of Resistance*; Feierman, *Peasant Intellectuals*; Feierman and Janzen, *The Social Roots of Health and Healing in Africa*; Livingston, *Improvising Medicine*; Geissler, *Para-States and Medical Science*.

2. See, e.g., Barello, Graffigna, and Vegni, "Promoting Patient and Caregiver Engagement"; Carman et al., "Patient and Family Engagement"; and Domecq et al., "Patient Engagement in Research."

3. These phrases are, respectively, *emirimu gy'abajjajja* or *emirimu gy'abakulu* and *ebintu eby'obuwangwa*.

4. See, e.g., Feierman, *Peasant Intellectuals*; Schoenbrun, *A Green Place, a Good Place*; Gunderson, *Sukuma Labor Songs from Western Tanzania*.

5. Feierman makes this point emphatically in "Struggles for Control," 74–78.

6. Tantala, "The Early History of Kitara in Western Uganda," 45; Kodesh, *Beyond the Royal Gaze*, 29, 48, 65–66.

7. Feierman, "Colonizers, Scholars, and the Creation of Invisible Histories," 189.

8. Schoenbrun, *A Green Place, a Good Place*, 197. Schoenbrun cites Renee Tantala and three precolonial sources on this point.

9. See, e.g., Vernaschi's articles "The Man behind RACHO" and "Babirye, the Girl from Katugwe."

10. Pulitzer Center, "Questions on Uganda."

11. Kalibbala, "Is Witchcraft on the Rise, or is the Press Blowing It Up?"

12. Berger, "The 'Kubandwa' Religious Complex of Interlacustrine East Africa"; Schoenbrun, *A Green Place, a Good Place*, 267; Kodesh, *Beyond the Royal Gaze*.

13. See Hoesing, "Nabuzaana Omunozzi w'Eddagala," 349.

14. See, e.g., Arnoux, "Le Culte de la Société Secréte des Imandwa au Ruanda." For a review of colonial-era perspectives on similar associations in Tanzania, see also Gunderson, "Musical Labor Associations in Sukumaland, Tanzania," 43–63.

15. Uganda Protectorate, *The Witchcraft Ordinance*, 2 (italics in original).

16. See, e.g., *New Vision*, "Kiryapaawo Warns Healers on Human Sacrifice"; *Religion News Blog*, "Child Sacrifice Is on the Rise in Uganda"; Kelly, "Child Sacrifice and

172 · Notes to Chapter 1

Ritual Murders Rise in Uganda as Famine Looms"; Ayebazibwe, "Child Sacrifice on the Rise"; Martel, "Uganda Prepares for Surge in Child Sacrifice by Witch Doctors as Election Nears." These articles have been published in such varied venues as *New Vision* and *Daily Monitor* (Uganda), the *Guardian* (United Kingdom), and *Breitbart* (United States).

17. Iliffe, *East African Doctors*, 144–49.

18. Iliffe, 164; now called the Natural Chemotherapeutics Research Institute (NCRI).

19. Iliffe, 165.

20. For a perspective on the place of music in this trend, see Barz, *Singing for Life*.

21. Uganda, Indigenous and Complementary Medicine Bill, 2015, 9–23.

22. Sarah Opendi, "Press Statement: Clarification on the Traditional and Complementary Medicines Bill, 2019."

23. Feierman, "Struggles for Control," 80–81.

24. See especially Barz, *Singing for Life*. See also Barz and Cohen, *The Culture of AIDS in Africa*.

25. Kasilo et al., "An Overview of the Traditional Medicine Situation in the African Region."

26. Tsing, *Friction*, esp. 3, 9–10.

27. WHO, *WHO Traditional Medicine Strategy, 2002–2005*; reiterated in WHO, *WHO Traditional Medicine Strategy, 2014–2023*, 27–29.

28. Anonymous interview with the author, March 30, 2009.

29. Bhabha, *The Location of Culture*, 53–56.

30. Bhabha, 51.

31. Hellweg, *Hunting the Ethical State*, 1–12, 14–16; see also Amselle, *Mestizo Logics*.

32. Tsing, *Friction*, 13.

33. See Janzen, *Ngoma*, esp. xi; see also the introduction to Feierman and Janzen, *The Social Roots of Health and Healing in Africa*.

34. *Ebintu eby'obuwangwa* and *bya bajjajja*.

35. Kodesh, *Beyond the Royal Gaze*, 14–15; Feierman, "Colonizers, Scholars, and the Creation of Invisible Histories," 203.

36. For examples of how these economic histories are bound up with technologies of money, gender and sexuality, and moral reasoning, see, e.g., Van Zwanenberg and King, *An Economic History of Kenya and Uganda*; Barbara Nyanzi et al., "Money, Men, and Markets"; Jörg Wiegratz, "Fake Capitalism?"

37. Uganda Ministry of Health, *Health Sector Development Plan*, 35. See also Opendi, "Press Statement," which estimates the "conventional practitioner" to patient ratio at "1:20,000 or even less."

38. For an excellent study of land and power, including spiritual power, in Buganda's history, see Hanson, *Landed Obligation*.

39. Hoesing, "*Nabuzaana Omunozzi w'Eddagala*," 364.

40. Janzen, *Ngoma*, 105.

41. Meinert, "Regimes of Homework in AIDS Care," 126.

42. Barz and Cohen, *The Culture of AIDS in Africa*.

Notes to Chapters 1 and 2

43. Barz, *Singing for Life*, 16.

44. Reed, "C'est Le Wake Up! Africa."

45. See, e.g., Feierman, "Struggles for Control"; Feierman, *Peasant Intellectuals*; Janzen, *Ngoma*; Feierman and Janzen, *The Social Roots of Health and Healing in Africa*.

46. McNeill and James, "Singing Songs of AIDS in Venda, South Africa," 194.

47. See especially Van Gennep, *The Rites of Passage*; Turner, *Drums of Affliction*.

48. Janzen, *Ngoma*, 88; Gluckman, *Essays on the Ritual of Social Relations*.

49. On ritual semiotics, see, e.g., Turner, *The Forest of Symbols*; Turner, *Dramas, Fields, and Metaphors*; Perman, *Signs of the Spirit*. The literature on resistance is vast, but see, e.g., Comaroff, *Body of Power*; Fry, *Spirits of Protest*; Lan, *Guns and Rain*; Ranger, *Dance and Society in Eastern Africa*. For an efficient review of literature at the intersection of ritual, resistance, and structural reform, see also Hellweg, *Hunting the Ethical State*, 7–8.

50. Yahaya Sekagya, interview with the author, November 18, 2008.

51. SEYA T. M. Consultancy Firm, "Kampala District Traditional Healers' Directory," 6.

52. SEYA T. M. Consultancy Firm.

53. Yahaya Sekagya and Charles Kiggundu, interview with the author, December 12, 2008; Uganda Ministry of Gender, Labour, and Social Development, "Traditional Medical Practitioners and Human Sacrifice" summit, February 20, 2009.

54. WHO, *WHO Traditional Medicine Strategy, 2014–2023*, 27–29; Abdullahi, "Trends and Challenges of Traditional Medicine in Africa," 116; see also Uganda Ministry of Health, *Health Sector Development Plan*," 35.

55. HOPE is not used as an acronym, but it consistently appears in PROMETRA literature in all capital letters, perhaps to emphasize the importance of associated activities for people living positively.

56. Barz, *Singing for Life*, 77–106.

57. Real Doctors, "Mpereza Engabo Yange."

2. Ecologies of Well-Being

1. Strathern, *Reproducing the Future*, 10.

2. See Blokland, "Kings, Spirits, and Brides in Unyamwezi, Tanzania," esp. 36; see also Boddy, *Wombs and Alien Spirits*, 70, 72–74.

3. Hoesing, "Nabuzaana Omunozzi w'Eddagala," 352–54.

4. Niane, *Sundiata*, 8n1; see also Hoesing, "Nabuzaana Omunozzi w'Eddagala," 359–67.

5. Waalabyeki Magoba, pers. comm.

6. This summary of twinship and its meanings in Kiganda ontology synthesizes information from several interviews and multiple rituals: Centurio Balikoowa and Nassuna Proskovya, interview with the author, November 8, 2008; Umar Ndiwalana, interviews with the author, November 27 and December 4, 2008; Nakigozi Nabawanuka, interview and performance at Ndejje, March 28, 2009; Kabona Wamala Muga-

lula, interview with the author, April 8, 2009; Jjajja Kabona Mutale and Nakayima, interviews with the author, May 11–12, 2009; Kabona Jjumba, *Okubasiba Abalongo* rite, March 8–9, 2010; Ssematimba Frank Sibyangu, interview with the author and analysis of *balongo* songs from Kirowooza, May 19, 2010.

7. Kraemer, "The Fragile Male."

8. See also Nannyonga-Tamusuza, *Baakisimba: Gender*, 69–70.

9. Ssematimba Frank Sibyangu, interview with the author, March 18, 2010. See also Kodesh, *Beyond the Royal Gaze*, the core argument of which is that linkages like this helped Buganda achieve political complexity that permeated the farthest reaches of the kingdom.

10. Ssematimba Frank Sibyangu, interviews with the author, March 27 and May 19, 2010; see further Hoesing, "Nabuzaana Omunozzi w'Eddagala," 362.

11. Jjajja Kabona Jjumba, *Kusamira*, February 16, 2010; Ssematimba Frank Sibyangu, interview with the author, March 18, 2010.

12. Nannyonga-Tamusuza, *Baakisimba: Gender*, 63–70; Nannyonga-Tamusuza, "Baakisimba: Constructing Gender"; Kafumbe, *Tuning the Kingdom*, 25–60, esp. 56, 60.

13. *Ggwe musota kazaala baana*. Regarding the historical importance of python symbolism in Kiganda oral traditions and rituals, see also Kodesh, *Beyond the Royal Gaze*, 39–48.

14. Johnson, "Fish, Family, and the Gendered Politics of Descent along Uganda's Southern Littorals," 450, 459, 463, 465; see also Nannyonga-Tamusuza, "Female-Men, Male-Women, and Others."

15. For other interpretations of the -*buga* stem related to motherhood and land, see Stephens, *A History of African Motherhood*, 140–41; and Schoenbrun, *The Historical Reconstruction of Great Lakes Bantu Cultural Vocabulary*, 34, 71–72.

16. Turino, "Signs of Imagination, Identity, and Experience," 226, 229; Turino, "Peircean Thought as Core Theory for a Phenomenological Ethnomusicology," 213.

17. Kodesh, *Beyond the Royal Gaze*, 5.

18. Kafumbe, *Tuning the Kingdom*, 117.

19. Ray, *Myth, Ritual, and Kingship in Buganda*, 127–28; Kagwa, *Ekitabo kye Mpisa za Buganda*; Trowell and Wachsmann, *Tribal Crafts of Uganda*, 372, 377; see also Kagwa, *The Customs of the Baganda*.

20. Nakigozi Nabawanuka, interview with the author, March 28, 2009.

21. Ray, *Myth, Ritual, and Kingship in Buganda*, 105.

22. See, e.g., Roscoe, *The Baganda*, 273–75; Kagwa, *Empisa za Buganda*, 112–16; Mair, *An African People in the Twentieth Century*, 232; and Hanson, *Landed Obligation*, 72–75.

23. Cohen, *The Historical Tradition of Busoga*, 19–20.

24. Kodesh, *Beyond the Royal Gaze*, 27–66.

25. Luganda: *Sembeza, sembeza, sembeza, emisambwa*.

26. "Munkuukuulu kitegeeza nti mu . . . akakuukuulu, akakiiko; akanyoolagano kiri 'circus' oba 'chaos' nga bw'olabye." Ssematimba Frank Sibyangu, interview with the author, June 26, 2010.

Notes to Chapters 2 and 3

27. Hoesing, "Nabuzaana Omunozzi w'Eddagala."

28. Gulere, "Riddle of Self-Identity," 7–14.

29. Kodesh, *Beyond the Royal Gaze*, 36–48.

30. Cohen, *The Historical Tradition of Busoga*, 18–20.

31. Anonymous group interview with the author, January 17, 2009, Munamaizi; Andrew Mwesige, Rehema Lukowe, and Kyambu Ntakabusuni, interview with the author, February 8, 2009.

32. Gulere, "Riddle of Self-Identity," 10. See also Gulere, *Lusoga–English Dictionary*, 23; Nabirye, *Eikwanika ly'Olusoga*, 28, 104, 541. This bird appears to have many names, but Gulere and Nabirye's references to it are consistent with a ground hornbill.

33. Cohen, *The Historical Tradition of Busoga*, 136. Cf. Nabirye, *Eiwanika ly'Olusoga*, 393; Gonza, *Lusoga–English/English–Lusoga Dictionary*, 203. Both Nabirye and Gonza have prayer as the primary meaning of this verb, but in Gonza's dictionary, the term does carry a connotation of "making an offering," which is consistent with Cohen's narrative of gatherings for sacrifice at Buwongo.

34. Gulere, "Riddle of Self-Identity," 10.

35. For more on public perceptions of ritual sacrifice in Uganda, see chapter 1.

36. For a video clip of this song, see Hoesing, *Birth of an Ancestor*, at 9:55.

37. For an excellent analysis of the emergence of the Mukama narrative, see Cohen, *The Historical Tradition of Busoga*, 124–39.

38. Minah Nabirye, interview with the author, April 2, 2009.

39. Andrew Lukungu Mwesige Kyambu, *Nswezi*, January 18, 2009.

40. This is a rough forage shrub, *Sida schimperiana*, per Gonza, *Lusoga–English/English–Lusoga Dictionary*, 83.

41. For a spirited defense of conceptualizing Nyanja Nalubaale as a sea rather than a lake, see Johnson, "Eating and Existence on an Island in Southern Uganda," 7–9.

42. Kajolya, *Witchcraft, Divination, and Healing among the Basoga*, 156–95; PROMETRA staff, pers. comm.

43. Kasumba Umar and Mzee Erukaana Waiswa Kabindi, interview with the author, 23 December 2010; Kabona Mutale and Kabona Kapere, *Okuwanga Amayembe*, June 19, 2010.

3. Possessing Sound Medicine

1. Stoller, *The Taste of Ethnographic Things*, 55.

2. For the Kitala example, see Cunningham, *Uganda and Its Peoples*, 172; the image is reproduced on the cover of Kodesh, *Beyond the Royal Gaze*.

3. Kinobe, *Kamungolo Language Guide*. This explanation formerly appeared on kinobemusic.com, but the page has since been redesigned.

4. Kinobe, "Kamungolo."

5. In Kinobe's translation: "Kamungolo musajja muwanvu," "Kamungolo musajja mulungi," and "Kamungolo musajja mugonvu" (Kinobe, *Kamungolo Language Guide*).

6. See, e.g., Steven Friedson, *Dancing Prophets*; Jankowsky, *Stambeli*; Kapchan,

176   *Notes to Chapters 3 and 4*

Traveling Spirit Masters; Roseman, *Healing Sounds from the Malaysian Rainforest*; see also Koen, *Beyond the Roof of the World*, 59–91.

7. Strathern, *The Gender of the Gift*, 178, 185; Bourdieu, *The Logic of Practice*, 53. For a Ugandan example of such a scenario, see Hoesing, *Birth of an Ancestor*.

8. Marriott, "Hindu Transactions," 111; Evans-Pritchard, *Nuer Religion*, 281. For a more thorough critical review of the "dividual" concept in anthropology, see Schram, "A Society Divided," 319–23.

9. Wagner, "The Fractal Person," 162–63; Wagner, "Analogic Kinship," 626–27.

10. "Tuwaye: Dr. Yahaya Sekagya, Prometra Uganda," at 5:30; PROMETRA, "Nakifuba," diagnosis sequence, November 12, 2008.

11. Nakifuba is a pseudonym.

12. They used the term *okusumulula* (to untie or unbind).

13. An alternative translation could refer to things from a place called Nkoola. This translation relies on eyewitness interviews from those who were present at the performance.

14. "Jjajja ow'eddaluddalu, mbayita mbagala! Ooooh Kigozi! Jjajja azze!" A more complete translation here is: "Wildly powerful grandparent, I call them and love them! Oh, Kigozi, the grandparent has come!"

15. "Weebale kukola n'okuuma, jjajja."

16. "Waliwo omulwadde, Jjajja . . . Jjajja nga be baliwo tubayita nga tubaagala."

17. Shifting pronouns might be confusing here: I translated the song with female pronouns to reflect a female medium, but the spirit engaged in this process of diagnosis was a male spirit.

18. Umar Ndiwalana, interview with the author, November 12, 2008.

19. "Owulidde ejjembe endala, Ssaalongo?"

20. Jjajja Kabona Mutale and Nakayima, interviews with the author, May 11–12, 2009.

21. Heidegger, *Being and Time*, 34; Friedson, *Dancing Prophets*, 36; see also Dreyfus, "Between Technē and Technology."

22. Lévi-Strauss, *The Savage Mind*, 30–33.

23. Friedson, *Dancing Prophets*, 36.

24. Piot, *Remotely Global*.

4. Sacrifice and Song

1. This information was corroborated by multiple observations and informal encounters, but also in three formal interviews: Umar Ndiwalana, interviews with the author, November 12, 2008, and January 28, 2015; Ssematimba Frank Sibyangu, interview with the author, May 25, 2010.

2. In Luganda, the verb used here is *kuwayo* (to give); in Lusoga, it is *kusenga* (to pray), with a connotation of offering something in prayer.

3. Ronald Bwette and Umar Ndiwalana, interview with the author, December 31, 2008.

Notes to Chapter 4   177

4. Crothers, *Queen of Katwe*; Nair, *Queen of Katwe*.

5. For example, *kulika omwaka* is the idiomatic expression congratulating someone on the year gone by, much in the same manner as one congratulates a person on having safely traversed roads (*kulika amakubo*) or conquered studies (*kulika okuwangula omusomo*).

6. In favor of clarity and brevity, subsequent references to this place with two names will be truncated to simply Kisuze.

7. Sacrifice at Nakawuka, June 23, 2010.

8. Prayers at Ndejje, March 28–29, 2009; year-end celebration at Nakawuka, January 1, 2010; *Okugabula Nnyama*, June 23, 2010.

9. "Banjula nte nga Byuma, ate Byuma agenda kutuwa nte. Banjula ebitta by'omwenge ne mata n'ebirabo birala byonna by'abantu abamuleese Byuma n'ababaleese ku bajjajja balala." Umar Ndiwalana, speaking at the first of several rituals at Nakawuka, January 1, 2010.

10. As with my use of the term *index* in this book, this use of the phrase *rhythmic symbol* draws on semiotic discourse in Turino's work, specifically "Signs of Imagination, Identity, and Experience"; "Peircean Thought as Core Theory for a Phenomenological Ethnomusicology"; and *Music as Social Life*, 5–16.

11. See, e.g., Turner, "Betwixt and Between"; Turner, *The Ritual Process*, 94–130.

12. Turner, *From Ritual to Theatre*, 41.

13. For a contrasting perspective on spirit mediums relative to substance abuse, see Scherz, "His Mother Became Medicine."

14. Lisa Nakawuka, interview with the author, January 7, 2010.

15. Harunah Mbogga, interview with the author, January 4, 2010.

16. PROMETRA staff, interviews with the author, November 12, 2008; Yahaya Sekagya, interview with the author, November 20, 2008; Umar Ndiwalana, interviews with the author, November 27 and December 2–3, 2008.

17. Muka Ndawula, interview with the author, January 4, 2010.

18. Lisa Nakawuka, interview with the author, January 7, 2010; Umar Ndiwalana, interview with the author, January 29, 2010.

19. Nakayima, *Kawumpuli*, April 6, 2009; Nakayima and Jjajja Kabona Mutale, *Emisomo gy'obuwangwa*, May 11–12, 2009; Umar Ndiwalana, interview with the author, January 29, 2010.

20. "Bwette agenda azaala abalongo! Bweeza!"

21. Cf. chapter 2, "Invoking the Twins."

22. Umar Ndiwalana, New year's rituals, December 31–January 5, 2010.

23. Friedson, *Dancing Prophets*, 100; Reed, *Dan Ge Performance*, 350.

24. "Bweeza, Jjajja!"

25. "Abakyala baagala nnyo ebintu, wololo!"

26. Arafat Nsubuga, commentary to the author during the performance, January 4, 2010.

27. Waalabyeki Magoba, pers. comm.; Deo Kawalya, pers. comm.

178 *Notes to Chapters 4, 5, and Conclusion*

28. The larger sequence of rites is the subject of a documentary film; see Hoesing, *Birth of an Ancestor*.

29. Cf. Jennifer Kyker, "Carrying Spirit in Song."

30. Sylvia Nantongo, interview with the author, November 3, 2008.

31. Parus Nabwiire, Lovisa Logosi, and Kibale Logosi, interview with the author, June 22, 2015.

5. From Tea and Coffee Berries to Beer and Meat

1. Evans-Pritchard, *Nuer Religion*, 281. See also my discussion of "partible" or "fractal" persons in chapter 3.

2. For more on blood pacts in the region, see Williams, "Blood Brotherhood in Ankole"; White, "Blood Brotherhood Revisited."

3. The early part of a week-long postmortuary ritual in Busoga revealed this brewing procedure to be quite similar in process and purpose to those I have seen in Kiganda *kusamira* rituals. See Hoesing, *Birth of an Ancestor*.

4. The generic name of this role in any clan is Ow'Akasolya, literally the one at the roof apex of the household of that clan. For more on how this relates to the Kabaka as roof apex of the kingdom, see chapter 2. See also Kafumbe, *Tuning the Kingdom*, 2–5.

5. Both Baganda and Basoga describe beer in terms of its age: *mwenge muto* (lit. "young beer," not yet fully fermented) and *mwenge mukadde* (lit. "mature beer").

6. Harunah Mbogga and Lisa Nakawuka, pers. comm.; see also chapter 2.

7. "Kaakanno, bwe mbamaze okunywa musaayi gwange, ekibumbira omuzzukulu wange, owulira baaba?" Interview with Jjajja Kasajja, March 23, 2010.

8. See, e.g., Janzen, *Ngoma*; Dijk, Reis, and Spierenburg, *The Quest for Fruition through Ngoma*.

9. Hopkins, *The Greatest Killer*.

10. Hoesing, "Sound and the Social Aesthetics of Religious Pluralism in Southern Uganda."

11. See Durkheim, *Elementary Forms of Religious Life*, 31, 245–51.

Conclusion

1. See Green, *Rethinking AIDS Prevention*, 141; See also Iliffe, *The African AIDS Epidemic*, 91, 130.

Bibliography

Interviews and Other Primary Sources

Balikoowa, Centurio, and Erukaana Waiswa Kabindi. Seasonal rituals, 22–24 December 2008, Itanda. Digital video.

Balikoowa, Centurio, and Nassuna Proskovya. Interview by authors, 8 and 15 November 2008, Kampala. Digital recordings.

Bujagali, Nabamba. Interview by author, 1 August 2006, Jinja. Digital recording.

Buyego, Mumbejja. *Kusamira*, 6 April 2009, Buyego.

Bwette, Ronald. Interview by author, 22 January 2010, 23 June 2010, Nakawuka. Digital recordings.

———. *Okugabula Nnyama*, 23 June 2010, Nakawuka.

Bwette, Ronald and Umar Ndiwalana. Interview by author, 31 December 2008. Digital recording.

Janat, Akita, and Kizza Sulaiman. Interview by author, 30 March 2009, Kakooge. Digital recording.

Jjajja Ndawula Community. *Kusamira*, 23 and 30 March 2009, 17–18 April 2010, Kakooge. Digital video.

Jjumba, Jjajja Kabona. *Kusamira*, 2 February 2010. Kirowooza. Digital recording.

———. *Kusamira*. 16 February 2010, Kirowooza. Digital recording.

———. *Okubasiba Abalongo*, 8–9 March 2010, Kirowooza. Digital recording.

———. *Omukolo gwa Lubowa*, 27–28 March 2010, Kirowooza. Digital recording.

Jjumba, Mukyala Proskovya. Interview by author, 2 February 2010, Kirowooza. Digital recording.

———. *Kwanjula*, 28 February 2010, Kasankala. Digital recording.

Kabindi, Erukaana Waiswa. Interview by author, 7 August 2006, 10 and 11 February 2009, 20 April 2010, Itanda. Digital video and recordings.

———. *Okwaza*, 27–28 January 2009, Kyabakaire. Digital video.

180   *Bibliography*

———. *Okwaza*, 28–29 January 2009, Wairama. Digital video.

Kajura, Methuselah. Interview by author, 26 April 2009, Mubende. Digital recording.

Kasajja, Jjajja. Interview by author, 23 March 2010, Kotwe. Digital recording.

Kawalya, Deo. *Ssemasomo wa Luganda e Makerere*, 25 June 2010, Kampala. Digital video.

Kiggundu, Charles. Meeting of traditional medical practitioners, 18 December 2008, Kampala. Digital recording.

Kijogwa, Robert James. Interview by author, 14 December 2008, Iganga Lambala. Digital recording.

Kinobe, Herbert. "Kamungolo." *Dambe Project* (website). Archived page from 2002, accessed November 5, 2020. https://web.archive.org/web/20020826204510/http://www.dambe.org/kamungolo.html. Original site is discontinued.

———. *Kamungolo Language Guide*. N.p.: Kinobe, 2008. Originally available on http://kinobemusic.com/, but the site has been redesigned.

Lubowa, Hassan. Interview by author, 30 January 2010, Nateete.

Lubowa, Hassan, and LUTHA. *Kusamira*, 5–6 February 2010, Walugondo. Digital recording.

———. LUTHA *Lukiiko*, 7 February 2010, Walugondo. Digital recording.

Lutaaya, Dennis. Interview by author, 9 May 2009, Kampala. Digital recording.

———. *Olumbe*, 16 May 2009, Bombo.

———. *Omukolo gwa Lubaale lw'ekika*, 16–17 May 2009, Bombo. Digital video.

Magoba, Waalabyeki. *Ekyoto*, 29 November 2008, Kampala. Tape recording.

———. Interview by author, 22 November 2009, Kampala. Digital recording.

———. *Kwanjula*, 6 February 2010, Kawuku.

Matovu, Ssaalongo Deziderio Kiwanuka. Interview by author, 23 June 2010. Digital recording.

Mbogga, Harunah. Interview by author, 4 January 2010.

Mugalula, Kabona Wamala. Interview by author, inclusive of the *Bemba Omusota* tradition, 8 April 2009, Kitala.

Musanje, Kyabagu. Interview by author, 19 February 2009, Kampala. Digital recording.

Mutale, Jjajja Kabona, and Nakayima. Interview by author, 11–12 May 2009, Joggo. Digital recording.

Mutale, Jjajja Kabona, and Jjajja Kabona Kapere. *Okuwanga Amayembe*, 18–19 June 2010, Makandwa. Digital video and recording.

Mwesige, Andrew Lukungu Kyambu, Rehema Lukowe, and Kyambu Ntakabusuni. Interview by author, 8 February 2009, Nawandyo. Digital video.

———. *Olumbe*, 8–11 January 2009, Irondo. Digital video.

———. *Nswezi*, 16–21 January 2009, Munamaizi. Digital video.

Nabawanuka, Nakigozi. Excursion, 26–28 May 2009, Ssese Islands.

———. *Okulambula e Bakka* and interview by author, 28 March 2009, Bakka.

———. Saturday evening prayers and songs, 28 March 2009, 2 May 2009, Ndejje. Digital video.

Bibliography

Nabirye, Minah. Interview by author, 2 April 2009, Kampala. Digital recording.

Nabwiire, Parus, Lovisa Logosi, and Kibale Logosi. Interview by author, 22 June 2015, Irondo Village.

Nakanwagi, Erinah Pinky. Interview by author, 12 January 2010, Kampala. Digital recording.

Nakawuka, Lisa. Interview by author, 7 January 2010, Kampala. Digital recording.

———. *Kusamira*, 20–23 January 2010, Nakawuka. Digital recording.

———. *Omukolo gwa Muwanga*, 6 March 2010, Nabisunsa. Digital recording.

Nakayima. Interview by author, 23 March 2009, Kampala. Digital recording.

———. *Kawumpuli*, 6 April 2009, Buyego.

———. *Kusamira*, 21–23 March 2010, Kotwe. Digital recording.

———. Prayers at the tree, 14 April 2009, Mubende. Digital recording.

———. Walumbe and Kayikuzi, 9 April 2009, Tanda.

Nakayima, and Jjajja Kabona Mutale. *Emisomo gyʼobuwangwa*, 11–12 May 2009, Joggo. Digital video and recording.

———. Interview by author, 12 May 2009, Joggo. Digital recording.

Nakifuma Super Dancers. *Embuutu yʼEmbuutikizi*, 7 March 2010, Kampala.

———. *Olumbe*, 8–9 January 2010, Wabikookooma. Digital recording.

———. Rehearsal, 4 and 5 March 2010, Nakifuma.

Nalubega, Resty. Songs at the tree, 25 April 2009, Mubende. Digital recording.

Nambatya-Kyeyune, Grace. Interview by author, 28 May 2010, Kampala. Digital recording.

Nantongo, Sylvia. Interview by author, 3 November 2008.

Ndawula, Muka. Interview by author, 4 January 2010.

Ndiwalana, Umar. Interview by author, 12, 19, and 27 November 2008, 2–3 and 4 December 2008, 29 January 2010, Buyijja and Kampala. Digital recordings.

———. New yearʼs rituals, 31 December 2008–2 January 2009, Kisuze. Digital recording.

———. New yearʼs rituals, 31 December 2009–5 January 2010, Nakawuka. Digital recording.

———. Phone interview by author, 28 January 2015.

Nsubuga, Waalabyeki. Interview by the author, 17 December 2008, Buyijja. Digital recording.

Ntakabusuni, Kyambu. Interview by author, 30 November 2008, 31 January 2009, and 23 April 2010, Nawandyo. Digital video and recordings.

Ntakabusuni, Kyambu, and friends. *Nswezi* demonstration, 30 November 2008. Digital video.

PROMETRA. End of term, 17 December 2008, Buyijja. Digital video.

———. *Kusamira*, 26 November 2008, 2–3 and 10 December 2008, Buyijja. Digital video.

———. "Nakifuba" diagnosis sequence, 12 November 2008. Digital video.

PROMETRA Staff. Interviews by author, 12 November 2008.

Real Doctors. "Mpereza Engabo Yange" (Send Me My Shield). Written and posted

182   *Bibliography*

by Kasirye Ahmed (Moto Man). YouTube video, 3:22. Uploaded March 25, 2009. https://youtu.be/ROQUqxaccIs.

Rehema, Nnaalongo Lukowe. Interview by author, 1 February 2009, Nawandyo. Digital video.

Sekagya, Yahaya. Interview by author, 11, 18, and 20 November 2008, 12 December 2008, Kawempe and Buyijja. Digital recordings.

Sekagya, Yahaya, and Charles Kiggundu. Interview by author, 12 December 2008, Kawempe. Digital recording.

Sendijja, Matthias. Interview by author, 10 December 2008, Buyijja. Digital recording.

Sibyangu, Ssematimba Frank. Interview by author, 10, 18, 25, and 27 March 2010, 25 May 2010, 26 and 27 June 2010, Nakifuma and Kampala. Digital recordings.

———. Interview and song analysis of *balongo* songs from Kirowooza, 19 May 2010.

———. *Okubasiba Abalongo*, 7–8 May 2010, Kiwafu. Digital recording.

———. *Okulambula*, 16 June 2010, Dindo/Kasawo. Digital video.

———. *Okulambula*, 17 June 2010, Jjumba. Digital video.

———. *Okulambula*, 21 June 2010, Ssezibwa. Digital video and recording.

———. *Okusalira Amayembe*, 5–6 March 2010, Nakifuma. Digital recording.

———. *Okwaza Lubaale*, 28–30 May 2010, Namusaale. Digital recording.

———. *Olumbe*, 24–25 April 2010, Bukasa. Digital recording.

Ssempeke, Albert Bisaso. Interview by author, 29 January 2010, Kampala. Digital recording.

Ssenkulu, Kyoyagala. Interview by author, 17 May 2009, Nampunge. Digital recording.

Ssenyonga, Richard Mbuutu. Interview by author, 29 April 2010, Kampala. Digital recording.

Sulaiman, Kizza. Interview by author, 16, 23, and 30 March 2009, Kakooge. Digital recording.

Uganda Ministry of Gender, Labour, and Social Development. "Traditional Medical Practitioners and Human Sacrifice" summit. 20 February 2009, Kampala. Digital recording.

Uganda n'Eddagala Lyayo. Annual meeting, 25 February 2009, Mengo Social Centre, Kampala. Digital video.

Umar, Kasumba, and Mzee Erukaana Waiswa Kabindi. Interview by author, 23 December 2010.

Secondary Sources

Abdullahi, Ali Arazeem. "Trends and Challenges of Traditional Medicine in Africa." *African Journal of Traditional, Complementary and Alternative Medicines* 8, no. 5, supplement (2011): 115–23.

Amselle, Jean-Loup. *Mestizo Logics: Anthropology of Identity in Africa and Elsewhere.* Stanford, CA: Stanford University Press, 1998.

Arnoux, Alex. "Le Culte de la Société Secréte des Imandwa au Ruanda." *Anthropos: International Review of Ethnology and Linguistics* 7 (1912): 273–95, 529–58, 840–75.

Bibliography

Ayebazibwe, Agatha. "Child Sacrifice on the Rise." *Daily Monitor*, January 25, 2013.

Barello, Serena, Guendalina Graffigna, and Elena Vegni. "Promoting Patient and Caregiver Engagement in Self-Management of Chronic Illness." *Nursing Research and Practice* 2012, article 905934. https://doi.org/10.1155/2012/905934.

Barz, Gregory. *Singing for Life: HIV/AIDS and Music in Uganda.* New York: Routledge, 2006.

Barz, Gregory, and Judah Cohen, eds. *The Culture of AIDS in Africa: Hope and Healing through Music and the Arts.* New York: Oxford University Press, 2011.

Behrend, Heike, and Ute Luig, eds. *Spirit Possession: Modernity and Power in Africa.* Madison: University of Wisconsin Press, 1999.

Berger, Iris. "The 'Kubandwa' Religious Complex of Interlacustrine East Africa: An Historical Study, c. 1500–1900." PhD diss., University of Wisconsin–Madison, 1973.

Berliner, Paul. *The Soul of Mbira: Music and Traditions of the Shona People of Zimbabwe.* Chicago: University of Chicago Press, 1993. Originally published 1975.

Bhabha, Homi K. *The Location of Culture.* New York: Routledge Classics, 2004.

Bilton, Tony, Kevin Bonnett, Pip Jones, David Skinner, Michelle Stanworth, and Andrew Webster. *Introductory Sociology.* 3rd ed. London: MacMillan, 1996.

Blacking, John. *The Anthropology of the Body.* London: Academic Press, 1977.

———. "The Context of Venda Possession Music: Reflections on the Effectiveness of Symbols." *Yearbook for Traditional Music* 17 (1985): 64–87.

Blokland, Henny. "Kings, Spirits, and Brides in Unyamwezi, Tanzania." In *The Quest for Fruition through Ngoma: Political Aspects of Healing in Southern Africa*, edited by Rijk van Dijk, Ria Ries, and Marja Spierenburg, 12–38. Oxford: James Currey, 2000.

Boddy, Janice. *Wombs and Alien Spirits: Women, Men, and the Zar Cult in Northern Sudan.* Madison: University of Wisconsin Press, 1989.

Bourdieu, Pierre. *The Logic of Practice.* Translated by Richard Nice. Stanford, CA: Stanford University Press, 1990.

———. *Outline of a Theory of Practice.* New York: Cambridge University Press, 1977.

Carman, Kristin L., Pam Dardess, Maureen Maurer, Shoshanna Sofaer, Karen Adams, Christine Bechtel, and Jennifer Sweeney. "Patient and Family Engagement: A Framework for Understanding the Elements and Developing Interventions and Policies." *Health Affairs* 32, no. 2 (2013). https://doi.org/10.1377/hlthaff.2012.1133.

Chatora, R. "Traditional Medicine: Our Culture, Our Future." *African Health Monitor*, January–June 2003.

Cohen, David William. *The Historical Tradition of Busoga: Mukama and Kintu.* New York: Oxford University Press, 1986.

Comaroff, Jean. *Body of Power, Spirit of Resistance: The Culture and History of a South African People.* Chicago: University of Chicago Press, 1985.

Crothers, Tim. *Queen of Katwe.* New York: Simon and Schuster, 2012.

Cunningham, J. F. *Uganda and Its Peoples.* London: Hutchinson, 1905.

Dijk, Rijk van, Ria Reis, and Marja Spierenburg, eds. *The Quest for Fruition through Ngoma: Political Aspects of Healing in Southern Africa.* Oxford: James Currey, 2000.

184   *Bibliography*

Domecq, Juan Pablo, Gabriela Prutsky, Tarig Elraiyah, Zhen Wang, Mohammed Nabhan, Nathan Shippee, and Juan Pablo Brito, et al. "Patient Engagement in Research: A Systematic Review." *BMC Health Services Research* 14 (2014): article 89. https://doi.org/10.1186/1472-6963-14-89.

Doyle, Shane. "The Cwezi-Kubandwa Debate: Gender, Hegemony and Pre-Colonial Religion in Bunyoro, Western Uganda." *Africa: The Journal of the International African Institute* 77, no. 4 (2007): 559–81.

Dreyfus, Hubert L. "Between Technē and Technology: The Ambiguous Place of Equipment in *Being and Time*." In *Heidegger: A Critical Reader*, edited by Hubert L. Dreyfus and Harrison Hall, 173–85. Oxford: Basil Blackwell, 1992.

Durkheim, Émile. *Elementary Forms of Religious Life*. Translated by Carol Cosman. Oxford: Oxford University Press, 2001. Originally published 1912.

Emoff, Ron. *Recollecting from the Past: Musical Practice and Spirit Possession on the East Coast of Madagascar*. Middletown, CT: Wesleyan University Press, 2002.

Evans-Pritchard, E. E. *Nuer Religion*. Oxford: Clarendon, 1956.

Feierman, Steven. "Colonizers, Scholars, and the Creation of Invisible Histories." In *Beyond the Cultural Turn: New Directions in the Study of Society and Culture*, edited by Victoria E. Bonnell and Lynn Hunt, 182–216. Los Angeles: University of California Press, 1999.

———. *Peasant Intellectuals: Anthropology and History in Tanzania*. Madison: University of Wisconsin Press, 1990.

———. "Struggles for Control: The Social Roots of Health and Healing in Modern Africa." *African Studies Review* 28, no. 2–3 (1985): 73–147.

Feierman, Steven, and John M. Janzen, eds. *The Social Roots of Health and Healing in Africa*. Berkeley: University of California Press, 1992.

Feld, Steven. "Communication, Music, and Speech about Music." *Yearbook for Traditional Music* 16 (1984): 1–18.

———. *Sound and Sentiment: Birds, Weeping, Poetics and Song in Kaluli Expression*. Philadelphia: University of Pennsylvania Press, 1982.

———. "Sound Structure as Social Structure." *Ethnomusicology* 28, no. 3 (1984): 383–409.

Friedson, Steven. *Dancing Prophets: Musical Experience in Tumbuka Healing*. Chicago: University of Chicago Press, 1996.

Fry, Peter. *Spirits of Protest: Spirit-Mediums and the Articulation of Consensus among the Zezuru of Southern Rhodesia*. Cambridge: Cambridge University Press, 1976.

Geissler, P. Wenzel, ed. *Para-States and Medical Science: Making African Global Health*. Durham, NC: Duke University Press, 2015.

Gluckman, Max. *Essays on the Ritual of Social Relations*. Manchester: Manchester University Press, 1962.

Gonza, Richard Kayanga. *Lusoga–English/English–Lusoga Dictionary*. Kampala: MK Publishers for the Cultural Research Centre of Jinja, 2007.

Good, Byron. *Medicine, Rationality, and Experience: An Anthropological Perspective*. Cambridge: Cambridge University Press, 1994.

Bibliography

Green, Edward C. 2003. *Rethinking AIDS Prevention: Learning from Successes in Developing Countries*. New York: Praeger.

Gulere, Cornelius Wambi. *Lusoga–English Dictionary*. Kampala: Fountain, 2009.

———. "Riddle of Self-Identity: The Fundamentals of the Clan System in Busoga." Unpublished thesis, Makerere University Department of Literature, n.d.

Gunderson, Frank. "Musical Labor Associations in Sukumaland, Tanzania: History and Practice." PhD diss., Wesleyan University, 1999.

———. *Sukuma Labor Songs from Western Tanzania: "We Never Sleep, We Dream of Farming."* Leiden: Brill, 2010.

Hanson, Holly. *Landed Obligation: The Practice of Power in Buganda*. Portsmouth, NH: Heinemann, 2003.

Harris, Rachel, and Barley Norton. "Introduction: Ritual Music and Communism." *British Journal of Ethnomusicology* 11, no. 1 (2002): 1–8.

Heidegger, Martin. *Being and Time*. Translated by John Macquarrie and Edward Robinson. New York: Harper and Row, 1962.

———. *The Question Concerning Technology and Other Essays*. Translated by William Lovitt. New York: Harper and Row, 1977.

Hellweg, Joseph. *Hunting the Ethical State: The Benkadi Movement of Côte d'Ivoire*. Chicago: University of Chicago Press, 2011.

Herzfeld, Michael. *Cultural Intimacy: Social Poetics in the Nation-State*. New York: Routledge, 1997.

Hoesing, Peter, dir. *Birth of an Ancestor*. 2014. Documentary film, 26 min. https://video .alexanderstreet.com/watch/birth-of-an-ancestor-songs-of-death-and-social -responsibility-in-eastern-uganda.

———. "*Kubandwa*: Theory and Historiography of Shared Expressive Culture in Interlacustrine East Africa." Master's thesis, Florida State University, 2006.

———. "*Kusamira* Ritual Music and the Social Reproduction of Wellness in Uganda." PhD diss., Florida State University, 2011.

———. "*Nabuzaana Omunozzi w'Eddugulu*: Hearing Kiganda Ecology in the Music of *Kusamira* Ritual Healing Repertories." *History in Africa* 45 (2018): 347–71.

———. "Sound and the Social Aesthetics of Religious Pluralism in Southern Uganda." *Nova Religio* 21, no. 1 (2017): 31–59.

Hopkins, Donald R. *The Greatest Killer: Smallpox in History*. Chicago: University of Chicago Press, 2002.

Iliffe, John. *The African AIDS Epidemic*. Oxford: James Currey, 2006.

———. *East African Doctors: A History of the Modern Profession*. Cambridge: Cambridge University Press, 1998.

Jankowsky, Richard. "Music, Spirit Possession, and the In-Between: Ethnomusicological Inquiry and the Challenge of Trance." *Ethnomusicology Forum* 16, no. 2 (2007): 185–208.

———. *Stambeli: Music, Trance, and Alterity in Tunisia*. Chicago: University of Chicago Press, 2010.

186 Bibliography

Janzen, John M. *Lemba, 1650–1930: A Drum of Affliction in Africa and the New World.* New York: Garland, 1982.

———. *Ngoma: Discourses of Healing in Central and Southern Africa.* Berkeley: University of California Press, 1992.

———. *The Quest for Therapy in Lower Zaire.* Berkeley: University of California Press, 1978.

———. "The Social Reproduction of Health." In *Essays in Medical Anthropology,* edited by Ruth Kutalek and Armin Prinz, 91–109. Vienna: Wiener ethnomedizinische Reihe, 2009.

Johnson, Jennifer L. "Eating and Existence on an Island in Southern Uganda." *Comparative Studies of South Asia, Africa, and the Middle East* 37, no. 1 (2017): 2–23.

———. "Fish, Family, and the Gendered Politics of Descent along Uganda's Southern Littorals." *History in Africa* 45 (2018): 445–71.

Kafumbe, Damascus. *Tuning the Kingdom: Kawuugulu Musical Performance, Politics, and Storytelling in Buganda.* Rochester, NY: University of Rochester Press, 2018.

Kagwa, Apolo. *The Customs of the Baganda.* Edited by May Mandelbaum. Translated by Ernest B. Kalibala. New York: Columbia University Press, 1934.

———. *Ekitabo kye Mpisa za Baganda* (The Book of Customs of the Baganda). Kampala: Uganda Printing, 1918.

———. *Empisa za Buganda* (Customs of Baganda). Kampala: Uganda Printing, 1918.

Kajolya, John B. Ngobi. *Witchcraft, Divination, and Healing among the Basoga.* Jinja, Uganda: Cultural Research Centre, 2003.

Kalibbala, Gladys. "Is Witchcraft on the Rise or Is the Press Blowing It Up?" *New Vision,* February 12, 2009.

Kapchan, Deborah. *Traveling Spirit Masters: Moroccan Gnawa Trance and Music in the Global Marketplace.* Middletown, CT: Wesleyan University Press, 2007.

Kapferer, Bruce. "Ritual Dynamics and Virtual Practice: Beyond Representation and Meaning." In *Ritual in Its Own Right: Exploring the Dynamics of Transformation,* edited by Don Handelman and Galina Lindquist, 35–54. New York: Berghahn, 2005.

Kasilo, Ossy M. J., Jean-Marie Trapsida, Chris Ngenda Mwikisa, and Paul Samson Lusamba-Dikassa. 2010. "An Overview of the Traditional Medicine Situation in the African Region." *African Health Monitor,* August 2010. https://reliefweb.int/report/world/african-health-monitor-special-issue-african-traditional-medicine.

Kasooha, Ismail. "Girl Beheaded in Ritual Murder." *New Vision,* February 24, 2009.

Kelly, Annie. "Child Sacrifice and Ritual Murders Rise in Uganda as Famine Looms." *Guardian,* September 5, 2009.

Kiingi, Kibuuka Balubuliza. *Enkuluze Ya Oluganda Ey'e Makerere* (The Makerere Treasury of Luganda). 2nd ed. Kampala: Fountain, 2009.

Kodesh, Neil. *Beyond the Royal Gaze: Clanship and Public Healing in Buganda.* Charlottesville: University of Virginia Press, 2010.

Koen, Benjamin D. *Beyond the Roof of the World: Music, Prayer, and Healing in the Pamir Mountains.* New York: Oxford, 2009.

Bibliography

Kraemer, Sebastian. "The Fragile Male." *British Medical Journal* 321 (2000): 1609–12.

Kyker, Jennifer. "Carrying Spirit in Song: Music and the Making of Ancestors at Zezeru Kurova Guva Ceremonies." *African Music* 8, no. 3 (2009): 65–84.

Lan, David. *Guns and Rain: Guerrillas and Spirit Mediums in Zimbabwe*. London: James Currey, 1985.

Lévi-Strauss, Claude. *The Savage Mind*. Chicago: University of Chicago Press, 1966.

Livingston, Julie. *Improvising Medicine: An African Oncology Ward in an Emerging Cancer Epidemic*. Durham, NC: Duke University Press, 2012.

Mair, Lucy P. *An African People in the Twentieth Century*. New York: Russell and Russell, 1965. Originally published 1934.

Marcus, George, and Michael Fischer. *Anthropology as Cultural Critique*. Chicago: University of Chicago Press, 1999.

Marriott, McKim. "Hindu Transactions: Diversity without Dualism." In *Transaction and Meaning: Directions in the Anthropology of Exchange and Symbolic Behavior*, edited by Bruce Kapferer, 109–42. Philadelphia: Institute for the Study of Human Issues, 1976.

Martel, Frances. "Uganda Prepares for Surge in Child Sacrifice by Witch Doctors as Election Nears." *Breitbart*, June 18, 2015.

Masquelier, Adeline Marie. *Prayer Has Spoiled Everything: Possession, Power, and Identity in an Islamic Town of Niger*. Durham, NC: Duke University Press, 2001.

McNeill, Fraser G., and Deborah James. "Singing Songs of AIDS in Venda, South Africa." In *The Culture of AIDS in Africa: Hope and Healing through Music and the Arts*, edited by Gregory Barz and Judah Cohen, 193–213. New York: Oxford University Press, 2011.

Meinert, Lotte. "Regimes of Homework in AIDS Care." In *Making and Unmaking Public Health in Africa*. Edited by Ruth J. Prince and Rebecca Marsland, 119–39. Athens: Ohio University Press, 2014.

Nabirye, Minah. *Eiwanika ly'Olusoga: Eiwanika ly'aboogezi b'Olusoga n'abo abenda okwega Olusoga* (Dictionary of Lusoga: A Dictionary for Speakers of Lusoga and Those Who Would Like to Learn Lusoga). Kampala: Menha, 2009.

Nair, Mira. *Queen of Katwe*. Burbank: Walt Disney Pictures, 2016. Film, 124 min.

Nannyonga-Tamusuza, Sylvia A. "Baakisimba: Constructing Gender of the Baganda (of Uganda) through Music and Dance." *Women and Music* 5 (2001): 31–39.

———. *Baakisimba: Gender in the Music and Dance of the Baganda People of Uganda*. London: Routledge, 2005.

———. "Female-Men, Male-Women, and Others." *Journal of Eastern African Studies* 3, no. 2 (2009): 367–80.

New Vision. "Kiryapaawo Warns Healers on Human Sacrifice." August 1, 2000.

Niane, Djibril Tamsir. *Sundiata: An Epic of Old Mali*. Essex: Pearson, 2006. Originally published 1960.

Nyanzi, Barbara, Stella Nyanzi, Brent Wolff, and James Whitworth. "Money, Men, and Markets: Economic and Sexual Empowerment of Market Women in Southwestern Uganda." *Culture, Health, and Sexuality* 7, no. 1 (2005): 13–26.

Bibliography

Opendi, Sarah. "Press Statement: Clarification on the Traditional and Complementary Medicines Bill, 2019." Hon. Sarah Opendi, Minister of State for Health. February 14, 2019.

Peirce, Charles Sanders. "Logic as Semiotic: The Theory of Signs." In *Philosophical Writings of Peirce*, edited by Justus Buchler, 98–119. New York: Dover, 1955.

Perman, Tony. *Signs of the Spirit: Music and the Experience of Meaning in Ndau Ceremonial Life*. Champaign: University of Illinois Press, 2020.

Piot, Charles. *Remotely Global: Village Modernity in West Africa*. Chicago: University of Chicago Press, 1999.

Pulitzer Center. "Questions on Uganda: Child Sacrifice." Pulitzer Center. April 21, 2010. https://pulitzercenter.org/blog/questions-uganda-child-sacrifice.

Ranger, Terence O. *Dance and Society in Eastern Africa, 1890–1970: The Beni Ngoma*. Berkeley: University of California Press, 1975.

Ray, Benjamin C. *Myth, Ritual, and Kingship in Buganda*. New York: Oxford, 1991.

Reed, Daniel. "'C'est Le Wake Up! Africa': Two Case Studies of HIV/AIDS Edutainment Campaigns in Francophone Africa." In *The Culture of AIDS in Africa: Hope and Healing through Music and the Arts*, edited by Gregory Barz and Judah Cohen, 180–92. New York: Oxford University Press, 2011.

———. *Dan Ge Performance: Masks and Music in Contemporary Côte d'Ivoire*. Bloomington: Indiana University Press, 2003.

Religion News Blog. "Child Sacrifice Is on the Rise in Uganda." August 16, 2006. https://www.religionnewsblog.com/15637/child-sacrifice-is-on-the-rise-in-uganda.

Rice, Timothy. *Ethnomusicology: A Very Short Introduction*. New York: Oxford University Press, 2014.

Roscoe, John. *The Baganda: An Account of Their Native Customs and Beliefs*. London: MacMillan, 1911.

Roseman, Marina. *Healing Sounds from the Malaysian Rainforest: Temiar Music and Medicine*. Berkeley: University of California Press, 1991.

Rouget, Gilbert. "Music and Possession Trance." In *The Anthropology of the Body*, edited by John Blacking, 233–39. London: Academic Press, 1977.

———. *Music and Trance: A Theory of the Relations between Music and Possession*. Revised and translated by Brunhilde Biebuyck. Chicago: University of Chicago Press, 1985.

Ruane, Paige, and Patrick Kearney. "Building Integrated Systems in Uganda and Kenya through Traditional Medicine." Unpublished paper, Integrative Medicine Foundation, n.d.

Scherz, China. "His Mother Became Medicine: Drinking Problems, Ethical Transformation, and Maternal Care in Central Uganda." *Africa* 89, no. 1 (2019): 125–46.

Schoenbrun, David. "Ethnic Formation with Other-Than-Human Beings: Island Shrine Practice in Uganda's Long Eighteenth Century." *History in Africa* 45 (2018): 397–443.

———. *A Green Place, a Good Place: Agrarian Change and Social Identity in the Great Lakes Region to the 15th Century*. Oxford: James Currey, 1998.

Bibliography

———. *The Historical Reconstruction of Great Lakes Bantu Cultural Vocabulary: Etymologies and Distributions.* Cologne: Rüdiger Köppe Verlag, 1997.

———. "Pythons Worked: Constellating Communities of Practice with Conceptual Metaphor in Northern Lake Victoria, ca. A.D. 800–1200." In *Knowledge in Motion: Constellations of Learning across Time and Space,* edited by Andrew Roddick and Ann Brower Stahl, 216–46. Tucson: University of Arizona Press, 2016.

Schoenbrun, David, and Jennifer L. Johnson. "Introduction: Ethnic Formation with Other-Than-Human Beings." *History in Africa* 45 (2018): 307–45.

Schram, Ryan. "A Society Divided: Death, Personhood, and Christianity in Auhelawa, Papua New Guinea." *HAU: Journal of Ethnographic Theory* 5, no. 1 (2015): 317–37.

Seeger, Charles. "The Musicological Juncture: Music as Fact." In *Studies in Musicology 1935–1975,* by Charles Seeger, 45–50. Berkeley: University of California Press, 1977.

SEYA T. M. Consultancy Firm. "Kampala District Traditional Healers' Directory." Kampala: Integrated Forum for Traditional Health Practitioners and PROMETRA Uganda, 2004.

Ssemakula, Mukasa E. "The Christian Martyrs of Uganda." *The Buganda Home Page* (website). Accessed December 28, 2010. http://www.buganda.com/martyrs.htm.

Stephens, Rhiannon. *A History of African Motherhood: The Case of Uganda, 700–1900.* Cambridge: Cambridge University Press, 2013.

Stoller, Paul. *The Taste of Ethnographic Things: The Senses in Anthropology.* Philadelphia: University of Pennsylvania Press, 1989.

Stoller, Paul, with Cheryl Olkes. *In Sorcery's Shadow: A Memoir of Apprenticeship among the Songhay of Niger.* Chicago: University of Chicago Press, 1987.

Strathern, Marilyn. *The Gender of the Gift: Problems with Women and Problems with Society in Melanesia.* Berkeley: University of California Press, 1988.

———. *Reproducing the Future: Essays on Anthropology, Kinship, and the New Reproductive Technologies.* New York: Routledge, 1992.

Tantala, Renee. "The Early History of Kitara in Western Uganda: Process Models of Religious and Political Change." PhD diss., University of Wisconsin–Madison, 1989.

Trowell, Margaret, and Klaus P. Wachsmann. *Tribal Crafts of Uganda.* London: Oxford University Press, 1953.

Tsing, Anna Lowenhaupt. *Friction: An Ethnography of Global Connection.* Princeton, NJ: Princeton University Press, 2005.

Turino, Thomas. *Music as Social Life: The Politics of Participation.* Chicago: University of Chicago Press, 2008.

———. "Peircean Thought as Core Theory for a Phenomenological Ethnomusicology." *Ethnomusicology* 58, no. 2 (2014): 185–221.

———. "Signs of Imagination, Identity, and Experience: A Peircean Theory for Music." *Ethnomusicology* 43, no. 2 (1999): 221–55.

Turner, Victor. "Betwixt and Between: The Liminal Period in *Rites de Passage.*" *Proceedings of the American Ethnological Society,* 1964, 4–20.

190   *Bibliography*

———. *Dramas, Fields, and Metaphors: Symbolic Action in Human Society*. Ithaca, NY: Cornell University Press, 1974.

———. *Drums of Affliction: A Study of Religious Processes among the Ndembu of Zambia*. Oxford: Clarendon Press for the International African Institute, 1968.

———. *The Forest of Symbols: Aspects of Ndembu Ritual*. Ithaca: Cornell University Press, 1967.

———. *From Ritual to Theatre: The Human Seriousness of Play*. New York: Performing Arts Journal Publications, 1982.

———. *The Ritual Process: Structure and Anti-Structure*. Chicago: Aldine, 1969.

"Tuwaye: Dr. Yahaya Sekagya, Prometra Uganda." Uploaded January 19, 2017, by Akawungeezi. YouTube video, 45:41. https://youtu.be/1hKeuAFWLb8.

Uganda. "The Indigenous and Complementary Medicine Bill, 2015." Bills Supplement no. 2 to the *Uganda Gazette*, no. 7, vol. 108 (February 13). Entebbe: UPPC by Order of the Government, 2015.

Uganda Ministry of Health. *Health Sector Development Plan, 2015/16–2019/20*. Kampala: Republic of Uganda Ministry of Health, 2015.

Uganda Protectorate. *The Witchcraft Ordinance*. Entebbe: Government Printer, 1957.

Van Gennep, Arnold. *The Rites of Passage*. 1909. Translated by Monika B. Vizedom and Gabirelle L. Caffee. 2nd ed. Chicago: University of Chicago Press, 1960.

Van Zwanenberg, R. M. A., with Anne King. *An Economic History of Kenya and Uganda, 1900–1970*. London: Macmillan, 1975.

Vernaschi, Marco. "Babirye, the Girl from Katugwe." *Child Sacrifice in Uganda* (series). Pulitzer Center. April 16, 2010. https://pulitzercenter.org/reporting/uganda-babirye-girl-katugwe.

———. "The Man behind RACHO." *Child Sacrifice in Uganda* (series). Pulitzer Center. April 16, 2010. https://pulitzercenter.org/reporting/uganda-man-behind-racho.

Wagner, Roy. "Analogic Kinship: A Daribi Example." *American Ethnologist* 4, no. 4 (1977): 623–42.

———. "The Fractal Person." In *Big Men and Great Men: Personifications of Power in Melanesia*, edited by Maurice Godelier and Marilyn Strathern, 159–73. Cambridge: Cambridge University Press, 1991.

White, Louise. "Blood Brotherhood Revisited: Kinship, Relationship, and the Body in East and Central Africa." *Journal of the International African Institute* 64, no. 3 (1994): 359–72.

Wiegratz, Jörg. "Fake Capitalism? The Dynamics of Neoliberal Moral Restructuring and Pseudo-Development: The Case of Uganda." *Review of African Political Economy* 37, no. 124 (2010): 123–37.

Williams, F. L. "Blood Brotherhood in Ankole (Omukago)." *Uganda Journal* 21 (1934): 33–41.

World Health Organization (WHO). *WHO Traditional Medicine Strategy, 2002–2005*. Geneva: WHO, 2002.

———. *WHO Traditional Medicine Strategy, 2014–2023*. Geneva: WHO, 2013.

Index

abalongo b'embuga (twins of the royal enclosure), 79
"Abalongo twabazaala" song, 77
abamuleerwa (birth attendants), 45
abasawo ab'ekinansi (traditional healers), 7
abatabuzi b'eddagala (herbalists), 45
abayunzi (bonesetters), 45
abazaalisa (birth attendants), 45
ab'emitwe (mentalists), 45
ab'empewo (spiritual healers), 45
abundance, 32, 153, 166; performing idioms of, 65–82
affliction, cults of, 2, 25, 28, 47–48
African Union (AU), 40
agriculture, 6
AIDS. *See* HIV/AIDS
alienation, spiritual, 118
allopathic medicine, 28, 33, 118, 119, 164
amassabo (shrines), 38, 79; as sanctuaries of tradition, 109–11
animal life. *See* flora and fauna
Arafat, 135, 136
archiving of medicinal knowledge, 43
associations of traditional healers, 36, 37, 38, 41
audibility of traditional healers' practices, 36, 37, 42
autochthon, use of term, 84

baakisimba rhythms, 16, 78
Babirye, name for a sibling, 64
badingidi (one-string fiddle player), 131

bad things, 151; eradication of, 43–44. *See also* binding: of bad things; *ebibi* (bad things)
bag, 111–12
Baganda people, 4, 5, 16, 26, 62, 64, 85, 104, 107, 110
bagole (mediums), 78
Bakka, 110; hill at, 156
balalu spirits, 162
Balikoowa, Centurio, 10
balongo (twin), 62, 63
bampologoma (lion people), 98
Bamweyana (a spirit), 138
banana beer, 117, 120, 133, 149, 153; brewing of, 31, 129, 150, 155–56, 157; gifting of, 155–58
banana fibers, destruction of, 158
banana groves, 97, 157; burial in, 136, 150, 151, 152; as dumping places, 64
bananas (*Musa acuminata*) 6, 99, 151. See also *matooke*
banana trees: leaves of, 141, 156; planting of, 56; in urban environment, 167
bark, growing new, 24
barkcloth, 111, 112, 122, 132; gifting of, 129; planting of trees, 56
barrenness, 86, 87, 88, 100
Barz, Gregory, 46, 48; *Singing for Life*, 46
basamize (people of *kusamira*), 4–8, 135, 144, 149, 152, 153, 155, 157; assessment and development of resources, 108–9, 125–26; and bagole (spouses), 78; and Christian

communities, 120–25, 164; compared with *baswezi*, 4–5, 7, 22–25, 43, 51; and ecologies of well-being, 59, 82, 84–85, 89, 91–94, 97; effectiveness of, 42; and heterophony, 22; and hospitality, 163; independence and interdependence of, 51; notions of illness, 25; performing diagnosis, 115–19; and positive intervention, 47; relationship to *baswezi* and repertories of well-being, 3, 35, 106, 164, 165–68; and sacrifice, 128–30, 149, 152–53, 158–60; and shrines, 110–11; and spirits, 25, 85, 88–92, 104, 162; terminology, 3, 24; tools of, 126–27; training, 55; understanding of sea and sky, 101–5; worldview of, 4, 59, 120

Basiki subgroup of the Basoga, 87

Basoga people, 4, 5, 17, 26, 27, 28, 64, 84, 85, 87, 98, 107, 155, 156

Bassekabaka, 109

baswezi (people of *nswezi*), 82; assessment and development of resources, 108–9, 125–26; and binding/unbinding, 7, 157; compared with affliction/resistance model, 47–48, 51; compared with *basamize*, 4–5, 7, 22–25, 43, 51; cosmologies of, 4; and ecumenical mutual aid, 164; in the ex-colonial "third space," 42–43; and hospitality, 163; and imitation of Luganda songs at *nswezi* rituals, 17; instruments used by, 20; notions of illness, 25; relationship to *basamize* and ecologies of well-being, 59, 82, 84–85, 89, 91–94, 97; relationship to *basamize* and repertories of well-being, 3, 35, 106, 164, 165–68; and sacrifice, 128–30, 149, 152–53, 158–60; and shrines, 110–11; tools of, 126–27; understanding of sea and sky, 101–5

bazzukulu (grandchildren, ritual attendees), 159

beer, offered to spirits, 129, 158

Berliner, Paul, 29

Bhabha, Homi, 41

biggwa (shrine), 111

binding, 32, 59, 63, 156–57; of bad things, 7, 25, 60–61, 97, 115, 126, 129–30, 152, 157, 165; of twins' umbilical cords, 43. *See also* twins, tying of

biodiversity, maintenance of, 151–52

birds, 87, 98, 99

birthing, 60, 65, 85, 88, 144, 145, 167; in breech, 65

birth rate in Uganda, 60, 164

bisoko motifs, 17, 76, 78, 81

Blacking, John, 28, 29

blessings, 63, 118, 130–34, 152; equitable distribution of, 132. *See also* unbinding: of blessings

Blokland, Henny, 60

blood, sacrificial, 89, 121, 123, 127, 153; drinking of, 92, 136, 148; foreheads marked with, 139; spilled onto grave, 151; washing of items in, 151, 152

blood pacts, 26, 27, 129, 155; duality of, 158

bombo plant, 84, 94, 96, 97, 110, 157; as spiritual binding agent, 97

bonesetting, 60; training in, 52

Breitbart (news outlet), 37

brewing, association with binding/unbinding, 156–57

bricolage, 124–25

buffalo, 146, 147

Buganda, 5, 27, 28, 29, 36, 61, 83, 84, 89, 109, 149, 153

bukyokolo (a covering), 144

Bulamu (a spirit), 141

burying the dead, 136. *See also* graves; mourning

bushbuck (antelope), 104

bushbuck clan, 104

Busoga, 5, 10, 12, 29, 36, 82, 83, 84, 87, 89, 90, 93, 94, 99, 104, 126, 149, 153, 155

Buwongo, 87, 88, 98

Buyijja, 52, 115, 126, 162

Buyijja Traditional Healers' Association, 50, 51–52, 118

Bwette, Ronald, 130–31, 132, 134, 136, 138–39, 143

Byuma (a spirit), 137

cancer, 163

carrying pad, 101, 102

cassava, 6, 100

charlatan practices, 35, 36

chicken, 99. *See also* sacrifice: of chickens

chicken pox, 140

children, 12, 25, 88; learning capacity of, 133–34; playing with instruments, 145

Christianity, 120, 122, 123, 124, 126, 152, 164; conflict with, 163; missionaries, 9; missionaries' opposition to traditional healing, 35

civet cat clan, 156

clans, 11, 27, 29, 45, 61, 86, 89, 104, 156; alienation from, seen as illness, 27; as basic

Index

social unit, 7; as basis for naming, 7–8; guardian of, 26; leadership of, 109
clapping, 116
cleansing, 158–62
clothing, 24, 55, 139
coffee berries, 91, 100, 154; gifting and sharing of, 76, 129, 131, 142, 155–58; used in blood pact, 129
Cohen, David William, 86, 87
Cohen, Judah, 46
community, reproduction of, 154
cooking pot, 60
counseling, 60
cow, 132; horn of, 91; sacrifice of, 133
cowrie shells, 91
crowns, making of, 157
cults of affliction, 2, 25, 28, 47–48
cwezi spirit, 7

dance, 32, 54–58, 81, 83, 84, 114, 116, 117–18, 163; archiving of, 168; benefits of, 164
dance groups. *See* music: dance and drama troupes
dances, hip-centered, 162
dancing, 91, 108, 133, 149; with spirits, 162–64
Ddungu the hunter, 85, 92–94, 134, 135, 136, 163
death, 6, 102, 107, 150; boundary between life and, 142; confrontation with, 142
Decade of African Traditional Medicine, 40
demons. *See* spirits: malevolent
development, discourses of, 3
Deziderio, Ssaalongo Matovu Kiwanuka, 131
diagnosis, 28–30, 129
dicent (semiotics), 79
diversity, celebration of, 163
dividual, 154; use of term, 114
divination, 26, 28–30, 31; techniques of, 29
dog, Ddungu's, 93
dowry, exchange of, 158
drama, use of, in health education, 46
drummers, 126, 144, 145
drumming, 8, 11, 133, 134, 139
drums, 1, 29, 42, 81, 95, 113, 114, 116, 121, 145; as focal point of unity, 60; gendered aspects of, 78; personified as womb, 60; relevance of, 3; rhythms of, 4; sounding of, 81, 83, 96, 97, 129, 149, 150, 156
"drums of affliction" model, 90
duality, 61, 79, 83, 107; of blood pact, 158; in Kiganda ontology, 155

dwelling places for spirits, 110; building of, 55–56, 90, 100, 101, 110, 121, 122, 126, 152

ebibi (bad things), 7, 43–44, 89, 92. *See also* bad things; binding: of bad things
ebintu ebyobuwangwa (things of tradition), 108
ebyuma (metallic things), 131
ecologies of well-being, 58–107, 108, 128
ecology, 82–88, 92; and heritage, 167; local, 31–32
economic misfortunes, 88
ecumenical pluralism, 121
eczema, 25, 162
edutainment, 48, 54; in health sphere, 46, 47
ekibumba (cow liver), 159
ekifundikwa (belt), 111
ekigali (gift of special significance), 120
ekijjula (feast), 160
ekyombo (ship), 141
elders, respect for, 163
emikisa (blessings), 7, 92; promotion of, 43–44. *See also* blessings; unbinding: of blessings
Emoff, Ron, 29
empandi (legume), 100
engo (leopard), 62
engole (small crowns), 78
enitobo (emptiness), 141
enkata (carrying pad), 102
entebe (chair), 138
ethnography: Africanist, 33, 41; of healing, 11, 41, 124, 166; sensuous, 30
ethnomusicology, 12; of *kusamira* (see *kusamira*); of *nswezi* (see *nswezi*); of trance, 28–29, 30
Evans-Pritchard, E. E., 114
exchange, importance of, 158
exogamy, 8, 156

father of twins, 62, 65, 76, 77, 78, 79, 81, 82. *See also* Ssaalongo
fauna. *See* flora and fauna
feasting, 6, 44, 111, 133, 153, 154–64
fecundity, 144; human, 135–36
feeding, 130–34
Feierman, Steven, 30, 35, 40, 47, 51
Feld, Steven, 23
fertility, 88, 132, 139–41, 144, 150, 152, 158
ffumbe (civet cat), 156
fieldwork, context of, 4–8

Index

fire, 103, 137, 138, 141; eating of, 105; kept burning, 139

Fischer, Michael, 30

flora and fauna: domains of, 31, 59; people and, 25, 84; of ritual practice, 94–99, 120; spirits residing in, 7. *See also* forests; trees; *and specific animals*

food, 60, 154; gifting of, 10, 31, 44, 141; sharing of, 32, 93. *See also* ghee; groundnuts

forests, 92, 99, 135

fraudulent healers. *See* charlatan practices

"frictions of encounter," 42

Friedson, Steven, 124, 125, 142

"functions," ritual gatherings as, 126

funding agencies and networks, 38–39, 49, 52

funerals, 11, 94. *See also* mourning

Gaboggola (a spirit), 122, 123

garments. *See* clothing

gender, ambiguity of, 80

genitals, references to, 65–66. *See also* phallus; vagina

geographic context of research, 4–8

ggono (pleasing inflection), 3–4

Ggulu (a sky dweller), 104

ghee, 143, 145

gift economies, 44

gifting, 44–45, 133, 151; of food, 10, 31, 44, 141. *See also* coffee berries: gifting and sharing of

Global Health Council, 49

Gluckman, Max, 47

goats, 102. *See also* sacrifice: of goats

Good, Byron, 24

gourd rattles, 12, 16, 20, 29, 91, 95, 112, 114, 116, 121; relevance of, 3; washing of, 151. See also *nnhengo*; *nsaasi*

gourds, for drinking, 91, 111, 112, 117, 163

grandchildren (devotees), 133, 141, 153, 159, 162

grandparent/grandchild relationships, spiritual, 45

grandparents, 112, 131–32, 134, 142, 143, 144, 148–49

gratitude, 158–62

graves, mourning rituals at, 150–51

ground hornbill, 87

groundnuts, 6, 100, 154; gifting of, 141, 145, 155–58

Gulere, Cornelius Wambi, 86, 87

handclapping, 16

Hanson, Holly, 84

Harunah Mbogga, 138, 141

headbands, 96, 97

healers, 30; fraudulent (*see* charlatan practices); mediating role of, 31; medicinal knowledge of, 127; public, become invisible, 35

healers, traditional, 1, 7, 24, 25, 46, 57, 164, 166; agency of, 48; associations of, 36, 37, 38, 41; concern for flexibilities, 115; death of, 149; demands of, 129; devaluing of, 167; directory of, 50; foreign investment and, 37; peer education of, 49; professional, 113; professionalization of, 40, 41, 44, 48; public perceptions of, 36; public scrutiny of, 9; registration of, 37, 39, 51; regulation and self-regulation of, 39–41; statistical ratio to general population, 45; training program for, 52; visibility of, 36, 37, 42; wary of government control, 41

healing: as central to functioning of kingdom, 27; public, historiography of, 34–35; ritual, 1, 33–34; as a social process, 2

healing, traditional, 24, 154; conflated with witchcraft, 37; dismissal of, 166; efficacy of, 2; expressive contours of, 2; forms of, 5; professionalization of, 34, 38; social marginalization of, 2; in times of AIDS, 46–48; treated with suspicion, 35

health: definition of, 30; social basis of, 43–45; spiritual components of, 162

health care: primary, 1, 44–45; provision of, 52; public, 167; resistant to change from above, 40; as social process, 40–41, 47

Heidegger, Martin, 124

Herzfeld, Michael, 30, 31

heterophony, 11–12, 165; definition of, 20

hippopotamus, tooth of, 91

HIV/AIDS, 25, 39, 40, 118, 153, 162; ABC slogan, 166; culture of, 46; "living positively," 46–48, 54, 57, 115

hoe, iron, 99–100, 101, 150

HOPE activities, 54

hospitality, 29, 32, 44, 111, 117, 151, 153, 154–64

hunting, 92–94, 134–37

hybridity, 42

hymns, Christian, 122–23

illness, 25, 31; concepts of, 1, 3, 11, 33, 41, 43, 57; etiology of, 24–25; folk model of, 24

incense, 110, 138–39, 141

indigenous knowledge, 3, 36

innovation, 166

insanity, 28, 100

Irondo village, 94, 153; post-mortuary rites in, 149–52
Isegya (a spirit), 95, 97, 102, 150
Isegya Wamunogga, 100, 101
Islam, 125, 164; imams' opposition to traditional healing, 35

James, Deborah, 47
Jami-Tiiba Society, 39
Jankowsky, Richard, 23, 29, 30, 31
Janzen, John M., 11, 29, 42, 46, 47
Jjajja Byuma. See Byuma
Jjajja Ddungu. See Ddungu the hunter
Jjajja Gaboggola. See Gaboggola
Jjajja Kapere. See Kapere
Jjajja Mutale. See Mutale
Jjajja Nakavuma. See Nakavuma
Jjajja Ndawula. See Ndawula
Jjajja Ndawula Community, 54
jjembe (a working spirit), 89–90, 103, 146–47
Jjumba, Kabona (a healer), 27–28, 125
Johnson, Jennifer L., 105

Kabaka, 27, 77, 83, 109
kabanni (incense), 138–39
Kabindi, Erukaana Waiswa, 10, 90
kabona (title), 125
kadingidi (drum), 20; rhythms of, 21–22
kaffulu (a master across several domains), 126
Kafumbe, Damascus, 78, 81
Kaggwa (name for a sibling of twins), 64
Kagwa, Apolo, 83
kagwala instrument, 20
kalanga (invasive plant), 135, 140
Kalisa (a spirit), 95
Kalondoozi (a spirit), 90
Kalulu (a spirit), 145–46
"Kamungolo" song, 111–13
Kamya (name for a sibling of twins), 64
kanyoolagano (struggle), 142
Kapere (a healer), 91, 92, 122, 124
Kapferer, Bruce, 23, 29
Kasagga (a jjembe), 137, 138
Kasajja (a spirit), 135, 146, 149, 159, 160
kasiba nte plant, 100, 101, 102
Kasirye "Moto Man" Ahmed, 54–55
Kasolya, 109
Kato (name for a sibling of twins), 64
Katonda (creator), 6
Katwe, 143
Katwe Kagezi, 131
Kawalya, Deo, 10

kawojjolo (butterfly, reference to vagina), 136
kawowo (pleasant odor), 4
Kawumpuli (a spirit), 140
Kellogg Foundation, 49
khat (Catha edulis), 145
Kibuuka Mumbaale (a spirit), 104, 160, 161
Kifaalu Mumbaale (a spirit), 103, 104
kiggwa (shrine), 109, 121
Kigongo (name for a sibling of twins), 64
Kimera, Kabaka, accession of, 83
kingships, abolition of, 37
Kinobe, Herbert, 111–12
Kirowooza village, 66, 161
Kisuze, 130, 135, 136, 141, 144, 145, 153, 159, 162
Kitala, 110
Kiteera (name for a sibling of twins), 64
kitone (talent), 3
Kitooke, name for a sibling of twins, 64
Kiwanuka (a spirit), 61–63, 83, 103–5, 138, 140, 141, 155, 158; depicted as white or albino, 163; power of, 138; rite of, 138
Kizuuzi (a spirit), 149
Kizza (name for a sibling of twins), 64
knowledge, composing of, 108–27. See also indigenous knowledge
Kodesh, Neil, 26, 27, 30, 35, 80, 82, 83, 84–85, 86
Kookola, 110
Kotwe, 159
kubandwa (spirit mediumship), 8, 9
kugaba (to give), 161
kugabula (serve a feast), 161
kulagula (prophecy), 26
kulanya (form of introduction), 10
kulungoosa (cleansing), 159
kumansira process, 101
Kungu, 110
kusamira, 47, 55, 58, 63, 81, 97, 108, 121, 124, 126, 127, 157, 162; and brewing, 155; contextual situating of, 1–32; dismissed as superstitious, 167; historical trajectories of, 36; and hospitality, 139, 151; lessons of, 165–68; portrayed as insanity, 28; related to nswezi, 4–9; relation to ethnographic theory, 23–28, 42–43, 54; relation to trance, 23, 128; and sacrifice, 128–31; transformational nature of, 24, 164; use of term, 9
kusenga, performance of, 100
kusiba abalongo (twin-tying ritual), 137
kusula (to spend the night), 130

Index

kuwemula (vulgar language), 76
kuwulira (sensory concept), 4
kuwumbirawumbira (reassembly of things), 159
kuwuuba (possession), 98
Kyabakaire, 90
Kyambu, Andrew Lukungu Mwesige, 97, 100
Kyambu, Ntakabusuni, 97, 100

labor and delivery, training in, 52
landlord, 83, 139, 142
languages, 3; agglutinative nature of, xi; Eastern Lacustrine Bantu, 8, 26; Luganda, xi-xii, 4, 5, 8, 17, 23, 64, 93, 104, 113; Lusiki dialect, 87; Lusoga, xi-xii, 4, 5, 23, 98
leopard, 61, 76, 80, 81, 98, 99, 133, 134, 136, 137, 162; fear of, 62
Lévi-Strauss, Claude, 124
libations, pouring of, 150
lightning, 105
liminality, contours of, 134-37
lion, 104, 133; as manifestation of Mukama, 98-99
Lisa Nakawuka, 11, 143, 144-45, 146-49
listening, ethnographic, 167
liver, cooking and consumption of, 159
living positively. *See* HIV/AIDS: "living positively"
lubaale (guardian spirits), 7, 26, 61, 84, 96, 104, 105, 106, 138, 140, 148
lubiri (royal enclosure), 77
Lubowa (a spirit), 138, 143, 146, 147, 148, 149
Lubowa Traditional Healers' Association, 54
Lukowe (a fertility spirit), 88, 95, 96, 97
Lukowe Kotilida Bibireka, 149-52, 157
Lukowe Namwase, 100-101, 102
Lukowe Rehema, 97, 101, 102
lungfish clan, 85, 121, 130, 143
lweeza plant, 84, 94, 110; bathing with, 159-60

Magoba, Waalabyeki, 10, 62, 64, 79
Magobwe (a spirit), 55, 56, 61, 63, 76, 78, 81, 117, 142
majiini (*jinns*, spirits), 7
Makandwa village, 90, 92, 108, 120, 121, 123, 124, 126, 152
Makerere University, 38; Klaus Wachsmann Audio-Visual Archive, 168
malaria, 40, 162; prevention of, 167
Marcus, George, 30
marijuana, smoking of, 138

marriage, 8, 94; choices of alliance, 156. *See also* weddings
Marriott, McKim, 114
marwa (fermented liquid), 156, 157
Masquelier, Adeline Marie, 30
matooke, 141, 152; gifting of, 129
Mayanja (a spirit), 61, 62, 142, 63, 76, 81, 98, 135
mayembe (sing. *jjembe*, working spirits), 7, 76, 88-92, 103, 106, 116, 119-20, 145, 148, 162; fierceness of, 124; installation of, 92, 121-22; invocation of, 89; rite of, 146
mbuutu drum, 12, 13, 126; rhythms of, 16-17
McNeill, Fraser, 47
meat, 6, 101, 131, 137, 149, 151; distribution of, 161-62. *See also* liver
Médecins sans Frontières (MSF), 39, 49
medicinal plants, 7, 43, 47, 59, 61, 157; knowledge of, 45; listing of, 105-6; regulation of, 107; research into, 37-38; use in training traditional healers, 106; use with power objects, 84
medicines, 34; legitimacy of traditional, 60
mediums and mediumship. *See* spirit mediums; spirit mediumship
Meinert, Lotte, 46
mental health, 100
mental illness, training in, 52
messing around, 81-82
meter, 17, 20
methodology of research, 8-11; use of interviews, 9; use of music lessons, 9-10
mibala (drum slogan), 81
midwife spirit, 106
migration to cities, social costs of, 167
Ministry of Gender, Labor and Social Development (of Culture), 40, 50, 119
Ministry of Health, 40
minyolo sticks, 14, 20
misambwa spirits, 7, 26, 61, 76, 84-86, 106, 137, 138, 162; rite of, 138
missionaries, Christian, 9; opposition to traditional healing, 35
mizimu (ancestral ghosts), 7, 26
mmamba clan, 11
mmwanyi (coffee berries), 155
money, gifting of, 129
monitor lizard, 15
mother of twins, 62, 82. *See also* Nnaalongo
mourning, 94, 95, 96, 97, 150-51, 157
mpuunyi drum, 13
Mubende, 110

Index

197

mubissi (juice), 156
mufumu (healer), 8
mukago, 155
Mukama (a spirit), 98–99
"Mukame wange," use of phrase, 77
Mukasa (a sea spirit), 84, 145, 155
mukose (sesame seed), 86
Mukose patriline, 87
mukugu (master), 126
Munamaizi village, 55–56, 82, 88, 89, 90, 100, 103, 104, 126
music, 3–4, 9, 10, 23, 43, 44, 59, 108, 110; in ancient Greece, 4; archiving of, 168; as central to ritual performance, 114–15; as channel for understanding of illness and wellness, 41; dance and drama troupes, 54–55; instrumentation and idioms of, 11–12; lack of term for, 3–4; popular, 168; as ritual work, 33; in time of AIDS, 46–48; used to invoke spirits, 28
musical instruments, 126–27
musical repertories, 97, 165
musical socialization of spiritual power, 119–20
musicians, 9, 157; ritual work of, 31; role in therapy management, 30; role in traditional healing, 2
musicking: as ritual work, 54–58; role of, in well-being, 154
musiige (caretaker for shrine), 130
Muslim imams. *See* Islam
Musoke (a spirit), 61, 62, 63, 83, 140, 155
mutabaganya food mix, 100, 102
Mutale, Kabona (a spirit medium), 90–91, 92, 120, 121, 122–24, 125, 126; as interreligious peacemaker, 124
mutual aid, 58, 113, 119, 154, 164
Muwanga (a spirit), 161
muyonza (one who moves people), 126
muzimu (ancestral spirit), 88, 91, 114
mwenge (beer), 120
mwenge muganda (banana beer), 117
Mwesige, Andrew Lukungu, 10, 101

Nabawanuka, Nakigozi (a medium), 83
Nabuzaana (a spirit), 85
NACOTHA, 39, 48, 50, 51
Nakaggwa (name for a sibling of twins), 64
Nakamya (name for a sibling of twins), 64
Nakasujja (a spirit), 144
Nakato (name for a sibling of twins), 64
Nakavuma (a *jjembe*), 122, 123

Nakawuka, 130–31, 137
Nakayaga (a spirit), 138, 144
Nakayima (a traditional musician), 11, 63
Nakifuba (a woman seeking guidance), 115–19, 126
Nakityo (name for a sibling of twins), 64
namagga (landlord), 91–92, 123
Namayanja (a spirit), 142
Nambaga (a spirit), 138, 144, 146, 148, 149
namunjoloba drum, 13–14, 17
Namunobe (wife of Buwongo), 86, 87, 100
Namusisi Waititi clan, 86
nannyinimu (landlord / landlady), 66, 92
Nannyonga-Tamusuza, Sylvia A., 78
Nansukusa (name for a sibling of twins), 64
National Chemotherapeutic Research Laboratory (NCRL), 38
National Council of Traditional Healers and Herbalists Associations (NACOTHA), 39, 48, 50, 51
National Culture Policy, 50
National Integrated Forum, 51
Ndawula (a spirit), 139–40, 141, 163
Ndiwalana, Umar, 110, 33, 142
net, for hunting, 92, 94
networks, in traditional healing, 2, 119
new life, rituals of, 139–41
ngalabi drum, 13–14, 15, 16, 17
nnhengo (gourd rattles), 12, 14, 17
Niane, Djibril Tamsir, 62
Nile (river), 104
nkukuulu grass, 85
nkuni, first-comer spirits, 7, 85, 86, 88
Nnaalongo (mother of twins), 62, 64, 65, 66, 77
nnankasa rhythm, 16–17, 18–19
Nnyanja Nalubaale (Lake Victoria), 6, 11, 100, 104–5, 110, 139, 151, 155
nnyimba (songs), 3
non-governmental organizations (NGOs), 166, 167; employment of rural health workers, 46; promoting traditional medicine, 37
nsaasi (gourd rattles), xii, 12, 14
"Nsula-nkola" (I spend the nights struggling), 55–57, 58
nswezi, 58, 164; contextual situating of, 1–32; and development discourse, 47; and ethnographic theory, 31, 41–42; in ecologies of well-being, 61, 82, 97–98, 100, 105; lessons of, 165–66; and medicinal knowledge, 108, 114, 127, 162; related to

198 *Index*

kusamira, 4, 41; and sacrifice, 128–31, 139, 151, 155, 157
Ntakabusui, Kyambu, 10
ŋoma (drum), xii, 8, 11, 27, 42, 60, 90, 162, 167

Obote, Milton, 37
obukotolo (roasted offering), 145
obulamu obulungi (the good life), 25, 165
okukoona (to knock), 135
okuŋŋana (gathering), 155, 159, 164
okusamira, meanings of, 23–24
okusamiza (process of initiation), 24
okusiba ebibi (binding of bad things), 7
okusumulula (unbinding), 118
okusumulula emikisa (unbinding of blessings), 7
okutta omukago (cutting a pact), 129
okuwanga amayembe ritual, 92
okuwemula (vulgar language), 66
okuwumba (organization), 159
okuzina (dancing), 66
okuzina abalongo (dancing the twins), 62
okwabya olumbe (chasing away death), 81, 150, 156–57
okwaza (searching for spirits), 55, 115–19
olubiri (royal enclosure), 61
omugongo (back), 64
omukongozzi (a carrier of spirits), 113–14
omunozzi weddagala (gatherer of medicine), 85
omunyumungufu (adept person), 3
omutwe (the head), 114
one who opens doorways, ritual of, 141–44. *See also* Sserugulamilyango
open doors, rituals of, 139–41
oral narratives, hearing of, 35
other-than-human beings, 151, 167; use of term, 2

pad, carrying, 101, 102
palliative care, 46, 47, 57
partible persons, 114
Peirce, Charles Sanders, 79
people, as resources, 113
personhood, beyond individuality, 114
phallus, 76, 78, 140
Piot, Charles, 125
pipes. *See* tobacco pipes
plants. *See* flora and fauna; medicinal plants
play, ritual seriousness of, 122–24
playing around, 81

pluralism, religious, 121, 122, 163
poetry, rhythms of, 4
polio, 140
polyrhythmic music, 165
possession, 5, 8, 9, 23, 34, 60, 98, 108, 114, 124, 134, 142, 143; during church services, 121; ethnomusicology of, 28–30; measuring of brain waves during, 164; signs of, 116
postmodernity, 125, 165
post-mortuary rites, 149–52
potatoes, 6
power objects, 32, 63, 92, 97, 106, 108, 112, 120–22, 125–27, 151; associated with working spirits, 91; creation of, 123, 152; manufacture and sale of, 89
prayers, 132, 138, 165; saying of, 130–34
pre-Christian practices, demonization of, 35
prefixes, use of, xi–xii
primary health care. *See* health care: primary
productive frictions, 41
Promotion des Médecines Traditionelles (PROMETRA), 10, 39, 45, 48–49, 51, 54–57, 106, 115, 118, 119, 126, 133, 153; Institute of Traditional Medicine, 52; registration of Uganda branch, 49
proximity, model of, 52
Pulitzer Center, 35–36
python, 61, 76, 78, 80, 81; carved on drum, 83

Queen of Katwe, 131

Radio Maria, 122
rats, 151
Ray, Benjamin C., 83
reciprocity, human-spiritual, 151
recording: of songs, 146; of sound, 68
Red Pepper, 35
Reed, Daniel, 47, 48, 142
relationships, restoration of, 88
religious pluralism in Uganda, 121, 122, 163
repertories (term), 2
repertories of well-being, 1–32, 33, 60, 107–10, 153, 154–64
resistance, 48
resources, gathering of, 108–27
rice, 6
risk, 153, 166; performing idioms of, 65–82
ritual innovation, 124–25
ritual practice, fauna and flora of, 94–99

ritual work, 33–58
rivers, 102–6
Rockefeller Foundation, 39, 49
rolling on the ground, 149
Roscoe, John, 26
Rouget, Gilbert, 28, 29
royal accession to throne, 83
royal court, 16
royal enclosure, 65, 80
royalism, 61
royal shrine, 77

sacrifice, 25, 31, 32, 88, 89, 101, 107, 121, 123, 124, 126, 134–37, 138, 153, 158–59, 168; burning whole animal, 158; chaos of, 148–49; of chickens, 90, 97, 100, 104, 133; of children, alleged, 35, 37; of cows, 133; cultural logic of, 130–34; debris of, 149; of goats, 92, 131, 133, 136, 137, 145, 146, 147, 151; of humans, alleged, 35; negotiation of, 129; of sheep, 139, 141; and song, 128–53; specifications regarding, 44
sanitation, 167
Schoenbrun, David, 2, 26, 35
sea and sky, understanding of, 101–5
Sekagya, Yahaya, 10, 48–49, 50–51, 52, 115, 118, 119
sesame seeds, 86, 87, 100; gifting of, 129, 141, 145
sexual frigidity, 27
sexuality, 82, 85, 134–37
sexually transmitted infections, 25, 136
sexual safety, 167
shaking, as sign of possession, 98
shield, 110, 140
shrines, 32, 38, 42, 79, 109–12, 115, 126, 127, 137, 141, 158; as means to an end, 113; as space for cooling spirits, 124; urban, 167; violent destruction of, 163–64; visits to, 25
Sibyangu, Ssematimba Frank, 11, 26–28, 76–77, 78, 85
singers, 89, 90, 114; good, definition of, 126; improvisational ability of, 132; known for motifs, 130; solo, 20
singing, 8, 11, 12, 91, 92, 97, 98, 116, 126, 129, 130–34, 135, 139, 149, 150, 156, 163; benefits of, 164; choruses in, 20; as a means to seek answers, 115
skin diseases, 139, 140, 162, 163
sky, understanding of sea and, 101–5
smallpox, 140, 163
snakes, 55, 79, 99, 162

song and songs, 61, 62, 91, 119, 139, 160–62; about bag and drinking gourd, 111–13; for blessing, repertories of, 44; connected to natural elements, 86–87, 100, 103, 105; about Ddungu, 93; for deceased medium, 94–96; as form of ritual work, 31, 54–58, 90, 106; improvised elements of, 132; as indices, 158; invoking animals, 98; invoking spirits, 140, 143–44, 146–49; at liminal moments, 137; about possession, 98; and power objects, 123, 127; in repertories of well-being, 3, 7, 12, 16–17, 20, 166; role of, in shaping transcendent occasions, 110, 153; role of, in traditional healing, 3, 34, 37, 42, 44; and sacrifices, 128–53; styles of, 12; as technologies of well-being, 120, 125; of thanksgiving, 160–61. See also twin songs
sound: in healing processes, 108–27; technologies for recording and distributing, 68; thinking about, 167
spears 92, 94, 110
spirit mediums, 5, 6; as bearers of exchange communications, 130; chosen by spirits, 100, 121; death of, 94; demands for sacrifice, 146; and gathering resources, 113, 119; and ecology, 103, 104; in ethnographic theory, 30, 32, 41; farmer mediums, 99–100; flexible personhood of, 114, 154, 164; hard work of, 147; new, initiation of, 82, 105, 149, 151, 152; participation in performance, 12; possession of, 105, 143 (see also possession); and power objects, 126–27; terms for, 8
spirit mediumship, 8, 26, 30, 108, 109, 126, 144
spirits, 165; demonic, 35; associated with specific afflictions, 140; and ecologies of well-being, 84–5, 86, 92, 94, 97, 99–106, 115; exchange with, 32, 44; female, 144, 145; functioning of, 85, 165–66; influence on illness and well-being, 25–6, 28, 29, 43, 61, 88, 120; invocation of, in ritual, 76–7, 82, 117, 142–43; in liminal phase, 138, 139; malevolent, 35, 121; neglect of, 90; participation in ritual performances, 12, 24, 43, 44, 84, 122–24, 135; places of, 6–7; propitiation of, 27, 59, 90, 124; and ritual work, 34, 45, 55–6, 58, 89, 90–92, 126, 146–52; royal, 7, 26; and sacrifice, 132, 133. See also dwelling places for spirits; working spirits
spiritual alienation, 118
spiritual healing, training in, 52

200 *Index*

squirrel, 99
Ssaalongo (father of twins), 62, 64, 65, 77, 140
ssabo (shrine), 9, 92
Ssemaluulu John, 116–17
Ssemugumbe (a spirit), 146
Sserubwatuka (praise name for Kiwanuka), 105
Sserugulamilyango (a spirit), 142–43
"Ssewasswa" (a song), 62, 65, 135; tune of, 66–75
Stoller, Paul, 30, 108
Strathern, Marilyn, 59, 114
struggle, 56, 85, 106, 142, 148
sugarcane, 145
Sundiata epic, 62
surnames, not used, 7
sweet potatoes, 6, 90, 100

taboos 159, 160, 163; suspension of, 137, 138
Tantala, Renee, 35
tea, 154, 155
technē, 124, 125
technologies for recording and distributing sound, 68
technology: as art, 124–25; spiritual/ritual, 122, 123, 124
thanks, forms of, 161
THETA, 39, 48–49
things of tradition, 33, 34, 43, 58, 108, 109
Third Space, post-colonial, 41, 42
tobacco: gifting of, 129; smoking of, 29, 138, 145, 155
tobacco pipes 95, 112, 163; washing of, 151
Tonda (the Creator), 6, 130–31
top-down directives, 166
totems, 7–8, 81, 86, 87; table of, 87
Traditional and Modern Health Practitioners Together against AIDS (THETA), 39, 48–49
trance, 30, 60; ethnomusicology of, 28–30
trees, 102–6; relation to human fecundity, 136
trickster persona, 146
tromba spirit possession, 29
Tsing, Anna Lowenhaupt, 41, 42
Ttanda, 110
ttimba (drum), 83
Turino, Thomas, 79
Turner, Victor, 23, 25, 29, 137; *Drums of Affliction*, 29
twins, 62, 82, 84, 140; binding of umbilical cords of, 43; dancing of, 84; dumping feces of, 64; multiple associations of, 81; naming of, 63, 81; parenthood of, 66; of the royal enclosure, 77, 79, 80; tying of, 62, 63, 65, 78, 82, 94, 135, 137. *See also* father of twins; mother of twins
twinship, 106; invocation of, 61–64; trope of, 83
twin songs, 61, 63, 64, 77, 78, 82, 83, 85, 135, 140, 144

Uganda, 12
Uganda National Integrated Forum of Traditional Healers, 39
Uganda n'Eddagala Lyayo organization, 38, 39
umbilical cords, 65; meaning of, 62; of twins, 62, 97
unbinding/distribution, 32, 59, 156–57; of blessings, 7, 25, 60–61, 115, 126, 129–30, 157, 158, 165
UN Development Program, 49
urbanization, 167
US Agency for International Aid, 49

vagina, 80, 136
Venda, rituals of, 28
venues, for ritual performance, 108, 109
Vernaschi, Marco, 35
vulgarity, 66, 76, 78, 81, 135, 136–37, 138, 162

Wachsmann, Klaus P., 83
Wairama, 90
Waititi Buutu clan, 87
Walumbe (a spirit associated with death), 6, 102
waragi (spirit drink), 138
Wasswa (name for first-born twin), 64, 65
waters, 102–6
weddings, 10, 11
well-being, 32, 84, 106, 123, 166; beyond therapeutics, 162–64; concept of, 1; concept of, integrated into national health care, 41; in era of international development, 48; ontology of, 3; social basis of, 41, 43–45. *See also* ecologies of well-being; repertories of well-being
wellness, 7, 25, 31, 36; associated with fulfilment of responsibility, 26; concepts of, 11, 27, 33, 41, 43, 57; folk model of, 24
Western medicine, 48
wholeness of personhood, 26

witchcraft, 36–37; accusations of, 89; protection from, 25
Witchcraft Ordinance (1957), 36
womb, 80, 81
women: health of, 88, 150; rites of, 144–45
women's groups, 46
working spirits, 120, 123, 145; as discrete category, 89; rite of, 146–49; searching for, 91. *See also* spirits

"work of the ancestors," 34
World Health Organization (WHO), 166

yams, 6

ziizi grass, 135

PETER J. HOESING is Director of Sponsored Programs at Dakota State University and an adjunct assistant professor at the University of South Dakota Sanford School of Medicine.

The University of Illinois Press
is a founding member of the
Association of University Presses.

University of Illinois Press
1325 South Oak Street
Champaign, IL 61820–6903
www.press.uillinois.edu

Printed by Printforce, United Kingdom